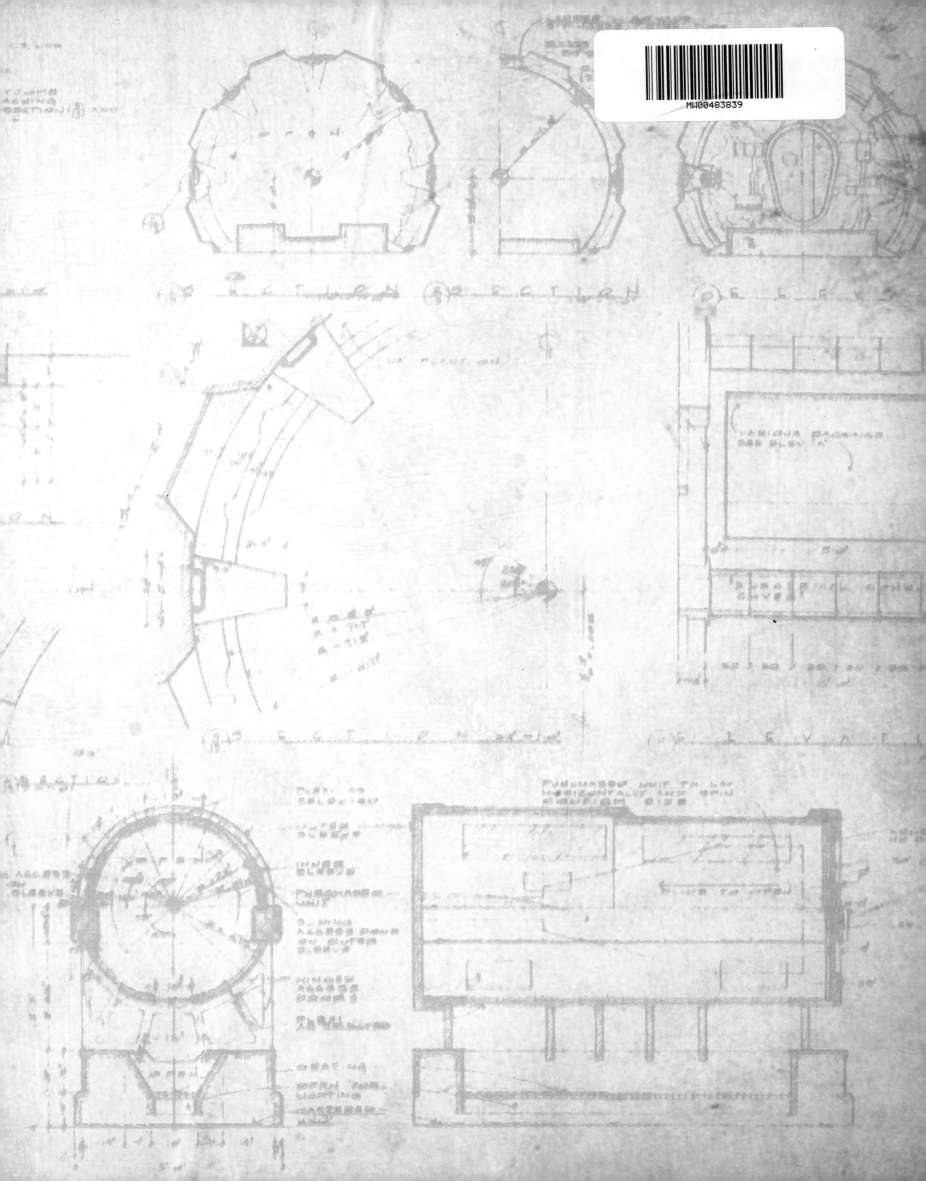

firefly

ENCYCLOPEDIA

FIREFLY ENCYCLOPEDIA

ISBN: 9781785655296

Published by Titan Books
A division of Titan Publishing Group Ltd.
144 Southwark St.
London
SE1 0UP

First edition: 2018
10 9 8 7 6 5 4 3 2 1

Based on the series created by Joss Whedon

Did you enjoy this book? We love to hear from our readers.
Please e-mail us at: readerfeedback@titanemail.com or write to Reader
Feedback at the above address.

To receive advance information, news, competitions, and exclusive offers online,
please sign up for the Titan newsletter on our website: www.titanbooks.com

A CIP catalogue record for this title is available from the British Library.

Printed and bound in Canada.

firefly ENCYCLOPEDIA

MONICA VALENTINELLI

TITAN BOOKS

CONTENTS

06

BOOK ONE:
THE STORY OF *FIREFLY*

100

BOOK TWO: BROWNCOATS,
THIEVES & PURPLE BELLIES

Serenity's Crew	102
Friends & Allies	136
Varmints & Villains	140
Them Pesky Alliance Folk	146

152

BOOK THREE: WIDE KNOWN 'VERSE

Big Gorramn Sky	154
Shuttles, Ships & Space Stations	176
Learning to Technobabble	190
Brimming with Culture	202
Chinese in *Firefly*	222

230

BOOK FOUR: SCRIPT EXCERPTS & ANALYSIS

256

ACKNOWLEDGMENTS & CONTRIBUTOR BIOS

book one

THE STORY OF *FIREFLY*

THE STORY OF *FIREFLY*

THE DEATH OF EARTH-THAT-WAS

The story of Malcolm J. Reynolds and his *Serenity* crew did not start in 2517; it began 500 years in the past. Back on Earth-That-Was, humankind grew and grew, draining all of Mother Nature's gifts the planet had to offer. At that pivotal moment, when food was scarce and water even more so, humanity had a choice: war with one another to fight for survival or search for a new home among the stars.

Every man, woman, and child in the 'verse knows that humanity chose hope over bloodshed. Their ancestors, many of whom had never set foot on an alien planet or moon, used all the scientific and technological achievements at their disposal to find a non-violent solution to their problems. Instead of building high-tech weapons they designed generational starships, terraformers and helioformers, gravity regulators, and atmosphere processing plants. If they couldn't find a habitable planet, they'd make one. And so they did.

Following their discovery of barren celestial bodies orbiting a nearby star called the White Sun (Bai Hu), humankind manufactured habitable planets and moons to create a galaxy made up of five star systems that would become humanity's future home. After the first group of earthlike planets were ready to be settled, those who had stayed behind on Earth-That-Was collected samples of plants, animals and the like, and prepared for the journey of a lifetime. Anyone and everyone, from the poorest beggar to the wealthiest politician, was invited to make

the trip to their new galaxy. Bai Hu was more than a destination; the white sun was a shining beacon in the blackness of space, a promise that humanity would survive.

As Shepherd Book said, "After the Earth was used up, we found a new solar system and hundreds of new Earths were terraformed and colonized. The Central Planets formed the Alliance and decided all the planets had to join under their rule. There was some disagreement on that point. After the War, many of the Independents who had fought and lost drifted to the edges of the system, far from Alliance control. Out here, people struggled to get by with the most basic technologies; a ship would bring you work, a gun would help you keep it. A captain's goal was simple: find a crew, find a job, keep flying."

FAR RIGHT: **Death of Earth-That-Was: the planet, once drained of all natural resources became barren, cracked and uninhabitable.**

BUILDING A NEW HOME

Not long afterward, the White Sun became the hub, the epicenter of the known 'verse, the Central Planets. The kernel of civilization was reborn on not one, but two bountiful planets, Sihnon and Londinium, built by Chinese and American superpowers who reigned supreme back on Earth-That-Was. Here in the Core, the two regimes worked in tandem with one another and their harmonious efforts formed a utopia in which all cultures, all pacifist beliefs, and all lifestyles were embraced and accepted.

Every aspect of society flourished in unexpected and surprising ways. For example, the population enjoyed a 94% literacy rate, the average lifespan was 120 years, and the concepts of volunteerism and public service were ingrained in daily life.

Helping others was something people did because they thought it was right, not because they were forced to do so. Even social mores evolved well past the 21st century mindset, leading to the legalization of drugs and the establishment of female owned-and-operated Companion Houses for sex workers.

Sooner or later, however, even the King of all Londinium had to make hard choices. In the Central Planets, the nascent governments never expected that the pioneers would outgrow their new homes so quickly, nor did they expect some settlers would not 'take' to a peaceful lifestyle. On the one hand, there were plenty of new planets and moons (even outside of the Central Planets) to live on. On the other, while there was lots of space, there weren't enough resources to go around. What's more, the terraforming process wasn't perfect, which meant that some planets and moons were toxic, infecting pioneers with rare diseases like Bowden's Malady.

A CRUMBLING UTOPIA

Fearing the violence of the past would **repeat itself, some settlers decided to strike out on their own, carving out simple lives on Border Planets in the Red Sun (Zhu Que) or Georgia (Huang Long) systems. To keep an eye on these adventurous folk, members of the social elite were offered land, titles, and all the sundries an anxious magistrate could want in return for bringing a bit of order and civility to these backwater moons. Folk who wanted to steer clear of government interference altogether flew past the Border Planets to the newly terraformed Blue Sun (Qing Long) or Kalidasa (Xuan Wu) systems. For those explorers, the two systems were wild, untamed, free. As long as the Border Planets supplied folk with the food they needed to survive, settlers could live however they wanted to.**

With little oversight, the pioneers who'd left the Central Planets lived a hard life on their own terms. Some folk formed small communities bound by faith or by trade, while others terrorized their neighbors for a bowl of rice. Soon, living outside of the Core became synonymous with an existence that was poor, unlawful, hardened... and independent.

Slowly but surely, leaders back on Sihnon and Londinium began to realize how fragile their utopia was. Despite the fact that humanity was thriving, bit by bit their castle in the sky was beginning to crumble because people were turning their back on their dream of a unified, peaceful population. Every morning, broadwaves over the Cortex—the 26th century version of the Internet—sent from the Border and the rim showed how lawlessness and chaos were escalating on a daily basis. Worse, the news was filled with problems the government couldn't fix: the Gen-Seed not taking to the soil; prospectors abandoning a silver mine for fear of contracting a rare disease; an outlaw on the run terrorizing a trading post. Soon, minor problems turned into major disasters, which disrupted the flow of supplies between systems, causing famine, disease, and many deadly skirmishes.

While settlers on the Border and rim struggled to survive, the Core's citizens faced their fair share of problems too. Many people were dissatisfied with the life politicians created for them because their privileged lives weren't enough. They wanted more power, more influence, more land, money—even sex. And the more people wanted, the less there was to go around. This problem formed what the first settlers had tried like hell to prevent: a precarious imbalance of power and resources that threatened to topple fragile ecosystems. If the Central Planets couldn't keep the peace, then how did anyone expect them to help their sisters and brothers on the Border or rim?

FORMATION OF THE ANGLO-SINO ALLIANCE

Strained relationships, combined with the fear of an interplanetary war, fueled the formation of a centralized government called the Alliance. The seat of the Anglo-Sino Alliance, which combined the planetary powers of Londinium and Sihnon, called itself 'Parliament', and sought to unify the Central Planets into one cohesive interplanetary nation. Representatives from each Central Planet, from Bellerophon to Osiris, sat in Parliament to advocate for their nation's best economic and political interests. Secretive to a fault, the newly birthed Parliament feared a revolution. To keep the peace, the Alliance began training and recruiting soldiers under the guidance of the Military Council.

As Central Planet representatives renewed trade deals and old alliances, the average citizen's life also improved. Gone, however, was the dream of shared understanding and peace, for power imbalances caused by human greed remained entrenched throughout the Core. Social mores sharpened, forcing citizens to look over their shoulder, avoid loud criticisms, and focus on decorum and status. Subconsciously, many citizens—like the Tam family from Osiris—understood the terrible price they paid for peace and security. Consciously, they would never admit who or what they'd sacrificed to preserve their dream of a perfect society.

Though many Core citizens remained blissfully unaware of Parliament's shadier activities, disgraced members and outspoken protesters were quietly removed from polite society and faced increasing mercilessness. Neighbors were encouraged to spy on one another, and volunteers were sought for the Border Patrol. Over time, Parliament's anxiety worsened and a darker side of the government emerged. Highly advanced programs operating outside of the Military Council's purview shattered the wall between what Parliament believed was best for humanity and what its citizens needed. While the military continued to depend on a show of force, Parliament developed new secretive initiatives.

Research into cutting-edge sciences and experimental technology relied on testing unethical procedures, medicines, and equipment on unwitting subjects lured into volunteering. Other programs proved even more insidious, as the once-autonomous Companion Houses were often used as training grounds for spies and assassins.

RIGHT: The brightest and best children are invited to train and learn at special schools, little knowing the dark truth hidden in such places. Recognized as a shining example of physical and intellectual prowess, River Tam was enlisted with the full consent of her parents, with only her brother suspecting something was wrong.

SEEDS OF PARANOIA

Parliament, desperate to keep its citizens from revolting, and the Border Planets from invading, even began experimenting on exceptional children like River Tam. To the paranoid heads of Parliament, their questionable initiatives were an improvement on an already perfect system that would one day define the future for all. So, rather than kidnapping gifted children like River, the Alliance founded an elite school called the Academy and opened the door for the Core's best, brightest, and youngest. To all its citizens, the Academy was labeled as a school for the gifted, a place where only the most talented and intelligent children could get the care and attention they needed. Once on campus, however, students were slowly indoctrinated into a secret government program to create the unstoppable: enhanced 'sleeper' assassins who could be controlled from afar with subliminally implanted commands.

Of course, the interplanetary war the Alliance sought to prevent did not start the way they expected it to. In fact, it didn't start at all. People on the Border and rim planets were too busy fighting for their survival, and they did not have the resources required to launch a full-scale assault on the well-armed, well-trained Alliance military. Most folk just wanted to be left alone, to own a modest cattle ranch or eke out a living on a farm. They didn't much care for the Alliance's looming shadow and assumed the Central Planets would stick to their own—what with their fancy dress, fine manners, riches and all. For many outside of the Core, they knew what Parliament represented, and they rejected it in mind, body and spirit.

Eventually Parliament took matters into its own hands and pledged to offer an 'improved life' to everyone outside of the Core. One by one, almost all the Core Planets fell in line with the Alliance's wishes—not knowing the full truth behind their desire for war. Sihnon and Londinium. Ariel and Osiris and Bellerophon. All the centralized planets and moons—excluding Persephone, whose orbit around Lux skated precariously close to the Border Planets—agreed their way of life was the better one, never realizing that Parliament's ever-increasing paranoia was the driving force that would lead humanity to war.

THE WAR OF UNIFICATION

The lives of millions had been doomed by the scarcity of resources and the fear of invasion in what became the deadliest conflict recorded in human history. The Unification War lasted over five years and was fought on dozens of planets and moons. Most battles took place outside of the Central Planets for, just as the Alliance expected, the volunteer armies and battalions of the Border and rim did not possess military might and could not strike at the Core. Despite this, the Alliance's enemy, who called themselves Browncoats, did have something more valuable than firepower: the desire to live free from the yoke of a government bent on subjugating everyone to their will.

Most Core citizens supported unification as an ideology. They believed the Alliance was offering Border and rim settlers the same way of life they enjoyed, replete with healthcare, education, fine arts, and social mobility. No one, not even members of Parliament, expected neglected colonists, petty thieves, and hungry farmers to shake a fist at the Alliance. And, since the Central Planets were separated from the battles raging on Border Planets like Hera and Shadow—apart from the occasional protest or grenade thrown at a military outpost—no one believed the Alliance was waging an unjust war. They had what Parliament demanded from all its citizens: faith that the government knew what was best for its people.

Of course, members of the Independent Faction like Malcolm J. Reynolds disagreed. Despite knowing full well what firepower and high-tech ships the Alliance had at its disposal, farmers, miners, and ranchers like Reynolds fought in the War anyway. They were convinced that freedom and the ability to make their own choices were worth dying for, and those beliefs led to the formation of a ragtag military comprised primarily of volunteers who had more heart than experience.

LEFT: Browncoats Rations Vouchers

ABOVE: Sergeant Reynolds: a key figure in the Unification War.

FIGHTING FOR INDEPENDENCE

Reynolds, a bright-eyed kid from the planet Shadow in the Georgia System, left his mother's ranch to join the Independent Faction. Five years later, the boy became a man; his innocence and naïveté had been beaten out of him by the devastating loss of his home world. Shadow had been bombed so heavily the land became uninhabitable, turning it into a 'black rock'. It seemed the Alliance wasn't taking no for an answer, and resistance proved to be deadly to everyone—even those who stayed home to raise their families, tend fields, and corral steers.

By that time, Malcolm Reynolds (Mal) had earned the title Sergeant of the 57th Overlanders—nicknamed the Balls and Bayonet Brigade—of the Independent Faction. An opinionated (if not downright sarcastic) individual, Sergeant Reynolds was the type of commander who was more comfortable fighting on the front lines than planning around a war table.

While the leaders of the Independents may not have fully appreciated Sergeant Reynolds' candor, the soldiers under his command—which included the comical Private Tracey Smith who stole Colonel Obrin's prized mustache—were utterly devoted to him.

Though Sergeant Reynolds had fought in other battles in the Border and rim, such as the winter campaign on New Kasmir in the Kalidasa System, two key skirmishes won him the respect of an entire army: the Battle of Du-Khang and the war-ending Battle of Serenity Valley.

BATTLE OF DU-KHANG

The Independent Faction's ranks were filled with young, scrappy volunteers like Privates Bendis and Smith, who often relied on veterans for their survival. Records show that at the Battle of Du-Khang, under the command of Sergeant Reynolds and Corporal Zoë Alleyne, Private Tracey Smith opened a can of beans, not realizing an Alliance soldier had snuck up on him. The enemy tripped on a rock but still had the drop on the young Independent. The Alliance soldier raised his weapon to strike just as Corporal Alleyne appeared behind him and slit his throat.

Corporal Alleyne lectured Private Smith and, during her review of battle protocols, gave him an overview of their position. Thirty Alliance troops armed with mortars were positioned behind them in nearby buildings. Thus far, they were unaware of the Independent Faction's position—thanks to Corporal Alleyne's takedown of two of their scouts. Suddenly Alleyne and Smith heard Sergeant Reynolds screaming at the top of his lungs. Arms flailing and dodging bullets, he crashed into their position.

The situation was grim. The Corporal expected tanks, or 'rollers', to enter the field of battle. Most members of their squad were either dead or missing. Vitelli was out of commission; the officer surrendered to the Alliance and exposed the northwest quadrant. Their Lieutenant, shortly before succumbing to shell shock, ordered the 57th to join up with the 22nd holed up at a school system—but it was clear the remaining squad members would have a tough time following orders.

Sergeant Reynolds, Corporal Alleyne, and the few remaining Independents took a break from the battle and discussed what to do next. Unfortunately, their hesitation cost them dearly: the Alliance fired a heat-seeking missile to attack their location. Reacting quickly, Mal lit a flare and tossed it high into the air. Drawn to the flare's heat, the missile exploded on contact in a shower of sparks and shrapnel that rained down on the soldiers below. Mal's back and arm were torn open, and Tracey sustained a cut to his leg.

Though the heat-seeking missile didn't kill them, Mal's stunt alerted the enemy to their presence. The Alliance had found them. Hoisting the injured Smith over his shoulder, Sergeant Reynolds told the Corporal to do the same. Just as Corporal Alleyne lifted the Lieutenant's catatonic body, an Alliance tank rolled through the area. Running for their lives, the pair saved two lives that day and managed to survive without incurring serious injuries.

War stories like these are the reason soldiers pledged their loyalty to Sergeant Reynolds. Almost everyone who fought with the Independent officer was infected by his optimism and his faith that the Independents could win.

Faith, however, can be shaken. Tested. Even broken.

THIS PAGE: Reynolds and Alleyne fought hard in the Battle of Du-Khang, while overseeing less able soldiers like Private Smith.

BATTLE OF
SERENITY VALLEY

Almost three years after the Battle of **Du-Khang, Sergeant Reynolds and Corporal Alleyne flew to join the Independent Faction's dwindling forces in Serenity Valley on Hera, located in the Georgia System. The planet Hera was crucial to the Alliance's plan to swiftly end the Unification War: not only was Hera positioned near a shipping lane it had also been so successfully terraformed that its crop yields were higher than average. To the Alliance brass, securing the Border Planet allowed them to do two things: control a key route and cut off a main source of food. They theorized that if the Alliance couldn't shoot their way through the plucky but determined Independents, then they'd starve and weaken their forces instead.**

Unlike the quick and decisive Battle of Sturges that had been fought in space over a rumored cache of money, the Battle of Serenity Valley lasted for seven long weeks. The Browncoats, nicknamed for the long leather trench coats they wore, dug their heels in, believing they could win the fight.

Tenacious to a fault, the Independent Faction waged war for almost two months. Sergeant Reynolds, one of the officers who saw the fight through to the end, commanded 2,000 soldiers to stand up to the smartly uniformed 'purple bellies'. Reynolds pressed for any advantage he could find, knowing that the Alliance's superior firepower was preventing Independent reinforcements from entering the theater. Unfortunately, though Reynolds was convinced the Independent Faction's High Command would send relief, his commanders were reviewing several options and considered surrendering to the Alliance.

In the heat of battle, Graydon, an Independent radio operator, told Sergeant Reynolds that air support was holding their position until they could confirm the ground forces' status; they required a clear shot at the advancing Alliance forces and a lieutenant's authorization code to carry out an attack. In response, Reynolds ripped the rank insignia from Lieutenant Baker's dead body and gave Graydon the codes he needed.

LEFT: **Despite leading and fighting with great bravery, Malcolm Reynolds saw victory turn to ultimate defeat.**

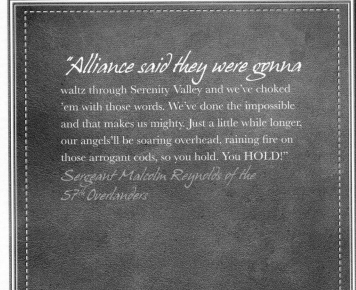

"Alliance said they were gonna waltz through Serenity Valley and we've choked 'em with those words. We've done the impossible and that makes us mighty. Just a little while longer, our angels'll be soaring overhead, raining fire on those arrogant cods, so you hold. You HOLD!"
Sergeant Malcolm Reynolds of the 57th Overlanders

After ordering a squad to higher ground, Sergeant Reynolds grabbed Corporal Alleyne and Private Bendis, planning to commandeer an Alliance anti-aircraft gun. Once Reynolds had control of the gun, he'd be able to shoot down a hovering Alliance skiff that was preventing reinforcements from arriving. Thinking he had the support he needed, the Sergeant dodged heavy fire to man the gun. Unfortunately, the young Private Bendis froze in panic and Graydon was shot and killed.

Reacting quickly, Corporal Alleyne stepped up and provided much-needed cover fire, allowing Reynolds to execute his plan. Reynolds fired on the skiff, and the ship exploded in an instant. It was a direct hit. Deadly pieces of shrapnel burst into the air and tumbled toward the ground. With no time to spare, Mal spotted the blistering fragments, abandoned the gun, and slammed into Alleyne. The soldiers dropped to the ground and rolled out of the way—just as a fiery shard of the wreckage spun over them and burst into flames.

Unbeknownst to Sergeant Reynolds, nothing he could do would change the outcome of the battle, for it had already been decided. The Independents' dwindling forces could only watch in horror as their ships—the 'angels' as Reynolds had called them—flew overhead without dropping their payload. Then, the unthinkable happened: High Command ordered the Independent soldiers to

surrender. Private Bendis was the first to follow orders, but the Alliance shot him not long afterward, proving that the government who professed they wanted nothing more than peace was not at all trustworthy.

Undaunted and undeterred, both Sergeant Reynolds and Corporal Alleyne did not 'negotiate', nor did they leave the field. Following the Independent High Command's surrender, the pair held the valley for an additional two weeks, until they were captured and held in Alliance-run prisoner-of-war camps. Though some Core citizens wanted to try the surviving Independents for war crimes, the Alliance set the infamous Browncoats free—along with their reputations.

In a twist of fate, Reynolds and Alleyne became legends. The Battle of Serenity Valley had a 68% casualty rate, and they were the only two members of the 57th Overlanders who had survived. The Captain even received a Commendation of Valor for his efforts. Of the two, however, only Alleyne escaped unscathed from the horrors of war; Reynolds lost something in the commotion that he has never regained: his faith.

RIGHT: The events of the Battle of Serenity Valley went on to shape the life and behaviour of Malcolm Reynolds in a profound way.

The Anglo-Sino Alliance's victory
expanded their powerful reach into four systems,
hundreds of worlds, and thousands of stars. Though
billions populated the Core, Parliament lacked the
personnel and resources required to fully occupy
every planet from Persephone to Deadwood. Most
citizens living in the Border and rim systems
understood that the Anglo-Sino Alliance did not have
the resources to commandeer every planet and moon
outside of the Core. Many former Independents
took advantage of the Alliance's weakness and
chose to remain on the move, living on the fringes of
civilization, flying in spaceships that gave them the
freedom they were desperate to protect.

EPISODE: OUT OF GAS

MAL: That's an awful lot of caveats and addendums there,
           Miss.
INARA: As I stated, I just want to be clear.
MAL: Well, I'll be sure and take all of that into
           consideration when I review the applications.
INARA: Don't be ridiculous. You're going to rent this shuttle
           to me.
MAL: Am I?
INARA: Yes. And for one quarter less than your asking price.

To 'civilized' folk, the Independent Faction represented
everything wrong with the Border Planets and the rim: the
people in those far-flung places preferred to end arguments with
a gun; they didn't want an education and didn't bother to speak
properly... Hell, many Browncoats were looters, thugs, thieves,
the kind of criminals who would be locked up or rehabilitated in
the Core. In fact, many former Independent soldiers, like Mal,
Zoë, and their friend Monty did choose to live on the fringes of
society, never giving in to the Alliance—no matter the cost. If
they required a permit to salvage, they didn't bother getting one.
If they needed an Ident Card or ship's papers, they falsified that
information, too.

While Monty's ship of choice was a freighter he could use
to smuggle and resell needed goods on backwater moons,
Malcolm Reynolds fell in love with an older model, a Firefly-
class ship he named *Serenity*. Zoë Alleyne, a career soldier who'd
fought with Reynolds in over a dozen campaigns for two and a
half years, became Captain Reynolds' First Mate. Their plan

was simple: stay out of Alliance trouble, keep *Serenity* in the air.
To that end, Captain Reynolds hired a talented (but annoying,
according to Zoë at the time) pilot by the name of Hoban
'Wash' Washburn. The three flew for some time until Zoë fell
madly in love with Wash—much to Mal's dismay—and were
married after a year. Eventually the small crew expanded to
include a ship's mechanic, Bester, who was replaced by the far-
superior engineering prodigy: the sweet, cheerful Kaywinnet
Lee 'Kaylee' Frye.

With a ship and a four-member crew, Captain Reynolds
possessed all he needed to become a smuggler—minus a pile of
credits, of course. To stay in the air his crew had to find work,
the kind of jobs most respectable people would not take on.
This forced the Captain to consider his options, and think about
hiring new crewmembers.

BELOW: Mal needed a variety of people on his crew to keep
Serenity **flying.**

To add legitimacy to his operation, the Captain decided to rent out Shuttle One. So, the next person to join was Inara Serra, a Companion who hailed from House Madrassa on the Capital Planet Sihnon in the White Sun System. Mal attempted to bargain with the shrewd Companion, but she stopped him cold. Inara, a Buddhist and supporter of Unification, understood the Captain needed her more than she required his services. With this leverage, she delivered her terms: complete autonomy from the Captain and the rest of the crew, the ability to keep her appointments, no one having the right to enter her quarters without her permission, and the Captain was to avoid calling her 'whore'. Shuttle One was to become Inara's home, and she was not interested in mixing her work and trade with whatever thievery the crew committed.

Having a Companion onboard proved to be advantageous as Serra's presence gave the crew access to Alliance-run territories, but Reynolds needed more muscle. Zoë and Mal were both good shots, but having an extra gun was mighty useful in a pinch. Always looking to gain the upper hand in a tough situation, Mal found his next crewmember during a robbery. Mal and Zoë had just finished hiding a fresh cache of loot on *Serenity* when they were held at gunpoint by a gang of three. Their leader was called Marco.

Marco, his partner, and a tough brute called Jayne Cobb demanded that Mal and Zoë hand over their cargo. Reynolds, impressed that Jayne had found them so easily, asked the mercenary how much Marco was paying him—and then bargained Jayne's interest away from the rest of the gang. Claiming he'd been underpaid with a measly 7% and a shared bunk, Mal offered Cobb a fair share of any income and his own room on the ship. Speaking the language Jayne understood—money—the mercenary shot Marco in the leg and joined the *Serenity* crew.

For six years following the end of the Unification War, Mal flew from one end of the 'verse to the other, sticking close to the Border Planets on the outskirts of the Core. Then, in 2517, his life took a darker, unexpected turn.

THIS PAGE: **For Mal, it was love at first sight.**

NOT YOUR USUAL CARGO

Though Reynolds managed to fly on **his own terms, credits were in short supply. So, determined to keep flying, Mal, Jayne, Zoë, Wash, and Kaylee were sometimes forced to take on odd jobs for unsavory folk that included Badger, a local crime lord who hailed from the Eavesdown Docks on the planet Persephone. At Badger's behest, the crew attempted to perform an illegal salvage operation on a derelict ship drifting in space—while doing their best to avoid the Alliance. The crew knew the Alliance had declared that salvaging ships for contraband was illegal, even if all the passengers were missing or dead. Since they didn't have a permit to salvage, the Alliance had just cause to arrest them if they were caught with stolen cargo.**

A nervous Wash scanned the radar, watching for Alliance trouble, while Mal, Jayne, and Zoë attempted to burn their way through a sealed door on the derelict ship using a hot, sticky gel. Once inside, the salvagers quickly retrieved unopened and intact crates flush with sellable cargo. Before their work was finished, however, Wash spotted the Interstellar Alliance Vessel (I.A.V.) *Dortmunder*, a Tohoku-class cruiser, closing in on their location. After alerting the salvage team, Wash told Kaylee to cut the ship's power. The *Dortmunder* crew wasn't fooled by this new development; their equipment picked up *Serenity*'s residual heat signatures, which prompted them to scan the ship with greater scrutiny and then deploy Alliance gunships to intercept and arrest them.

Though the Alliance cruiser loomed over them, the crew was reluctant to abandon a potential money-maker, and hauled the salvage back to *Serenity* as quickly as possible. To distract the cruiser, the Captain told Wash to release the Crybaby, a modified beacon that, when activated, mimicked a passenger ship in distress. Thankfully, the *Dortmunder* crew fell for the ruse, and abandoned their pursuit to answer the false distress signal, buying the *Serenity* crew precious moments to finish boarding and slip away.

As was often the case with the *Serenity* crew, however, things never went smoothly. Following the encounter, the Captain of the *Dortmunder* sent a flag to Interpol and an interplanetary bulletin over the Cortex to watch for a Firefly-class ship that was suspected of hauling stolen Alliance goods. Though there were 40,000 such ships in the Black, the flags plagued *Serenity* for several months. Their 'simple' salvage operation gave Mal yet another reason to steer clear of the Alliance.

Once the cargo was secure and *Serenity* was safe, Captain Reynolds inspected the crates more closely and found hundreds of uniformly shaped bars inside. Each bar had a government stamp pressed into the surface, which worried Mal. Would Badger accept the stamped cargo? Anticipating trouble, the crew hid the cargo in cubbyholes beneath the ship's internal panels, just in case the Alliance caught up with them.

DEAL GONE SOUTH

After contacting Badger with news that they'd completed the job, Captain Reynolds changed course to meet with him on Persephone, rendezvous with Inara, and pick up passengers. The paying passengers would add a little extra security by giving the impression *Serenity* was conducting legal business. The *Serenity* crew had planned to meet with Badger, unload the stamped cargo, get paid, and then fly to Boros in the Georgia System.

The crew separated after landing at Eavesdown Docks, leaving Kaylee behind to search for passengers. Mal, Zoë, and Jayne attempted to sell their Alliance-stamped cargo to Badger, but the crime boss rebuked them for running into the Alliance and refused to pay them. The *Serenity* crew pointed out they weren't identified in the bulletin, which made it harder for the Alliance to track down their Firefly-class ship. Badger disagreed: the cargo was not only hot, the molecular stamps were also traceable. In his mind, whomever was foolish enough to handle the cargo would wind up in an Alliance jail cell.

Badger's refusal to hold up his end of the bargain tested the *Serenity* crew's patience, but there was no chance the three of them could win in a firefight against Badger and his thugs. Outnumbered and outgunned, Mal, Zoë, and Jayne were forced to walk away and find another buyer.

BELOW: Mal and the crew often have to deal with criminals in "very fine hats" like Badger, often with unwished for results.

PASSAGE TO BOROS

Kaylee, sporting a colorful parasol, had
better luck on the Eavesdown Docks. Following Mal's
orders, the ship's mechanic found passengers to add
an air of legitimacy to the Firefly-class ship and earn
much-needed credits. First, she encountered an older
man named Shepherd Book. After a brief exchange
during which Kaylee noted the preacher was more
interested in the ships than their destinations, she
learned Book was from Southdown Abbey and had
recently decided to be in the world awhile. Charmed
by *Serenity* and Kaylee's sweet smile, Book decided to
come aboard, and was joined by two other travelers
seeking passage: a plainly dressed man named
Dobson and a rich doctor named Simon.

Under the guise of a friendly host, Mal informed the group
the Alliance had ordered them to deliver medical supplies to
Whitefall, the fourth moon of Athens located in the Georgia
System, before they could fly to Boros. This news was a half-
truth; the Captain had decided to sell the stamped goods
to an old contact on Whitefall named Patience—who had
threatened to shoot Mal if she ever saw him again. Never
mind the fact Captain Reynolds had a tumultuous history
with Patience, she was the one person he needed most: a
buyer for his high-risk cargo.

Before Wash broke atmo, Inara docked her private
shuttle with the ship and shared a brief conversation
with Mal, Book, and Kaylee. The Captain, true to form,
introduced the Companion by referring to her as an
'ambassador' and a 'whore', which earned him a sharp
rebuke. Though Mal explained the Companion's usefulness
to Book, his insults confused the inquisitive preacher, who
later sought Inara out in her private shuttle. The Captain
clearly cared for everyone on board, but had a funny way
of showing it.

After welcoming their new passengers, the *Serenity* crew
left the edges of the White Sun System and headed for the
Border Planets.

A MOLE IN PLAIN SIGHT

The trip to Whitefall gave the crew and their passengers an opportunity to palaver and get to know one another. Kaylee made good use of the spices, fresh vegetables, and strawberries Book brought with him from Southdown Abbey and cooked a fresh meal for the crew—a brief and welcome respite from the canned goods and protein bars they usually ate.

Following a tense moment of silent prayer, Simon Tam grew more curious about Mal's announcement and asked about the Alliance's relationship with *Serenity*. The Doctor's question sparked further discussion about the current political climate, but it also seemed a mite suspicious to Mal. What was a fancily-dressed doctor doing on board a ship like *Serenity*? Surely a wealthy man like Simon had enough credits to buy his own ship?

Often there was no serenity to be found on the ship for the crew. After Wash summoned Mal to the bridge, he learned that one of the passengers had contacted a Tohoku-class Alliance cruiser. Though Wash managed to scramble the message, they now knew that someone on board had hailed the Alliance and alerted them to *Serenity*'s position. The Captain assumed Simon Tam was a Federal Agent searching for their recently acquired contraband. Wasting no time, Mal headed straight to the cargo bay to confront him. Simon was right where Mal expected him to be; the Doctor was inspecting a large metallic crate. Before Simon had a chance to react, Mal punched Simon, pulled out his Liberty Hammer and called him a 'Fed'.

Mal and Simon were not alone in the cargo bay, however. On his way back to his quarters, Book emerged only to point out that Dobson was armed and perched above them. His cover as a Federal Agent blown, Dobson ordered Simon to stand down, that he was 'bound by law'. Agent Dobson was quick to accuse Mal and the *Serenity* crew of aiding and abetting a known fugitive, and wanted to investigate their questionable cargo further; while his true target was Simon Tam, the Fed wasn't buying their 'medical supply run' cover story either.

THIS PAGE: Taking on passengers can be a lucrative way to make money, but people are very rarely what they seem.

Both Mal and Book attempted to diffuse the situation, but the commotion drew more crewmembers to the cargo bay. Startled by their sudden appearance, Dobson shot Kaylee in the stomach and dropped her to the deck. Mal and Book overpowered Dobson as Simon, a doctor first and foremost, rushed to Kaylee's body to inspect her wound. Jayne considered shooting Dobson, but Shepherd Book positioned himself between the mercenary and the Fed to stop him. Zoë, who was the last to arrive at the scene, forced Jayne to follow her orders and tie Dobson up instead.

Captain Reynolds, facing piles of trouble, pondered Simon Tam's fate and threatened to hand him over to a nearby Alliance cruiser. The seemingly wealthy doctor from Osiris had other ideas. Desperate to remain free, Simon refused to treat Kaylee's wound if the Captain delivered him to the Feds. With Kaylee's life hanging in the balance, Mal reluctantly agreed and allowed Simon to treat her in the ship's infirmary. Though the Doctor was able to remove the bullet fragments, the mechanic was not out of the woods yet; her wound was so severe only time would tell if she'd survive.

Though the mole was revealed and secured, Mal wasn't satisfied. The Captain was no friend to the Alliance, and he didn't trust them either. What did the government want with Simon Tam? Why was a fancy citizen from Osiris so important to them?

THIS PAGE: Simon Tam agrees to tend to Kaylee, but not before using her condition as leverage.

FUGITIVES ON THE RUN

Mal, curious to a fault, returned to the cargo bay to open the crate Simon had been so eager to protect. Desperate to keep the box sealed, Simon tried to stop Mal, only to be restrained by Jayne. Mal opened the metal container and was amazed to find out that the box contained a naked, 'sleeping' girl. The act of removing the lid forcefully ended the cryogenic process that kept the teenager artificially unconscious; as her body heated up, she woke up and started to scream, adding to everyone's shock and surprise. Simon broke free from Jayne's grip, ran to her and did what he could to calm his 'patient' down.

> *"For two years I couldn't get* near her, but I was contacted by some men, some underground movement. They said she was in danger, that the government was playing with her brain. If I funded them, they could sneak her out in cyro, get her to Boros, and from there I could take her... wherever."
>
> *Simon Tam*

After tending to his patient, Simon returned to the mess hall to address the crew. He explained that the girl was his sister, River Tam, and that they were on the run from the Alliance. At fourteen years of age, River, a child prodigy, had been admitted to an elite, government-funded school. At first, the Academy seemed like a dream come true, for it was an environment that would allow River to nurture her many intellectual and physical talents, like dancing.

Unlike their parents, Simon, who had his own bright future in medicine working as an up-and-coming doctor in Capitol City on Osiris, was close enough to his sister to realize her life at the Academy was not what it appeared to be. River tried to warn Simon about her situation by using coded language in the letters she sent to their family home, writing about family events that had never happened. Simon's concern increased with each passing letter, and though he broached the subject with his parents, Gabriel and Regan, they brushed his fears aside. Simon, however, refused to abandon River to her fate.

Simon glossed over the details of River's rescue from the Alliance, not knowing if Mal would care about the money and time he spent to rescue River. He did, however, reveal a terrifying truth: the government was using River as an unwilling test subject. Simon did not know what the Alliance was doing to River or why, but it was clear they were experimenting on human subjects for some dark purpose—and he couldn't let that happen. Not to his sister. The cost was too high.

THIS PAGE: The discovery of a stowaway causes Jayne to revert to type and restrain the culprit.

After hearing this story, Mal responded not with compassion, but with a decision: Simon and River Tam would be left behind on Whitefall, and he'd throw them off the ship sooner if Kaylee did not survive surgery. Most of the other crewmembers, however, did not agree with the Captain, and Inara decided to leave if Mal kicked the pair off the ship. With a look of grim determination, Mal stayed the course and flew to Whitefall to rid himself of the stolen Alliance goods and newly discovered fugitives. Reynolds had had his fill of Alliance trouble, and would do everything in his power to be free of them.

Unfortunately for Mal, his plans always seemed to go awry. Ever the opportunist, Jayne Cobb entertained a bribe from Lawrence Dobson while interrogating him. The money wasn't good enough for Jayne—although the mercenary had no qualms about the principle of betraying the Captain or the rest of the crew. Dobson, however, took advantage of the situation and managed to slip out of his restraints.

En route to Whitefall, *Serenity* did not cross paths with an Alliance cruiser, but the ship was approached by something far worse: an old Trans-U cargo hauler. Though the ship was so old it was no longer in commission, Wash quickly noticed that its engines burned without a containment unit—something no sane pilot would ever do. This led him to identify the Trans-U as a Reaver ship. To most people in the 'verse, Reavers were the monsters right out of a fairytale; they were bogeymen, lurking in the depths of space, who preyed on passing ships by torturing, raping, and cannibalizing their crews.

Mal informed the crew of this grim news. Holding their breaths, all they could do was hope that the Reavers would allow them to pass. Luckily, inexplicably, they did.

THIS PAGE: The shock of River's discovery is tempered by Simon's demonstration of love for her.

DOUBLE-CROSSED ON WHITEFALL

Once they were safe and back on course,
Mal contacted Patience before landing on Whitefall. Expecting trouble, the Captain devised a plan to make sure she didn't shoot him during their meeting. Mal hoped to negotiate with Patience but assumed she'd have a scheme of her own. He knew their arranged meeting spot was in a valley, and the terrain was perfect for a sniper to shoot an unsuspecting target. Anticipating this, Mal sent Jayne to higher ground, ordering him to take out potential threats from long range. With Jayne Cobb protecting their backs, Mal and Zoë headed to a location of Patience's choosing to meet with her and her henchmen to conduct the sale.

As it turned out, the purloined bars were incredibly valuable—for health reasons. Each Alliance-stamped bar was filled with nutritious powder and immunizations, enough to feed a small family for an entire month; such products were rare in that part of the 'verse.

Just as Mal expected, Patience tried to take the bars and the money she promised them. Mal, Jayne, and Zoë were ready to thwart her plans to double-cross them. While they made quick work of her gang in a brief but intense shoot-out, Mal got shot in the arm. Worse, when Jayne rejoined the Captain, he had bad news to share: the Reavers had followed them to Whitefall.

BELOW: Being double crossed is a constant danger when dealing with folks in trying times.

REAVERS A COMIN'

Mal, Zoë, and Jayne rushed back to
the ship, not knowing that trouble was brewing there, too. Book had decided to check up on the imprisoned Federal Agent, but Dobson had other plans. After escaping from his quarters, Dobson attacked the preacher and knocked him out. Then the Fed tried to snatch River from the infirmary, only to be confronted by her brother, Simon. While struggling with Simon, Dobson grabbed a gun and pointed it at River. In a well-timed moment, Mal returned to *Serenity*, marched up the cargo bay ramp and shot the agent in the head before he caused any more damage.

With the Reavers hot on their tail, the crew dumped Dobson's body off the ship and ran back to their stations, anxious to break atmo as soon as possible. As a further precaution, the Captain told non-essential crewmembers to join Inara in her shuttle. Meanwhile Kaylee, who was awake but groggy, showed Book which wires and levers to push in the engine room to help Wash escape the Reavers. Wash, Kaylee, and Book performed a special, risky maneuver called a Crazy Ivan, which forced the ship to burn all its fuel in the atmosphere. There was a small chance that the move would cause a blowback and burn out *Serenity*'s interior, but the Crazy Ivan maneuver worked. The blowback from *Serenity*'s engines enveloped the Reaver ship in angry, hot flames, allowing the crew to escape again.

BELOW: Mal acts swiftly and ruthlessly—and in a way that Jayne would surely approve.

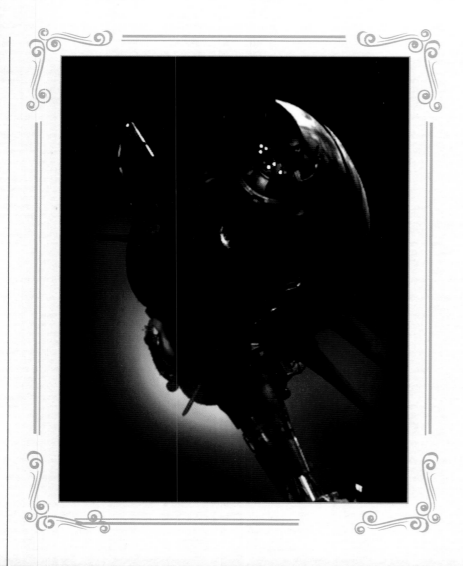

Once *Serenity* and her passengers were safe from the Reavers, the crew dealt with the fallout of the day's events in their own way. Shepherd Book, who had struck up a rapport with Inara, talked to the Companion for reassurance, while Simon comforted his sister, telling her that he'd find a safe place where the Alliance couldn't find them. Reunited after three long years, the siblings hugged, not knowing what the future held for them. For a brief, shining moment, the brother and sister had each other—and that was all that mattered. Thankfully Kaylee was well on her way to making a full recovery, which meant that Mal wouldn't kick the Tams off the ship after all.

Always vigilant, Mal suspected Dobson must have tried to bribe Jayne Cobb. After all, there was only one crewmember stupid enough to take the Alliance's money, and that'd be Jayne. The Captain confronted the mercenary, and learned that Jayne had decided that Dobson's offer wasn't worth the trouble. Mal wondered what might've happened if the offer *had* been good enough, but took comfort in the fact that the mercenary was the devil he knew.

Before sailing off into the Black, Mal advised Simon that they'd probably be safer if they were always on the move. Since having a doctor on board seemed like a good idea, the Captain then offered Doctor Tam a job, which he gratefully accepted.

THIS PAGE: A terrifying sight for any captain roaming the Black: the predatory outline of a Reaver ship.

A MAN CALLED NISKA

Always on the lookout for less-than-honest work, the crew received a tip that the crime boss Adelai Niska had a job offer. Niska, who has a reputation for cruelty, lived in a Skyplex orbiting the planet Ezra in the Georgia System. With Simon and River Tam on board, Mal chose his jobs even more carefully than he had in the past, which meant that honest work wasn't always available.

The Captain decided some risks were worth taking, however, and accepted the job without fully knowing the details. Niska, a wealthy crime boss, wanted them to rob a moving train while en route from Hancock to Paradiso on the planet Regina in the Georgia System. Niska did not divulge what the cargo was, and he expected Mal to not ask questions, either. Instead he issued one final warning by showing them the tortured body of his wife's nephew.

Mal knew that Niska wasn't the type of man to cross, but he took the job anyway. At the time, credits were more important than Niska's reputation—and it was clear the crime boss had a lot of them. Besides owning his own Skyplex, Niska possessed high-tech digital maps and displayed priceless Earth-That-Was artifacts in his office.

The train job itself did not seem difficult. Mal and Zoë would board the train in Hancock. Once *Serenity* caught up with the train, Mal and Zoë would enter a car used to store cargo, secure their booty, and open the roof. Then, Jayne would lower himself down from *Serenity*, grab the cargo with special equipment, then haul the crates, Mal, and Zoë back to the ship. After the cargo was secured, *Serenity* would fly off and rendezvous with Niska's representatives. The crew was to be paid half after accepting the job, and half after they delivered the goods.

Easy as lyin'.

> *"Do you know what a* reputation is? It's people talking, gossip, it's not... to hold, touch it, you can't. Not from gossip. Now I also have reputation, not so pleasant, I think you know."
> *Adelai Niska*

UNIFICATION DAY

Despite their lack of love for the government, *Serenity* and her crew did not avoid every Alliance outpost or bar filled with sympathizers, because it was impossible to do so. In the years that followed the end of the Unification War, the Alliance continued to extend its influence beyond the Core. To remind folks who was in charge, the government instituted a national holiday, Unification Day, to mark the end of the conflict between the Independent Faction and the Anglo-Sino Alliance.

Though they stuck to the Border Planets and the rim when they could, Mal, Zoë, and Jayne often visited a bar to 'celebrate' Unification Day on September 20th. This government-sanctioned holiday had its fair share of true believers on civilized planets and backwater moons. Not everyone, however, was happy about the War's outcome. Mal, for example, often took out his frustration by brawling with Alliance supporters like the reprobate Lund.

Though they boarded the train with no trouble at all, Mal and Zoë soon learned to their dismay that an armed squad of Alliance troops stood between them and the storage car. To get past the squad, they brazenly waltzed past twenty armed guards and swiped a key card to open the luggage car's door. Though the pair wasn't identified, one of the Feds began nosing about, suspicious of the strange noises he'd heard. Anticipating trouble, Zoë grabbed a smoke bomb out of Mal's bag, just in case she needed to distract the Fed.

The *Serenity* crew wasted no time and, while Jayne dangled from a hook, hauled the cargo up through the roof as quickly as they could. After successfully nicking the crates, Zoë and Mal tried to rejoin *Serenity*, but the nosy Alliance soldier managed to catch them in the act. Though the Fed didn't get a good look at their faces, the soldier shot Jayne Cobb in the leg just as he was hauled back up to *Serenity*. Their cover blown, Zoë and Mal were now stranded on the train with an armed squad of deadly Federal Agents between them and their freedom. To avoid getting arrested, Zoë pulled a catch on the smoke bomb and tossed it back into the Alliance-occupied car, distracting the soldier and the rest of his regiment. The car filled with smoke, allowing the Captain and his First Mate to safely slip past the Feds and return to the passenger compartment.

Following their eventful train ride, Mal and Zoë disembarked in the mining town of Paradiso. Sheriff Bourne and his deputy were questioning all the newly arrived passengers about the missing cargo. To avoid suspicion, Mal and Zoë pretended to be newlyweds—Mr. and Mrs. Raymond—who'd come to Paradiso to find mining work. They reported that their 'uncle' had suggested they talk to Joey Bloggs for an opening. The name checked out, but Sheriff Bourne didn't understand why the pair hadn't been told that Bloggs, a miner, had killed himself a few months back.

Mal and Zoë also learned from Bourne that all the miners who settled on Regina suffered from Bowden's Malady, a rare degenerative disease caused by a flaw in the terraforming process. Thankfully there was hope, for the painful disease was treatable with a drug called Pescaline-D. The bad news was the miners had expected another scheduled shipment, but someone had stolen all six crates right off the train.

Inara, who used her status as a Companion to free the hapless pair, claiming they were her escaped indentured servants, saved Mal and Zoë from the increasingly suspicious Bourne. Inara slapped the Captain across the face and told Sheriff Bourne to arrest Mal and and Zoë. After verifying the Companion's registration, Bourne cleared them to leave. He then asked Mal and Zoë for a retinal scan before resuming his investigation.

Mal, Zoë, and Inara rejoined the *Serenity* crew, but it was a bittersweet reunion. They had managed to successfully perform Niska's job and evade capture—but there was a hidden cost. By stealing the medicine, hundreds of people would suffer needlessly. So Mal did what his conscience demanded: he opted to thwart Niska and return the medicine to the miners in Paradiso.

Mal suspected what the crime boss would do to him as punishment, and he didn't have to wait long to explain his failure to deliver the cargo. Crow, one of Niska's henchmen, confronted him just outside the parked and idling *Firefly*. Crow refused to cancel the deal—even after Mal offered to return Niska's money—citing calls for his boss' vengeance. Faced with no recourse, Mal kicked the unflinching Crow into the whirring blades of one of *Serenity*'s intake valves, killing him instantly. This act was so sudden and merciless, the surviving henchmen surrendered. Mal ordered them to deliver news of what had happened, and the down-payment, to Niska back at his Skyplex.

Following their encounter with Niska's men, Mal and Zoë drove their transport, the Mule, to a spot just outside of town. The crewmembers would drop the medicine-filled crates and then notify the Sheriff of their location after they left. Sheriff Bourne, who'd put the clues together, was waiting for them with one of his deputies and six other armed men. The exchange was peaceable because, as Bourne admitted, times were hard for a lot of folk. Returning the valuable medicine to the needy proved Mal wasn't as heartless or bad as his name suggested.

HANDS OF BLUE

In their search for River Tam, the Alliance left nothing to chance. Two mysterious agents, who wore blue gloves, pursued every loose end by questioning Alliance officers and following cold trails. Simon and River Tam ran from the Alliance, but River was the only person who knew what deadly forces they were running from—which was why she was so afraid.

BELOW: River's mug shot used by the Hands of Blue.

OLD WAR WOUNDS

Unbeknownst to the Serenity crew,
Simon and River weren't the only passengers facing a heap of trouble. Turns out, some Independents were a mite upset after the Unification War ended on account of what happened during the Battle of Serenity Valley. Though High Command had decided to lay down arms of their own accord, some soldiers, like Toby Finn, took issue with their decision and refused to believe their side had given up. In fact, Finn had managed to drum up support for a dangerous notion: that his childhood best friend, Sergeant Malcolm J. Reynolds, was a double agent working for the Alliance. In Finn's mind, Mal was not only responsible for the deaths of the Independent soldiers in the war-ending Battle of Serenity Valley—he should be kidnapped and brought to justice, too.

ABOVE: The silver highways and buildings of Parsephone are a far cry from the dusty town and planets of the frontier.

During a milk run for supplies and chemicals on Persephone, Finn's men kidnapped Mal and forced him to fly Shuttle Two back to their hideout. Though the rogue Browncoats were powerful, stupid, and violent, they had a kind of code; Finn didn't want to outright kill Mal, he wanted to put him on trial for his life. Unlike Monty, Mal, and Zoë, this particular group of Browncoats hadn't moved on after the Unification War; they blamed the War for a bad hand at life's card table. Eventually, Mal realized that Finn was upset about something else entirely: his best friend was dying from injuries he sustained during the Battle of Serenity Valley—which, he insisted, Mal was directly responsible for.

The Captain's sudden disappearance did not go unnoticed. As soon as the *Serenity* crew realized he was missing, Zoë assumed command. Though the First Mate wanted to scour the Eavesdown Docks to find Mal, the chemicals they'd brought on board were highly unstable and had to be delivered within 72 hours before they began breaking down. Worse, Badger warned the crew that an Alliance detail had been alerted to their presence. To deliver the goods and avoid being captured or arrested, the crew needed to leave Persephone until the coast was clear. 'Captain' Zoë had few options open to her and quickly broke atmo to fly into the Black to search for Mal.

While the *Serenity* crew had their hands full of trouble, the trial of Malcolm J. Reynolds was about to begin. Mal tried to defend himself by recounting how he and Finn were recruited to fight for the Independent Faction—it was going to be a noble and exciting venture for a just cause. The best friends from Shadow were so young and idealistic; they left behind Jinny Adare, a girl they'd been rivals over. Not long after they enlisted, the soldiers quickly realized it took more than guts to win a battle. Turned out that the Unification War was the very definition of hell.

Though Mal and Finn left Shadow as equals, the War changed them in ways they didn't expect. Mal rose through the ranks faster than Finn. In fact, Sergeant Reynolds was Finn's superior when they were ordered back to Shadow to defend it from attack. No one was prepared for the brutal assault that left the planet in ashes. Browncoat spies discovered that

Alliance homing beacons had been planted in Independent hidden caches of munitions; the purple bellies blew those piles of weapons to smithereens—and Jinny was killed in the blast. Mal, who never knew what had happened to Jinny, blurted out, "They promised me she would be safe." Jamie and the rest of Jinny Adare's brothers promised Mal his girl would be safe as houses; Finn was convinced Mal was guilty, and took Mal's words to be a guilty admission.

Before Finn could pass sentence on Mal, the trial was interrupted by another familiar face: Jamie Adare. Turned out Jamie also joined the Independent Faction and was a highly decorated officer of the Unification War. After the Battle of Serenity Valley, he stuck close to his friends. They'd all fallen on hard times, and he'd help out where he could. Mal wasn't sure why Jamie joined Finn's band, but he was grateful to see him. Unlike Finn, Jamie kept his wits about him. He'd been out with some other Browncoats gathering supplies for the group and never noticed Finn had left. Jamie had no idea why Finn had kidnapped Mal, and insisted Mal was innocent. Finn, however, wasn't listening, not even when Mal prompted him to speak to Zoë. Mal looked at Jamie Adare. "Wave Zoë," he said. "She'll speak for me."

"She'll lie for you," Finn retorted. "String him up!"

Jamie managed to talk 'em down and get Finn's angry mob to disperse, but he and Mal both knew that Mal was running out of time.

Aboard *Serenity*, the crew had no luck finding the Captain. Worse, they hadn't dumped their cargo yet, and Kaylee reported that the chemicals were more volatile than they were led to believe—the crew had to get rid of them as soon as possible. To speed up their search, Zoë contacted Mr. Universe to scour the broadwaves to find Mal, but all he found was footage of the Captain being grabbed and taken away. With no leads to speak of, the crew was stuck. Should they deliver the dangerous cargo? Or, should they chase shadows trying to find their Captain?

Luckily, Jamie Adare sent *Serenity* a wave to tell them about Mal's 'trial'. Zoë told him she'd speak on the Captain's behalf, but before she could find out *where* Mal was being held, Finn knocked Jamie out and ended the wave. Unfortunately, Wash couldn't get a fix on Adare's location, either—the signal was pinging all over the 'verse. Zoë figured Mr. Universe had a better chance of finding the source of the signal, so she sent him a wave. That time, the reclusive tech was able to use the data from Jamie's wave to trace his location.

Upset that Jamie had sent for help, Finn was so riled up he didn't notice that Mal had freed himself. When he turned around to take his frustration out on Jamie, Finn realized they were both missing and quickly started searching for them. Mal, who never left a man behind if he could help it, staggered down an exit tunnel carrying Jamie on his back. Finn caught up with Mal and mocked him; he pointed out that if Mal had left Jamie behind, he might have made it back to his shuttle. Finn had intended to rattle Mal, his former superior and best friend, but his words had an unintended consequence: Jamie Adare was popular amongst the Browncoats, and some began to turn against Finn and his vendetta against Mal.

Thanks to Wash's fancy flying, the *Serenity* crew managed to

reach Mal in the nick of time. With *Serenity* hovering at a safe distance away, Zoë and Jayne loaded volatile chemicals into Inara's shuttle and flew it to the hideout. To assure a swift (and safe) exit, they unloaded the cargo close to the Browncoats' getaway ship. Then, Zoë and Jayne snuck into the hideout and came face to face with Finn attempting to hang Mal; luckily, not everyone was happy about this turn of events, and a few Browncoats attempted to block the execution. Zoë and Jayne didn't bother swapping words with Finn—they wanted their Captain back. Pulling out their guns, they opened fire, and Mal's sympathizers followed suit.

During the firefight, Jamie Adare took a bullet aimed at Mal. Dying in Mal's arms, Jamie confessed that he was the traitor Finn sought. In exchange for the guaranteed safety of Jinny and their folks, Jamie placed Alliance homing devices in the Independents' weapon caches back on Shadow. After Shadow was turned into a black rock, Jamie just wanted the War to be over, so he sent fake reports to High Command telling them the Battle of Serenity Valley couldn't be won by the Independents.

After Jamie passed on, Mal, Zoë, and Jayne slipped away during the commotion and returned to *Serenity* in both shuttles. Finn and his remaining followers quickly realized Mal had disappeared and left the hideout to recapture him. Before they boarded their transport, however, the chemically unstable crates blew up and killed them instantly.

Mal shared a brief reunion with the *Serenity* crew before breaking atmo. Though they pressed him for details, he didn't tell them what Jamie Adare had told him right before he died. The War's over and lost. To him, the hard choices Jamie made didn't matter now. What was done, was done.

ANOTHER SALVAGE GONE AWRY

Though they were still afloat, the crew had to take whatever jobs they could get—whenever and wherever they could find them. This time, the crew was headed back to the planet Persephone. The Eavesdown Docks offered a solid source of work for them all, including Inara. While en route, Wash crossed paths with a derelict transport ship that had been traveling from Bernadette to Newhall, the fate of her passengers unknown. As he studied the wreck, Wash did not have to wait long to find out what happened; a dead body hit the ship's cockpit with a loud thud, startling the pilot.

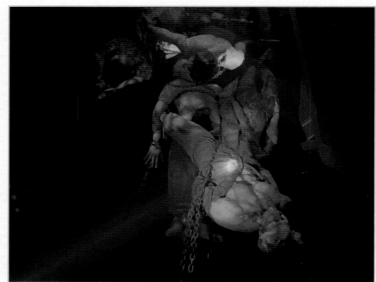

Mal decided to dock with the ship; he knew that derelict vessels often bore valuable cargo—goods that could be resold to the right buyer. The crew opted to loot the ship and found a cache of settlers' supplies: Gen-Seed, protein bars, and additional sundries that could provide for a mid-sized colony. Unfortunately, the crew found something else on board, too: evidence that Reavers had attacked the ship.

The signs the ship had been hit by Reavers were as plain as day: the defiled bodies of the passengers had been strung from the ceiling; a booby trap had been rigged to the cargo bay door; and a single witness had been left behind. This man, the sole survivor, was physically whole but bereft of his humanity, for he had been driven mad by the horrors he had witnessed.

After the survivor attacked Jayne in the derelict ship's galley, Mal knocked him unconscious. Fearing what he'd become—a Reaver—Mal, Jayne, and Simon moved the survivor to the medical bay. Simon patched up his wound, but when the survivor came to he was clearly delirious, muttering about "cattle for the slaughter". Mal gave Simon an order to drug the survivor, which put him into a semi-conscious, docile state.

With the threat contained, the crew refocused their efforts.

ABOVE: The crew make a gruesome discovery during a salvage operation.

Book held funeral rites for the tortured victims, Kaylee disabled the explosive device that had prevented them from detaching from the derelict vessel, and Jayne finished loading the remaining cargo. Before they could leave, however, they were intercepted by Commander Harken of the I.A.V. *Cronenberg*. Harken was responding to the bulletin for a Firefly-class ship that was suspected of harboring fugitives: a brother and sister.

Harken ordered his soldiers to arrest the crew and scour *Serenity* on the off-chance that she was the ship they were looking for. Before the Alliance troops arrived, Simon and River donned space suits and mag-boots, exited the ship, and then attached themselves to the hull. Peering inside through a window, the pair watched as Alliance soldiers searched the ship from top to bottom. The soldiers found the derelict ship's cargo and the lone survivor. The drugs Simon administered had worn off, and the survivor's deteriorating condition went from bad to worse: the man had cut flaps of skin on his face and pinned them back, exposing muscle and bone.

ABOVE: **The proto-Reaver finds a scalpal which he uses to scar himself to look more like his creators.**

Harken, who didn't believe in Reavers, assumed that Mal had disfigured and murdered all of the derelict ship's settlers in order to steal their cargo. The Commander didn't see the truth. He was convinced that Mal was a disgruntled Independent officer who'd attacked and tortured the survivor to finish what he'd started. Wasn't his sliced-up face proof of that?

During their puzzling exchange, which took place on board Harken's ship, Mal realized what was really happening. The lone survivor was a proto-Reaver, a monster in the making, whose mind was so far gone he felt compelled to mimic the murderous cannibals who killed his crew. After slashing the medical staff who were caring for him on board Harken's ship, the survivor pressed forward and escaped the cruiser. Mal, fearing what might happen next, offered his help to track down the proto-Reaver before he had the chance to murder anyone else.

Commander Harken reluctantly accepted Mal's help, but insisted on binding his hands in front of him. Harken still believed that Reavers were fairytales told to scare spacefarers and cover up brutal acts. Flanked by Alliance troops, the group searched for the survivor and found him on board *Serenity*. After attacking the Alliance scouting party, the proto-Reaver lunged for Harken—who'd be dead if it weren't for Mal. The Captain had anticipated the survivor's move, maneuvered behind the Alliance officer, and snapped the attacker's neck.

To show his gratitude, Commander Harken freed the *Serenity* crew and dropped all charges. Before firing on the derelict ship, the Alliance officer also confiscated the cargo, leaving the crew empty-handed.

RIVER'S NIGHTMARES

Though her brother had freed her from the Academy, River Tam's nightmare was just beginning. Her mind filled with confusing, fragmented thoughts that were difficult for her to process one day from the next. Her shattered mind, a result of the Alliance-run experiments, often led to unpredictable behavior and emotional outbursts. Each nightmare was a shard of cutting truth, offering a glimpse into the Alliance's illicit activities.

For many months, River was less of a crewmember and more of a patient, grasping the edges of lucidity until her brother, Simon, better understood her condition. Simon's inability to diagnose her mental state was further exacerbated by the fact they stuck to the Border Planets and rim, where sophisticated medical equipment was hard to come by.

BELOW: **Simon does his best to quiet River's troubled mind.**

USING FINESSE TO IMPRESS

After their disturbing encounter, the crew sailed on to Persephone. The planet, which orbits the protostar Lux, sits at the edge of the Core near the Border Planets. Its proximity to the Central Planets offered the crew a chance to rest, resupply, and connect with Badger or, in Inara's case, to charm clients like Atherton Wing. After landing on the Eavesdown Docks, the crew wandered Crius Road. Kaylee ogled a pink layer cake dress—a gown the mechanic didn't have the credits or the opportunity to wear. The Captain snapped at Kaylee, who returned to the ship with Zoë and Wash, disappointed for more than one reason.

As luck would have it, the Captain did have an opportunity to smooth things over with Kaylee. After confronting Badger in the street, they returned to his office where they smoothed over their differences enough for the small-time hood to tell the Captain about a potential client: Warwick Harrow. Harrow was a socialite with a reputation to protect and wouldn't deal with someone like Badger directly. Badger believed that Mal was the type of man who could convince Harrow to work with him; he thought that Captain Reynolds could put on airs and impress the socialite at a party later that night—one that required fancy suits and dresses. This time, the job didn't require a gun...at first.

ABOVE & LEFT: **The crew relish the opportunity to stretch their legs.**

ALL GUSSIED UP

Mal opted to bring Kaylee as his date, and bought her the fluffy layer cake dress of her dreams. Kaylee was delighted to attend the ball and forgave the Captain for his earlier rudeness. Once inside, the pair was announced as invited guests, not realizing that Inara and her date, Atherton Wing, were also attending the shindig.

At first, Mal ignored the Companion and concentrated on finding Harrow, allowing Kaylee to fend for herself at the buffet table. Surrounded by fresh food and mixed company, Kaylee was having the time of her life, despite Banning Miller and her friends, Cabott, Destra, and Zelle, who made fun of her store-bought dress. After being rescued by a kindly older man named Murphy, the ship's mechanic found she had more in common with the gentlemen attendees. Her love of ships and mechanical expertise made her the life of the party.

RIGHT: **Kaylee resplendent and radiant in the dress of her dreams.**

With Kaylee occupied, Mal tracked down Warwick Harrow and quickly realized why the man was so reluctant to associate with a criminal like Badger. Harrow was a minor noble, whose title 'Sir' spoke of his social and political status as a lord. An elite member of Persephone's ruling class, Harrow proved to be more forthcoming than Mal expected. Warwick possessed a strong mind and a powerful personality; he needed to be convinced, not persuaded, that Mal was trustworthy.

During their conversation, Inara's escort, Atherton Wing, approached Harrow and greeted him. Wing, a gentleman of some repute, knew Mal was an associate of Inara's and viewed him as a threat. Wing had asked Inara to leave *Serenity* and join him on Persephone as his personal Companion, providing the security and stability she often did not enjoy. Though Mal was not willing to express his true feelings for the Companion, he was secretly jealous of her date. Atherton Wing was everything Mal wasn't: loyal to the Alliance, wealthy, titled…and intimate with Inara.

Excusing himself from Harrow's company, the Captain asked Inara for a dance and whisked her to the floor where they discussed Atherton's proposal. Unable to stand idly by, Wing took a firm grip on Inara's arm and took her from Mal's side. The Captain told him that Inara didn't belong to anyone. This angered Wing, who took his frustration out on Inara, calling her a whore. Mal, in a misguided attempt to defend Inara's honor, punched Wing in the face. Wing took this as a challenge to a duel, which Mal happily accepted—until he found out the challenge could only be answered at the tip of a sword.

> *"Ath. Can I call you Ath?*
> Inara has spoken of you to me. She made a point of your generosity. Given that, I'm sure you won't kick if I ask Inara the favor of a dance."
> *Malcolm Reynolds*

Harrow was impressed by Mal's willingness to stand up to Atherton and indicated they might work together if he survived his morning duel at Cadrie Pond. Wing, an accomplished and trained swordsman who had killed a dozen men with his sword, had the advantage in the fight and everyone—including Badger—understood what Mal was up against. Expecting trouble, Badger and his men boarded *Serenity* to prevent the crew from launching a thrilling rescue. Even Inara, who snuck out of Wing's room, offered Mal the chance to escape.

After failing to convince the Captain to flee, Inara offered him tips on how to fight with a sword. The pair's late night conversation at the Plum Orchid allowed them to air old grievances even as they sparred. What was so different about Atherton Wing calling Inara a whore when Mal did the same thing? The Captain clarified that his name-calling was a remark on her profession, while Wing had no respect for Inara as a person. It was clear that Mal didn't like Atherton Wing but, at the same time, he knew he had no right to tell Inara what to do. Should he die during the duel, he asked her to refuse Wing's offer to become his permanent Companion.

While Mal trained for the fight of his life, the crew prepared to ambush Badger's men—but they needed a distraction. In a tense moment, River Tam wandered into the cargo bay, sliding into the role of a citizen who hailed from the Colony. The colony, which was located on Dyton, a moon orbiting the planet Greenleaf in the Red Sun System, was Badger's home world. The crew held their breaths, fearful that Badger would figure out who River really was, but the girl played her part with ease. She donned an accent and mannerisms so practiced the crime lord never once suspected who she was or why she was on board *Serenity*.

After a long night, Mal and Atherton faced one another at Cadrie Pond. Harrow, true to his word, fulfilled his pledge as Mal's second and stood by to watch the fight along with Inara. Once the fight commenced, Atherton showed his prowess as a trained swordsman. Mal, believing he could win, stubbornly lunged, unaware the master swordsman was merely baiting the Captain. Then, at a crucial moment, Atherton broke his opponent's sword. Wing moved to strike a deadly blow, but Inara distracted him by shouting "Atherton! Wait!" When Atherton hesitated, Inara seized the moment and promised to take him up on his offer if he spared Mal's life. Mal seized the moment and punched Wing with the hilt of his broken sword, then pinned the dandy to the ground.

To end the fight, Mal took Atherton's sword, cut his cheek open, then poked him twice. Instead of finishing the duel by killing him, Mal spared Atherton Wing's life, forcing him to live dishonorably. Defeated but defiant, Atherton threatened Inara, realizing she never would accept his offer. Inara stood up to her now-former client and reminded Atherton what rights he did not have: Atherton had "earned a black mark in the Companion registry," which prevented him from securing the services of a Companion ever again.

Sir Warwick Harrow was both impressed and amused by Mal's protective instinct. The noble had the proof he required and told the Captain he'd have his cargo delivered to his ship that same day for transport.

Mal and Inara returned to *Serenity* with a new client and a better understanding of their feelings for each other. Thankfully, the Captain's survival also triggered the release of the crew and the departure of Badger's men. Reunited once more, the crew breathed a sigh of relief before getting back to work. Simon tended to Mal's wounds, while the crew prepped the cargo bay to receive Warwick's valuable cargo: a herd of cattle.

THIS PAGE AND OPPOSITE: **The duel Mal seemed to have no chance of winning.**

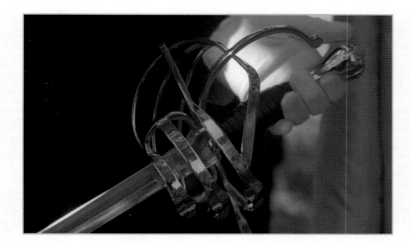

COWS IN THE CARGO BAY

The first part of Badger's job had been completed: Mal managed to convince Sir Warwick Harrow that he was honorable and trustworthy. The second part was a mite harder. The *Serenity* crew was to deliver Harrow's cattle to Jiangyin in the Red Sun System, get paid, and then fly back to Persephone to give Badger his share of the profits.

After landing on Jiangyin, the crew penned the herd. Mal, uneasy about River's erratic behavior, sent her and Simon into town. River's deteriorating mental state spelled potential trouble for the crew. To Mal, getting River out of the way, even temporarily, was the only way to ensure a nervous buyer wouldn't run off or refuse the sale.

Simon and River did catch up with Inara and Kaylee, but their friendships were strained. Kaylee always had a thing for Simon, but the Doctor was preoccupied with treating his sister and didn't pick up on her signals. Though Simon was slowly adjusting to life on the run, the Osiris native was used to luxury and wealth, and accidentally snubbed Kaylee's effort to flirt with him over a souvenir dish she secretly wanted to give him as a present. Feeling hurt by his snobbery,

Kaylee returned to the ship with Inara. Before Simon realized what he'd done, however, River had wandered off, forcing him to run after her once again.

While Simon searched for his sister, Mal, Jayne, Book, and Zoë met with the Grange brothers—Billy and Nathaniel—the buyers for Harrow's cattle. During their negotiation, a local law-enforcement officer and his men burst from the trees to arrest the brothers for the murder of Rance Durbin. The Grange brothers wouldn't go down without a fight, however, and drew their guns. The *Serenity* crew had no time to run and was caught up in the ensuing gunfight. They didn't want to get arrested either—and they had more to lose than the cattle.

The job went south fast as soon as the bullets started flying. Shepherd Book was shot, and his wound was so severe the crew worried he wouldn't survive without immediate medical attention. Simon wasn't anywhere near the ship, because he was busy chasing after River, who'd been drawn to a celebration just outside of town. River spun and twirled, dancing for the first time in years to the tune of 'The Sailor's Wife', not realizing they were being watched by a settler named Stark. River sensed Book's pain, and 'felt' him being shot. Distraught, she stopped dancing, but before Simon could ask why she was upset, Stark kidnapped him. River, who thought her brother was playing a game, was also captured and dragged off to a remote village on the other side of the forest.

In Simon's absence, Mal and Zoë tapped into their field training and stabilized the preacher by removing the bullet. While the former officers focused on Book, Wash searched for the Doctor but failed to find him. After hearing this piece of gloomy news, the Captain suspected that the local hill folk had snatched Simon and River to put them to work. Trapped between going to look for the ship's missing doctor or getting Book the medical help he required, Mal prioritized the preacher's life and decided to leave Jiangyin.

Meanwhile, Simon, River, and their kidnappers walked back to the isolated town and were welcomed by simple, superstitious folk. Despite their friendly demeanor, Simon was frustrated—especially after watching the tell-tale burn of *Serenity*'s engines as the ship broke atmo. Villagers like the schoolteacher, Doralee, treated Simon as best they could and gave him a house of his own, along with a makeshift hospital to tend to the sick. Settling in, Simon began seeing patients. Though the work was satisfying to a point, the Doctor was frustrated that the religious

community forced unsuspecting travelers to work for their benefit as slaves.

Back on board *Serenity*, Book's situation had not improved, and Mal was forced to consider an unlikely proposal. Inara, knowing the Alliance had the technology and medicine they needed, suggested they contact an Alliance cruiser on patrol in that sector of space. Reluctantly, Mal contacted the I.A.V. *Magellan*; their crew responded to the distress call and boarded *Serenity*. Following protocol, Mal presented falsified papers to the Alliance commander and explained their need. Mal was waved off—until a conscious-but-weakened Shepherd Book asked the Alliance Commander to check his Ident Card.

Following a quick scan of his personal details, the commander of the *Magellan* snapped to attention and immediately ordered his soldiers to help. This sudden change of heart confused the *Serenity* crew, forcing them to wonder what secrets Book carried. Who was Shepherd Book? And what was his connection to the Alliance?

NOT EVERY BOOK CAN BE READ

The Serenity crew knew Shepherd

Derrial Book was a preacher, but he was also something else: a man with a mysterious past. The truth about Book's history began several years ago when talk of war was brewing. Shepherd Book, who'd been born Henry Evans, was a rebellious young man from a broken, abusive home who volunteered to embed himself deep in the Alliance's ranks at the beginning of the Unification War.

To become an Alliance loyalist, Henry Evans sacrificed his former identity. First, Evans removed one of his eyes and replaced it with a cybernetic implant that would transmit images back to the Independents. Following this surgery, Evans murdered a man called Derrial Book and stole his identity. With the real Book dead, Henry Evans assumed the life of an Alliance loyalist and began infiltrating the enemy.

Before he became an Alliance officer, Henry Evans-turned-Derrial Book was a member of local law enforcement on Jiangyin in the Red Sun System. Alliance brass was convinced he was driven by a deep-seated desire to stomp out the Independent Faction, and they rewarded Book with promotion after promotion until he earned command of his own ship, the I.A.V. *Cortez*. Preferring to use his hands instead of sonic weapons, the anxious Alliance officer obsessively dogged the Independents to gain higher levels of access. In one operation, Book picked up Staff Sergeant Hope Claypool outside of their station on Dyton in the Red Sun System and interrogated her the old-fashioned way: with fear, intimidation, and his fists. Claypool was a means to an end, a way to prove his loyalty to the Alliance—and earn much-needed rewards.

During one of the officer's many operations, Book 'lost' the I.A.V. *Alexander* and her 4,000. For his apparent failure, Book's superior not only relieved him of command, he informed him there had to be a mole operating in the ranks—not knowing it was Book who was responsible for sabotaging the government's efforts. The Alliance had been hit hard by the Independents at the same time on six planets that were millions of miles apart—it was clear that someone was feeding intel to the Independent Faction. That someone was Henry Evans, posing as Derrial Book.

Book, who had been simultaneously accredited with impressive victories and the greatest failure in Alliance military history, was not given the opportunity to investigate the mole and continue his ruse. For the loss of the I.A.V. *Alexander*, the Alliance jettisoned him in an escape pod to the surface of a Border Planet. He was not expected to survive.

Thanks to the sacrifices that Henry Evans made, the Independents were able to mount an offensive, delaying the Alliance's victory. But Derrial Book quickly lost the will to fight following the loss of command. He had few choices available to him as a deposed military officer and veteran of the Unification War. So, instead of resuming his old identity as Henry Evans, the former double-agent sought a new, peaceful profession.

Book turned to an abbess at Southdown Abbey for answers and became a preacher devoted to a life of non-violence. Then, when Shepherd Book was ready, he rejoined the world and boarded *Serenity*, not knowing who or what awaited him. He'd seen enough bloodshed for one lifetime.

To the Independents, Book was an unsung war hero. To the Alliance, however, the man was a fiery legend who'd made a terrible mistake and paid the price for it. Now, with his wartime reputation intact and the truth of his identity protected, the Alliance was all too happy to help one of the pluckiest yet determined men to fight in the Unification War.

MOUNTING A GORRAMN RESCUE

With Book on the mend, Mal and the crew returned to Jiangyin to rescue Simon and River. The siblings continued to reminisce and share one another's company but, despite River's best efforts, Simon did not fully understand why his sister said the strange, cryptic things she did. Doralee, however, believed she knew the answer to River's eerie revelations. Doralee understood that River had a power she didn't understand.

After the sun went down, Doralee and Simon were surprised that River and a local girl named Ruby had left the sickhouse. River returned shortly with handfuls of hodgeberries, which she shared with Simon, and Doralee had found Ruby was not far behind. Simon was still upset that they had been captured to work in the town, and though Doralee quoted scripture, he was not convinced they'd be happy there. Doralee didn't know what to make of River; the schoolteacher understood she wasn't quite right and initially compared her to Ruby.

In fact, Doralee didn't make up her mind until River explained the reason why Ruby never spoke a word was because the girl's mother went out of her mind and murdered her sister before attacking her. At first, the simple schoolteacher treated this news as a miracle because she believed that River had finally managed to get the traumatized girl to talk. But, when River told Doralee that she understood Ruby despite the fact that the girl hadn't spoken a word, Doralee believed there was only one explanation for her

ability to read thoughts: River was a witch.

Panicked and fearful, Doralee roused the townsfolk in the dead of night, quoting Bible verses and announcing there was a witch in their midst. The village elder, referred to as the Patron, investigated the schoolteacher's claim, knowing how superstitious Doralee could be. River, who did not understand the ramifications of her actions, revealed the truth about the Patron's ambitious rise to power. Reading his mind, River described how he murdered the old Patron and took his place. This angered the white-haired man, who slapped her across the face and condemned her to death.

His decision clear, the Patron agreed that River should be burned as a witch and ignored Simon's protests. Whipped up into a frenzy, the villagers tied River to a stake. Simon refused to abandon his sister's side, and demanded that he be burned along with her. Before the villagers could light the fire, *Serenity* swooped in and launched a daring, last-minute rescue, which made the crew Big Damn Heroes once again.

AN UNUSUAL PAYDAY

With work in short supply, the Serenity crew visited a Border Planet called Triumph, which orbited the protostar Heinlein in the Red Sun System. Though their specialty was acting as middlemen to deliver cargo from one buyer to another, the crew occasionally wielded their muscle to put bullies in their place. Sometimes the crew even managed to have a little fun.

EPISODE: OUR MRS. REYNOLDS

BOOK: It says here, the woman lays the wreath upon her intended—which I do recall—which represents his sovereignty.

MAL: (To Saffron): That was you?

BOOK: And he drinks of her wine. This represents his obeisance to the life-giving blood of her—I'll skip this part—and then there's a dance, with a joining of hands. (closes book) The marriage ceremony of the Triumph Settlers, been so over eighty years. You, sir, are a newlywed.

After Jayne and a bonnet-wearing Mal successfully fended off bandits by shooting them all, the settlers on Triumph showed their gratitude by throwing them a party. Unlike the gala on Persephone, this celebration was the kind simple folk could afford. Drunk on bowls of wine, Elder Gommen rewarded Jayne Cobb with a symbolic stick, while the settlers danced around a large bonfire. Mal, on the other hand, was crowned with a wreath of flowers, offered a drink, and pulled to the dance by a beautiful red-haired woman.

Though the crew didn't earn credits on this job, they procured sundries like protein powder. While mechanical parts were in short supply—like a compression coil Kaylee needed to fix the engine—the *Serenity* crew had just enough to stay afloat. With Wash at the helm, the crew set sail for Beaumonde in the Kalidasa System. While Mal sorted through their fresh supplies in the cargo bay, he stumbled on an unusual find: the young and seemingly timid red-haired woman he'd danced with on Triumph, who now claimed to be his wife.

Confused, Mal asked Zoë to call Wash, but soon the entire crew joined the 'newlyweds' in the cargo bay. The uncomfortable situation required sensitivity and a soothing touch—neither of which Mal possessed. Stumbling through his words, the Captain disavowed his 'bride', who appeared to be terrified out of her wits. Looking to solve the mystery, Book used Simon's data sticks to research the customs of the Triumph settlers and learned that the Captain was in fact married, and divorce was hard to come by.

A NOT-SO-BLUSHING BRIDE

Mal tried to salvage the situation by having a private chat with Saffron. In his eyes, she was clearly frightened and submissive, promising to be a 'good wife'. Mal offered to return her to Triumph and try to secure a divorce, but that option was out of the question because one of the bandits Mal had gunned down was a prefect's nephew. If he returned, retribution for that act would follow. Instead, Mal hoped to reach Beaumonde and leave her behind. First, however, he had to convince his new 'wife' she was better off without him.

Saffron's presence on board and her strange marriage to Mal affected the crew in different ways. Wash envied how she cooked for her 'husband', which was something Zoë didn't do for him. Zoë, on the other hand, was dismissive of Saffron and her submissive desire to please the Captain in every way. Mal tried to avoid Saffron as best he could, and visited Inara's shuttle where he hoped she wouldn't find him. Inara didn't want to deal with Mal, so she complained about his irregular schedule and advised him to stick to his commitment. Jayne, on the other hand, clumsily offered to trade his beloved rifle, Vera, for Saffron. Frustrated, Mal returned to his quarters and convinced Saffron to find honest work on Beaumonde. She agreed, but not before she charmed the Captain, getting him to confide in her about his early life on Shadow.

Focused on the lovely, sweet side of Saffron, the crew eventually dropped their guard, not realizing they were being played. On their way to the Kalidasa System, *Serenity* floated past a high-tech camera mounted on an asteroid; the equipment transmitted pictures of the ship to a distant craft. Two men called Corbin and Breed analyzed the photos and decided to salvage the Firefly-class ship if she fell into their net.

The crew had no way of knowing they were heading into a trap on multiple fronts. Saffron tried to seduce Mal in his quarters, and while he was resistant, he was not immune to her charms. Locking lips with his 'wife', the Captain fell prey to a powerful narcotic present in Saffron's lipstick. After she knocked Mal out with the Goodnight Kiss, Saffron moved on to her next target in the cockpit: Wash. Deeply in love with his wife, Zoë, Wash babbled on and on about her to Saffron. Realizing seduction was not going to work, the con artist switched tactics and kicked the pilot out of the cockpit, knocking him unconscious. Free to sabotage the controls, Saffron deftly fixed *Serenity*'s destination and welded the doors shut.

Serenity's course was set. The cockpit doors had been fused shut. Mal and Wash were both unconscious. Saffron's next and final objective was to find a shuttle to flee in. Inara intercepted the saboteur as she made her way to the shuttles. Thinking quickly, Saffron tried to charm the Companion, too. Inara wasn't so easily fooled, however, and feigned interest in her advances to buy time. Though Inara prolonged their conversation, the pair was interrupted by the ship's alarm that forced them to drop their pretenses. After exchanging a few brief words, Inara tried to discover Saffron's real identity, but stopped cold after the con artist explained she was Malcolm Reynolds' widow.

After admitting this, Saffron punched Inara, but the Companion blocked her attack. Then the con artist kicked Inara, forcing her to roll out of the way. Instead of attacking, Saffron fled to Shuttle Two and blasted into space. Terrified that Saffron was telling the truth about Mal's death, Inara rushed to check on him. The Companion was so relieved to find him unconscious and alive, she kissed him passionately on the lips. Unfortunately, the narcotic Saffron used to attack Mal was still active on his lips. Collapsing to the deck, Inara fell prey to the Goodnight Kiss, only to wake up a few hours later.

THIS PAGE: **The success of Saffron's deception is down to her beguiling looks, her acting skills, ability to adapt to changing situations, ruthlessness and formidable intelligence.**

LURED INTO A NET

Their trajectory fixed by Saffron, the crew gathered in Mal's quarters to discuss the details of their situation. Though Saffron was an expert con artist and saboteur—who Inara thought may have been trained as a Companion—the crew had a fighting chance. After breaking into the bridge, Wash and Kaylee inspected what they called a 'masterful job of a muck up.' Though Saffron was an expert saboteur, Wash and Kaylee believed they knew how to undo the damage and restore power to the ship's navigation. Unbeknownst to them, the crew did not have much time to fix *Serenity*. Once they restored power to the monitors, the crew realized where they were headed: an electromagnetic net called a Carrion House.

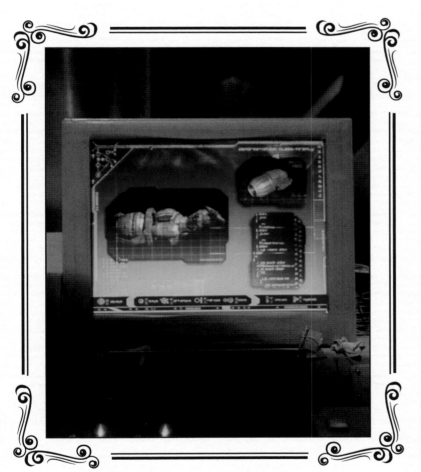

Saffron, Corbin, and Breed were thieves who wanted *Serenity* for her parts, and didn't care who they'd have to kill to get their hands on the illegal salvage. Any ship that passed through the electromagnetic net would be disabled and everyone inside electrocuted. To survive, the crew had to regain control of the ship and disable the net—but time was running out.

While Jayne took position at the rear of the ship, Kaylee rewired the controls to undo the damage Saffron had caused. As *Serenity* drifted toward the net, the electricity flared, reminding the crew they were in danger. Following Mal's orders, Jayne shot one of the breakers, which disabled the net and allowed *Serenity* to safely float through it. As they passed by, Jayne aimed for the salvagers' craft and shot at a key point, killing Corbin, Breed, and the rest of Saffron's crew.

Mal would not let Saffron's actions go unanswered. Not only did he want to reclaim Shuttle Two, he was curious about the con artist and felt he should confront her. Mal eventually tracked the con artist to St. Albans in the Red Sun System. The Captain located the shuttle, but he couldn't leave well enough alone and opted to face his 'wife' once again. After bursting into her cabin, Mal confronted Saffron and demanded answers. Saffron was evasive, even playful, and did not admit what her real name was. Saffron even went so far as to admit she worked with Elder Gommen, who was in on her schemes. To prevent her from following him, Mal knocked Saffron unconscious and left in Shuttle Two to rejoin *Serenity*.

MUD ON A MOON

Back in business, the Serenity crew flew to the Red Sun System to perform a high-paying job in the town of Canton on Higgins' Moon, which orbited the planet Harvest. Mal had agreed to pick up contraband from their contact, Kessler, and deliver the goods to Bernoulli later that week. Visiting the moon, however, required a little finesse. It was run by an overzealous politician named Magistrate Higgins who used slaves and indentured servants, called Mudders, as cheap labor. The clay found on Higgins' Moon was of such good quality it was used to manufacture everything, from ship parts to porcelain statues, and was the moon's one and only export.

Though the heist was guaranteed to be profitable, not everyone was happy about their destination. Jayne Cobb had a kind of history with the Magistrate and the town of Canton, one that he was a mite nervous about. The mercenary had many enemies, and feared his past would finally catch up with him.

After landing outside of Canton, the crew formulated a plan that would allow them to investigate the area without drawing undue attention to themselves. Mal tasked Simon Tam with a new job: pretending to be a wealthy buyer who wanted to tour the facility. Simon protested, but Mal was not concerned; they hadn't encountered any Alliance trouble in weeks and didn't know that the Hands of Blue were pursuing them. What's more, the role of a high-class buyer was perfect for Simon, due to the good manners and demeanor bred into him from his previous life on Osiris.

Simon Tam was a little nervous playing the part of a businessman fascinated by clay and often stumbled over his words. The Prod—their factory guide and middle manager—did not notice his awkwardness. The Prod was happy to show off the mud bogs to the right buyer, and didn't object when the crew left for town to find their contact. They reassured a poorly disguised Jayne he had nothing to worry about, and were convinced he was making a fuss for nothin'. Jayne, who wore a hooded coat and goggles, wasn't listening. The mercenary couldn't stop looking over his shoulder, because he was convinced someone would remember him—and his worries were quickly justified.

On their way into Canton, the crew passed by something that didn't make any sense; for some bizarre reason the Mudders had erected a life-sized statue of Jayne Cobb that stood watch over the town.

Once the crew got over their shock at seeing a life-sized statue honoring the town's 'hero', Jayne Cobb, they wandered into the local watering hole and shared a drink called Mudder's Milk, an alcoholic but nutritious liquid bread brewed to keep the workers satisfied and sleepy. While drinking, a gentleman approached them to share bad news. The crew's middleman, Kessler, had been brutally murdered and his body was tossed into a bog. What started out as an easy job was growing more complicated with every passing second. To get past Magistrate Higgins, the crew needed more time to figure out a plan without drawing attention to themselves.

Staying low was out of the question because, as they'd just discovered, Jayne Cobb was a household name. During the crew's conversation with their anonymous contact, a busker started to sing 'The Hero of Canton'. Soon, the entire bar jumped in to sing a rousing ballad about Jayne Cobb.

With each passing 'verse, the town's admiration for the mercenary became clear. Some time ago Jayne and a man named Stitch Hessian had stolen bags of cash from Magistrate Higgins. The politician, however, prevented their escape by firing anti-aircraft missiles. Jayne realized his ship was too heavy to gain height, so he dumped whatever he could—including a pile of stolen credits—to dodge the missiles. The Mudders interpreted Jayne's selfishness as an act of charity; when he dumped the stolen money, the credits rained down on the town.

Jayne's presence in the Canton Tavern did not go unnoticed. During the singer's performance, a young boy recognized him. When the *Serenity* crew emerged from the bar, they were surprised to see a crowd had formed to cheer for their returning hero. Anxious, Jayne ran back into the bar, but the patrons congratulated and celebrated with him there, too. The Mudders, who didn't have much in the way of worldly possessions, shared their finest whiskey with the man they believed had stood up to the Magistrate.

At that point, the crew's contact was anxious and expressed his dislike for their definition of laying low, but Mal reassured him he had a new plan. The Captain hoped to use the town's admiration for Jayne to their advantage. Mal and Wash returned to the ship to loop Zoë in on his plans, leaving Simon, Kaylee, and Jayne in the Canton Tavern to settle in for the night.

EPISODE: JAYNESTOWN

MAL: Jayne?

JAYNE: Yeah?

MAL: You want to tell me how come there's a statue of you here, starin' at me like I owe him somethin'?

JAYNE: Wishin' I could, Cap'n.

MAL: No. Seriously, Jayne? You want to tell me how come there's a—

Unbeknownst to Mal, the Magistrate had plans of his own. After learning from the factory foreman that Jayne Cobb had returned, the politician confronted a prisoner who'd been confined to a 'hot box' for four long years. That man was none other than Stitch Hessian, Jayne Cobb's old partner. The Magistrate, who wanted to kill Jayne for the crime he'd committed four years earlier, put a loaded gun in Stitch's hand, knowing that the disgruntled mercenary would do his dirty work for him.

The next morning, the Captain returned to the Canton Tavern and found Simon and Kaylee lying together on a couch in the bar. Simon, oblivious to Kaylee's interest in him, tried to explain that nothing happened, which insulted the mechanic once again. Frustrated and angry, Kaylee helped the Captain pull Jayne out of the bar, leaving Simon behind to eat breakfast by himself. Determined to confront Jayne, Stitch Hessian cornered Simon and decided to use him as bait to draw Jayne out in the open.

While the crew was doing a little crime, Inara met with Magistrate Higgins, who had hired her on behalf of his son, Fess. The Magistrate—a hard, shrewd man—looked down on his gentle-natured son who, at twenty-six years old, was still a virgin.

The domineering politician even went so far as to invade Inara's private shuttle. Once inside, the Magistrate loomed over her and Fess, bullying them both. Fortunately, the Companion had dealt with brutish men before and knew how to diffuse the tension. Politely but firmly, Inara asked Fess' father to leave. To Inara, her shuttle was a sacred space she had created to bless the union between herself and her clients. Magistrate Higgins was simply not welcome.

After the Magistrate left, Inara turned all her attention to her client and reassured the young man she was there to be with him and not his father. To Inara, the distinction was important. Fess didn't need to please his overbearing father; he just had to be himself. Fess was sweet and naïve—everything his father wasn't.

Though the young man enjoyed his time with Inara, their time was cut short when his father summoned Fess to a criminal hearing. The Magistrate was hell-bent on trying and capturing Jayne. Fess, on the other hand, admired the man who had not only stood up to his father, but had also given the stolen funds to the poor. At first, Inara believed Fess was describing the Captain as a Robin Hood-like figure, and was shocked after hearing the Hero of Canton was none other than Jayne Cobb.

JAYNE THE FOLK HERO

The Captain's plan involved giving **the people of Canton what they wanted: the opportunity to meet their hero, Jayne Cobb. Then, when everyone was focused on Jayne, Mal, Zoë, and Wash would haul the cargo across town and load it back on *Serenity*. Mal and the rest of the *Serenity* crew had no idea Magistrate Higgins was setting a trap for Jayne.**

Jayne gave a moving speech to the Mudders. For a moment the mercenary enjoyed the attention he was getting, but it didn't last long. During his speech, Stitch Hessian fired a shot into the air, drawing attention to him and his hostage, Simon, who he quickly tossed aside.

The crowd dispersed, giving Stitch room to address them. Stitch wasted no time and told the crowd what really happened four years ago. Jayne wasn't a good man. In fact, Jayne had pushed Stitch out of the ship from a height of thirty feet *before* he'd dumped the money. Jayne wasn't a hero or a Robin Hood-like thief. He was a snake who'd betray his best friend just to survive.

The Magistrate hadn't set Stitch free just to set the record straight; after telling the truth, Stitch aimed and fired at Jayne' Cobb—but a young Mudder named Meadows sacrificed his life for the 'Hero' of Canton by flinging himself into the path of the bullet. Jayne, reacting quickly, threw his knife at his

"As far as I see it, you people have been given the shortest end of a stick ever offered a human soul in this crap-heel 'verse... But you took that end, and you, you know... Well...you took it. And that's... I guess that's somethin'. "
Jayne Cobb

former partner, hitting him in the center of his chest. Jayne responded by lunging at his opponent, and the two grappled. Hessian, weakened by his injuries, was dying—but not fast enough. In a fit of rage, Jayne bashed the back of Stitch's head against the statue of his likeness again and again.

The threat over, Jayne Cobb was filled with powerful emotions. Anger. Frustration. Confusion. Even gratitude. The mercenary shouted at Meadows' body, wondering why he'd sacrificed his life for him, then yelled at the crowd for their stupidity. His words had no effect. The Mudders were unable to see Jayne as anything but a hero. Disgusted, Jayne turned to the statue erected in his honor and toppled it. Though the Mudders believed in the legend of Jayne Cobb, the mercenary understood he was no hero.

For once, the plan to retrieve precious cargo did go as planned and the *Serenity* crew managed to maneuver back to the ship unnoticed. Once everyone was back on board, however, they found they couldn't leave. The Magistrate had ordered the Port Authority to land-lock the ship, preventing Wash from taking off. Luckily, the digital lock released after a few moments, thanks to a new order given by the Magistrate's son, Fess Higgins, who had finally stood up to his father.

Back in the air, Simon and Kaylee had a heart-to-heart, ironing out the wrinkles in their relationship. Jayne, too, had a rare moment of honesty and talked to Mal about what happened. Why did a Mudder sacrifice his life for him? Why wouldn't they respond to the truth? The Captain wisely said that the Hero of Canton wasn't really Jayne Cobb the person; it was a legend created because that's what the Mudders needed—but the mercenary didn't understand what he meant.

THIS PAGE: **The Mudders saw Jayne as a hero—even after he proved not to be the man they thought. and wanted, him to be.**

DOWNTIME ON *SERENITY*

Though the crew was always concerned about credits, they often spent their downtime working out, reading, playing pool, Tall Card for chores, or shooting hoops. Games often helped the crew pass the time, and they also offered a bit of fun. Sometimes, though, even an enjoyable night out wasn't trouble-free. After playing a game of pool on Santo, Mal discovered their opponents were slavers flush with cash after a recent sale, men who supplied cheap labor needed for the deadly terraforming process in the Border Planets and rim.

The Captain showed his displeasure by stealing from Wright and Holder—the slavers in question—and starting a brawl. 'Course, for the happily married Zoë and Wash, downtime allows them to enjoy one another's company, sharing a love the other crewmembers had yet to experience.

DANGEROUSLY SHORT ON PARTS

The events of the past several weeks reinforced the *Serenity* crew's commitment to one another. Simon, River, and Book had been accepted into the fold, and were growing closer despite their differences. En route to Greenleaf in the Red Sun System, the crew exchanged funny stories during dinner and enjoyed each other's company. Kaylee, who'd ironed out her issues with the Doctor, even 'baked' him a birthday cake molded out of chocolate protein powder. The mechanic presented it to him in front of the entire crew, but the power failed before Simon could blow out the candles.

Right after the ship's power went out, the crew heard an odd sound, which prompted Kaylee to jump up and head straight to the engine room. River prophetically said, "Fire!" just before a fireball shot down the hallway heading straight for Kaylee. Acting on instinct, Zoë pushed the young mechanic out of the way and by doing so saved her life. The blast was so forceful it knocked the First Mate unconscious and threw everyone else to the ground. Mal shut the door to the mess hall to prevent the fire from spreading, but the danger was clear: the fire originated from the engine room and, if it wasn't contained, the ship's precious oxygen would run out. To end this immediate danger, the Captain remotely opened the cargo bay doors and allowed the ship's air—and the fire—to escape into space.

The mood was somber. The situation deadly. Zoë was unconscious, *Serenity*'s engines had stopped rotating, and the primary and secondary life support systems had failed and were not generating oxygen. Far from civilization, Mal forced the crew to remain focused on their situation and not their fear and concern for one another. First, he ordered Kaylee to investigate what had happened to the ship's engines. Simon concentrated on reviving Zoë and gave her a shot of adrenaline. Wash

hovered over his unconscious wife, worried she wouldn't make it, but Mal pulled him away. He needed Wash to man the bridge and focus on finding help—to be a pilot first and a husband second.

Unfortunately, Kaylee's assessment of the mechanical failure was filled with more bad news. *Serenity*'s life support system had utterly failed, and there were only a few hours of oxygen left. Worse, Kaylee couldn't fix the ship. The fire in the engine room had caused the auxiliary power to go out. They needed a new part, a replacement catalyzer, to fix the ship's compression coil that had finally failed.

The dwindling air affected the crew in different ways. Simon grimly recanted the stages of suffocation. Shepherd Book turned to find comfort in his faith. River attempted to console the preacher by telling him they'd die from icy cold temperatures before suffocating. Wash, on the other hand, turned to anger instead of nervousness. He blamed Mal for their situation, because their flight path had been devised to sail unnoticed through the Black. The clearer-headed Captain suggested the pilot divert the nav sats to the transmitter before dropping their distress beacon to boost the strength of the signal.

Mal's final order was to split the crew into two groups of four. Each group would fly a shuttle in opposite directions from *Serenity* to find help. The Captain decided to go down with the ship in the off chance the beacon's signal was answered. There was a glimmer of hope: if Mal was able to get help, he could call the shuttles back to the ship from the cockpit.

After sealing off the ship's bulkheads, Mal returned to the cockpit to wait for help. Bundled up, the Captain struggled to stay warm, not knowing if he'd die of hypothermia or from lack of oxygen. Eventually he fell asleep, only to be awakened by the Captain of a salvage ship dubbed the *Walden*.

Turned out, the newly arrived Captain was no stranger to thieves or pirates preying on salvagers in the Black. After the ships had docked, the armed crew of the *Walden* confronted Mal in *Serenity's* cargo bay. After learning that Mal was telling the truth about his desperate situation, the rival Captain seized the opportunity and shot Mal. Once *Serenity's* catalyzer was replaced, the Firefly-class ship could be sold or stripped down for parts.

Wounded but not out, Mal pulled out his Liberty Hammer and demanded the rival crew honor their original agreement. Now that Mal had the drop on them, the rival crew dropped the catalyzer on the deck and left. Though the *Walden* crew could have overpowered Mal, they didn't want to risk their lives. All they had to do was wait to see if the Captain survived, and if he didn't, they could return and salvage *Serenity*.

Wracked with pain, Mal collapsed to the deck. The Captain struggled to breathe, to move freely, to ignore the aching, bleeding wound in his belly. With no one to help him, Mal slowly inched his way to the engine room and tried to install the catalyzer—and couldn't get a grip. He dropped the precious part into the bowels of the engine and fell into a trance. Hearing phantom voices, the

Captain's memories overwhelmed him. The first time he saw *Serenity*. How he met Inara Serra. That lucky time he met Kaylee. The shrewd way he hired Jayne. Determined to the end, Mal eventually found the catalyzer and installed it, which instantly rebooted the ship's engines.

With *Serenity's* engines running again, the ship's systems and power were restored—but Mal was grievously injured. Though the life support systems began to generate oxygen again, his only chance to get medical help was to call back the shuttles. Making his way back to the bridge, the Captain reached for the recall switch and fell unconscious.

Hours later, the Captain slowly woke up in the ship's infirmary. The *Serenity* crew had returned—thanks to Zoë's stubborn refusal to abandon their Captain and her former Sergeant—and was busy helping where they could. Wash donated his blood to restore what Mal had lost, while Simon administered a higher dose of pain medication. Book, Jayne, Simon, Kaylee, and Inara were all present to reassure him, and they told Mal that Zoë's decision to ignore the Captain's orders saved his life.

Mal was conscious but in serious pain, so the Doctor shooed the crew away, telling them the Captain needed rest. He needed one more reassurance after his ordeal, however, and asked if they'd still be on board after he awoke. His faith shaken, Mal tried to grab Shepherd Book's hand. Book comforted him: the *Serenity* crew wasn't going anywhere, and neither was the Captain.

THIS PAGE: **In 'Out of Gas' we see the possibility of Mal losing everyone he cares about, as well as the circumstances in which he first met them, and how they became part of his crew.**

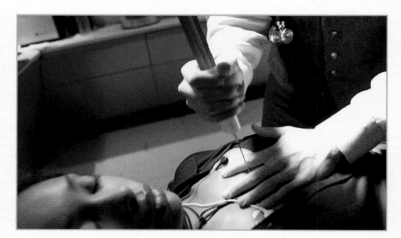

ANSWERS IN ARIEL CITY

With the danger passed, credits were at the forefront of the crew's mind. To keep *Serenity* flying they had to focus on maintenance and repair. Before they could find work, however, Inara had a mandatory appointment in Ariel City on the planet Ariel in the Core. Though Mal refused to get a license to salvage or deal with the Alliance in any way, Inara had to renew her Companion's license and undergo a physical examination if she wanted to remain registered. Visiting Ariel was risky because the planet was an important and well-guarded Alliance asset. Unlike the Border Planets or those on the rim, the Alliance had a strong foothold in the Core.

Ariel City boasted museums, fine restaurants, hiking trails, and a bioluminescent lake, but it was also crawling with Alliance patrols. So after landing, Mal gave an unpopular order: stay on board *Serenity* and out of sight. However, Simon knew that Ariel City possessed something he really needed: high-tech medical equipment that would allow him to examine his ailing sister. River's mental state was so unstable that she had slashed Jayne across the chest in response to his crude remarks about Simon. In the wake of the attack, Jayne demanded the Tam siblings be left behind on Ariel in exchange for a reward. Mal did not cave to Jayne's demands, but did tell Simon to keep River confined to quarters after noting her deteriorating condition.

Bored and broke, the crew passed the time by playing horseshoes in the cargo hold. Simon interrupted their game by telling them he'd found a client: himself. To illustrate the potential for a big payout, he pulled vials of medicine from his kit. Isoprovalyn, a common immunobooster, he said, sold for fifty platinum, maybe twenty credits, on the black market. Propoxin for eighty, hydrozapam for two-hundred. Medicine was hard to come by outside of the Core, and demand drove prices high. And, unlike the heist on Paradiso, St. Lucy's Medical Center was a well-funded and maintained institution that would not feel the pinch of stolen medicine.

ABOVE: The crew get to work on Simon's plan.

Simon's proposal was an interesting one. While the *Serenity* crew stole medicine from St. Lucy Medical Center's overflowing supply room, Simon would take River to the diagnostic ward to better understand her condition.

The government-run hospital possessed a 3-D neural imager, and the scan would provide a clear picture of River's brain. What's more, Simon had already devised a plan to get in. First, they needed an official-looking medical shuttle the crew could use to fly to the secure facility. Then, after landing, Mal, Jayne, and Zoë would roll 'dead' bodies—an unconscious Simon and River—past security. Once inside, the smuggled siblings would wake up and head to the diagnostic ward, while Mal and Zoë stashed dozens of vials in the recently emptied coffins.

To do the job, the crew also needed new ident cards, key cards, uniforms, and a fake MedVac shuttle—which proved easy to get. After greasing the right palms, Jayne secured the crew's disguises, while Wash and Kaylee flew to a local junkyard. After a quick search, the pair stumbled across an ambulance shuttle in rough shape. While Wash and Kaylee focused on repairing the ship, Mal, Zoë, and Jayne practiced what to say to the hospital staff to feign medical expertise, taking direction from Simon.

After applying a fresh coat of paint to the MedVac shuttle, the *Serenity* crew were ready to proceed with their plans. Simon administered drugs to himself and River, who was terrified of falling into a deathlike trance once again. Once everyone was on board, Mal vocalized his concerns that Jayne might take advantage of the situation, but the mercenary grudgingly admitted the Doctor's plan was a good (and profitable) one. Jayne didn't like Simon, and that wouldn't change, but getting paid did smooth things over.

Getting inside St. Lucy's Medical Center proved to be easier than the crew thought. Wash piloted the shuttle and landed on the EMT pad. After rushing into the emergency room, the admitting nurse directed Mal, Zoë, and Jayne to the morgue. Once inside, Mal started reviving Simon and River, then headed to the med vault to steal medicine. Jayne, who was supposed to be on the watch for Alliance trouble, did the one thing he said he wouldn't do: he contacted an Alliance officer. Promising to deliver Simon and River Tam, Jayne believed he'd get a big reward.

With the Feds on the way, Jayne handed the siblings their disguises, pretending to guard the fugitives until it was time to hand them over to the Alliance. Simon, wearing a doctor's uniform, wheeled his 'patient', River, through the post-op ward filled with recovering patients. Accompanied by Jayne, who continued to pose as an EMT, they stopped after River prompted Simon to check up on a hospital patient.

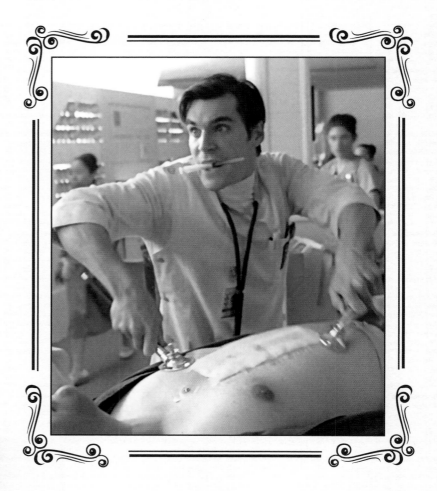

EPISODE: ARIEL

RIVER: You're going to suspend cerebral, cardiac, and pulmonary activity in order to induce a proto-comatose state.
SIMON: That's right.
RIVER: I don't want to do it.

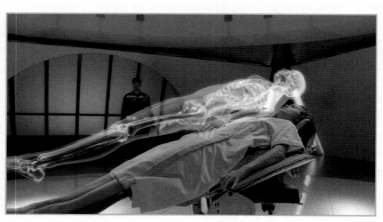

River, who urged her brother to help a patient being accidentally killed by a negligent doctor, was used to being ignored. Simon often downplayed her cryptic sayings and didn't respond until he heard a Code Blue. Rushing to the patient's side, Simon quickly discovered the doctor had forgotten that two medicines, alprazaline and dilavtin, would react badly to one another. After reviving and stabilizing the patient, Simon berated the physician as he left the recovery ward.

Meanwhile, Mal and Zoë rolled the gurneys down the hallway to the supply room, but were intercepted by a doctor who rebuked them for insubordination. To stop him from calling security, Zoë slipped behind the doctor, grabbed a set of wall-mounted defibrillator pads, and shocked him into unconsciousness. After stuffing the doctor's body into one of the coffins, Mal swiped his stolen keycard to open the storeroom but found it'd been demagnetized, so he used the doctor's ident card instead.

Just as Simon had said, the med vault was filled with so many medical supplies and medicines, Mal didn't know which drugs to take until he referred to a list written on his arm: romadyl, bipamomarinol, cepleyan, amirymadel, cimitriptilayn, hydrozapam, isoprovalyn, and fillioxalyn. After laying the doctor's body on the floor of the vault, Mal and Zoë stuffed the empty cases as full as they could, then made their way back to the shuttle for their rendezvous with Jayne and the Tams.

While Mal and Zoë raided the medical vault, Simon scanned River's brain using the high-tech 3-D neural imager and was shocked by what he saw. Someone had strategically cut into River's healthy brain, stripping her amygdala and the ability to suppress her emotions. Following this discovery, Simon and River were ready to leave, but Jayne steered them to a different exit point at the rear of the hospital, which kicked off an argument with Simon about the sudden change in plans. River, on the other hand, sensed the Feds were on the way and screamed. Her worst fears were finally coming true.

CAUGHT BY THE FEDS

Before Jayne, River, and Simon **reached the rear exit, Alliance soldiers, commanded by Agent McGinnis, arrested all of them. The mercenary assumed his arrest was a ruse—until it dawned on him he was being double-crossed by the Alliance officer who wanted the reward for himself. Captured by the Alliance, the three crewmembers were quickly taken into custody.**

Though he was handcuffed and secured, Simon expressed his gratitude to Jayne for tussling with the Feds. Unlike Mal, he never suspected the mercenary would betray him. River, meanwhile, was unable to cope with her impending capture, and babbled fearfully. Agent McGinnis separated her from the others, to transfer custody to higher-ranking officials who were already on their way. Following this, the Feds moved Simon and Jayne to a new holding facility, but during their transfer the prisoners fought their captors. The pair managed to kill one of the officers and knocked his partner unconscious.

Once freed, Jayne and Simon heard a terrified shriek and saw a blur of movement. River was sprinting away from them. Unaware that a deadly force, the mysterious Hands of Blue, had arrived, Jayne and Simon followed River. The screaming didn't stop, however, for the blue-gloved men left no survivors. They questioned Agent McGinnis and the officers on duty. Then, following a brief interview, they activated a high-tech sonic weapon and liquefied their brains.

Though they never saw the Hands of Blue, Simon and Jayne heard their victims' screams and ran to find River who'd found a way out: a locked door. Jayne tried to use his brutish strength to open the door, but it wouldn't budge. Luckily, Mal and Zoë blasted the lock open from the other side, and the crew escaped just before the Hands of Blue caught up with them.

Fleeing for their lives, the crew rushed back to *Serenity* and rejoined Inara and Kaylee. Anticipating pursuit, the Captain ordered Wash to leave as soon as possible, and told Jayne to stay behind and help him in the cargo bay. Though Simon and River were not aware that a member of the crew betrayed them, Mal's suspicions had been verified and the Captain had no choice: he had to put the mercenary in his place using language that only he understood. Violence.

Shortly after everyone left the cargo bay, Mal knocked Jayne out with a wrench, shoved him in an airlock with a radio, and waited for him to wake up. Once he regained consciousness, Mal tapped the window to have a 'friendly' chat with the mercenary. As *Serenity* continued to ascend, the Captain accused Jayne of betraying him and his crew. Jayne, fearful of Mal's wrath, feigned innocence until the last second. After professing his guilt and begging him not to tell the others, Mal explained that it didn't matter what Jayne thought. Simon and River were part of the crew, and an attack on them was a personal attack on the Captain. To underline his point, Mal left Jayne in the airlock but closed the outer door. He didn't kill the mercenary, but he did scare the wits out of him.

Sailing toward the Georgia System, Simon was able to make sense of what he'd learned in the diagnostic room and administered a new medicine. River, not fully understanding what was happening, wondered if she'd be put to sleep again. Her brother gently took her by the hand, telling her that: "No, mei-mei… It's time to wake up."

BELOW: The 'interesting day' when Jayne finally betrays Mal.

SELLING STOLE MEDICINE

Of course, River Tam's road to recovery was **just beginning. While en route to Ezra to sell the last of the medical supplies, Simon inspected the scans in the infirmary with Shepherd Book. Something about the surgeries bugged the Doctor, because they seemed brutal but precise. Book wondered if the Alliance had tortured River to test her, quoting a psychotic dictator named Shan Yu who fancied himself as a warrior poet.**

Thanks to her brother's treatment, River Tam's condition stabilized. The teenage girl's condition showed signs of improvement, but she wasn't fully healed. Not yet. Maybe not ever.

In a playful, lucid moment, River stole Kaylee's apple, a fresh and expensive treat courtesy of Jayne Cobb. Feeling guilty for his actions on Ariel, Jayne had donated his share of the take to buy a bushel of apples. The act was so out of character for the mercenary, Zoë and Wash couldn't help but wonder why he was acting so strangely. While enjoying the apples in the mess hall, Kaylee asked the First Mate why Zoë and Mal cut up their apples instead of biting into them. Zoë explained how apples were used in the War. Dubbed Grizwold Grenades, the Alliance embedded pressure-sensitive explosives into fresh apples. If an unsuspecting soldier bit into the apple, it'd trigger the grenade, and detonate inside their body. The Alliance had used them during the Battle of New Kasmir, and killed three of Mal's soldiers.

Wash, in a fit of jealousy, interrupted his wife's story. He knew that Mal and Zoë had a long history together, but felt left out. Unlike Mal, Wash wasn't a hardened soldier, and didn't understand the bonds of loyalty that form on the battlefield. To complicate matters, Mal told the pilot his plans hadn't changed; he'd honor his deal and sell the stolen medicine to a middleman, rather than dealing direct. By acting on information Wash shared privately with his wife, the pilot felt his privacy had been violated. Who was Zoë loyal to—her Captain or her husband?

After landing on Ezra, the crew readied the last of the stolen medicine, and Inara welcomed a mysterious, high-priority client in the cargo bay. The lady, known only as the Councilor, not only wielded political sway, she was also elegant and refined: two reasons why Inara felt her client was extraordinary. While the Registered Companion primarily accepted invitations from male clients, she did make appointments for women, too. For Inara, the Councilor wasn't just a client. She was also an opportunity, an exceptional person who allowed the Companion to relax and simply be herself.

After the cargo was loaded, Mal and Zoë were ready to meet with Bolles, their contact. Wash had other plans, however, and sabotaged the Mule, demanding that he go in Zoë's place on their mission. The pilot didn't just want to understand why Zoë was loyal to Mal, he wanted to end their camaraderie and return with stories of his own. Zoë, who normally supplied an extra hand and a gun, reluctantly agreed.

The Captain didn't expect any Alliance trouble but had no way of knowing if a different enemy was luring them into a trap: Adelai Niska. Niska, whose mobile base was on a Skyplex, sought revenge for what happened in Paradiso back on the planet Hancock. The crime boss had a long memory and a fearsome reputation to protect; he couldn't let Mal's defiance go unanswered. Thanks to information supplied by his assistant, Dalin, he wouldn't have to.

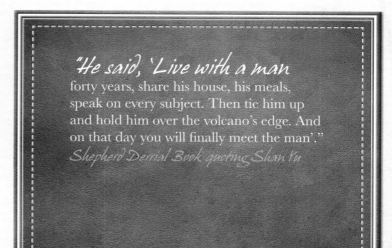

"He said, 'Live with a man forty years, share his house, his meals, speak on every subject. Then tie him up and hold him over the volcano's edge. And on that day you will finally meet the man'."
Shepherd Derrial Book quoting Shan Yu

CAPTURED AND TORTURED

What started out as a milk run—an easy
exchange between amicable parties—ended in
disaster. During their meeting in the desert, Mal,
Wash, Bolles, and his men were ambushed. Led by
Dalin, the attackers burst from their hiding places
beneath the sand, murdered the middlemen, and
kidnapped Wash and Mal. With no way of contacting
Serenity, they were flown back to Niska's Skyplex to
face the criminal's wrath.

"No power in the 'verse can stop me."

River Tam

On the Skyplex, Wash and Mal were bound and blindfolded.
After realizing who'd captured them, the crewmembers were
tied to a board and tortured. To keep Wash's mind from
fracturing, Mal prodded Wash and preyed on his jealous
instincts, ensuring he'd stay angry, awake, and focused on
anything but Niska and his torturer.

Unfortunately, their absence wasn't noted until after Mal
and Wash missed their rendezvous. Inara had just finished
saying goodbye to the Councilor, and the crew was anxious
to leave Ezra. Zoë, however, suspected something must have
gone wrong. Accompanied by Shepherd Book and Jayne
Cobb, the trio investigated the drop-off site. There, they found
crates full of valuable medicine; the tell-tale black trail of a
short-range craft; and precision shots from a 54R sniper rifle
with laser sights. The clues led Zoë to one conclusion: Mal
and Wash had been taken by Adelai Niska.

Wasting no time, Zoë opted to buy Mal and Wash's freedom. The First Mate understood that Niska was a businessman as well as a sadist and hoped he'd respond to bags of credits. After gathering what profits remained from the rest of the crew, Zoë flew to the Skyplex and tried to negotiate with Niska. Amused by this new turn of events, Niska forced Zoë to choose between rescuing Mal and Wash, but Zoë didn't flinch when Niska tried to get under her skin. Choosing Wash, she turned to leave, but the crime boss had the upper hand. Niska offered one more reminder of his brutality: Mal's severed ear, offered as a refund for overpaying him.

Leaving Mal behind, Wash and Zoë returned to *Serenity*. The pilot, who finally understood Mal and his connection to Zoë, knew that he was alive and mentally sound because of the Captain's quick thinking. Despite his injuries, Wash mounted a rescue with his wife. The crew, horrified by Niska's brutal 'gift', stepped up to rescue their Captain. Inara Serra wielded her influence and reached out to the Councilor to ask a favor. The Companion was unaware that Niska had bribed half of the World Council, and while her appearance at the Councilor's home was awkward, the world leader was only too happy to help. While Inara met with the Councilor, the rest of the *Serenity* crew grabbed guns and grenades, readying themselves for a full-scale assault.

Armed and angry, Wash powered down *Serenity* and breached the Skyplex's perimeter to surprise Niska's men. While Book, Simon, and Kaylee stayed behind to guard the entrance to Shuttle Two, Jayne, Zoë, and Wash searched for the torture chamber.

Niska, who wrongly assumed the *Serenity* crew wouldn't return, focused on breaking the Captain's spirit. Mal was so resistant to torture, the crime boss attached a torture device called the Spider to Mal's bare chest—this terrible device delivered so much pain it killed the Captain. But Niska had not finished torturing Mal, so he moved his body to a nearby table. After reviving the Captain, his torturers sliced his skin open with wire cutters. The crime boss wanted to prolong his death-by-torture over the next few days.

Once Niska's men were aware of the *Serenity* crew's presence they sounded an alarm and mounted an attack on the defenders.

Book, Simon, and Kaylee. Shepherd Book proved to be an excellent marksman, shooting their attackers in the kneecaps. Swiftly but surely, the Shepherd-with-a-past dodged oncoming bullets. During the fight, it became clear to Simon and Kaylee that Book had been in combat before. Kaylee, who wasn't used to the noise and terror of a gunfight, sank down behind a pile of cargo crates, fearing for her life. Suddenly, River appeared, grabbed Kaylee's pistol, and closed her eyes. Then she fired a single shot at each attacker, killing them instantly while Kaylee watched.

As alarms continued to blare, Niska became distracted and turned away from the Captain. Mal seized the moment, grabbed the Spider and used it on the torturer to temporarily disable him. Niska, fearing the Captain's wrath, started to slip away, but Mal slowed him down with his fists. At that point, the torturer came to and attacked the Captain, allowing Niska to escape. A weakened Mal and the torturer grappled until the torturer overpowered Mal and began to choke the life from him. Zoë, Wash, and Jayne arrived in the nick of time to rescue the weakened Captain and, at Mal's request, gunned Niska's torturer down.

After rescuing Mal, the crew returned to *Serenity*. Thanks to Inara Serra, Simon was able to reattach the Captain's ear using a dermal mender on loan from the Councilor. With the danger passed, Zoë cooked soup for her husband—a small but important sign of her affection. Mal teased Wash by feigning romantic interest in Zoë. Though he finally understood Zoë's loyalty to the Captain, Wash intervened and swept his wife back to their quarters.

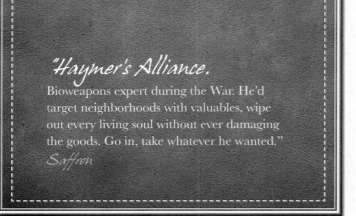

REST AND RESUPPLY

The crew, needing fresh supplies and ship **parts, left for a backwater moon to meet with an old war buddy named Monty. Monty, like Mal and Zoë, served for the Independent Faction during the Unification War. After the War was over, Monty bought himself a freighter, salvaged derelict ships for resources, and smuggled the rest. Often, the mustached Browncoat would set up shop to sell extra wares to like-minded folk, with the Alliance none the wiser.**

As the smuggler's crew unloaded his cargo, Mal and Monty swapped stories and introductions. Monty was excited to show off his new blushing bride, Bridget. Much to Mal's shock and surprise, however, 'Bridget' was none other than Saffron. The Captain immediately pulled out his gun, and Monty's 'wife' did the same. After disarming each other, the two came to blows until Monty separated them, unaware of the con artist's treachery. Exasperated, Mal explained to his friend that 'Bridget' was his wife and not Monty's. Saffron-Bridget challenged his claim, but while protesting her innocence made a simple mistake: she referred to Mal by name. Monty, after realizing Mal was telling the truth, cursed Saffron and left her stranded at the drop point.

With nowhere to go, Saffron attempted to seduce the Captain. When that didn't work, she tried teasing him, promising a profitable heist. Mal assumed Saffron would double-cross him, but a big payday sounded incredibly

attractive. After loading the cargo, along with Saffron, back on *Serenity*, the Captain met with Inara at her request. The Companion reminded him how difficult it was for her to find work flying nowhere near a civilized world. Then, Inara called Mal a petty thief, a cutting remark that bruised the Captain's ego, and chastised him for taking on small-time jobs like smuggling wobbly-headed geisha dolls.

Following Inara's lecture, Mal returned to the cargo bay, released Saffron, and allowed the con artist to address the crew—minus Simon and River Tam. A nervous Jayne, still feeling guilty about what happened on Ariel, kept watch over Simon and River while the rest of the crew played their parts to entertain Saffron.

Saffron had an elaborate plan to rob Durran Haymer, an insanely wealthy Alliance loyalist who owned an estate on Bellerophon, the wealthiest planet in the known 'verse. Haymer was a well-paid Alliance weapons manufacturer who collected priceless artifacts from Earth-That-Was, including pieces like the Lassiter, the first laser pistol ever created and the forerunner of modern weapons technology.

THIS SPREAD: Despite knowing Saffron is not to be trusted, Mal's crew are not ones to pass up the opportunity to earn at the expense of the Alliance.

Performing a heist on a secure Central Planet was incredibly difficult. Thanks to Saffron's intimate knowledge of Haymer's schedule and security detail, acquiring the weapon was easy. Getting off the estate, which was built on a floating island, would be far more challenging. Saffron couldn't complete the job on her own, not without help.

Due to their earlier encounter with the con artist, the *Serenity* crew was unhappy with Saffron's involvement. No one trusted her. After all, she had tried to kill them. The crew assumed she'd double-cross them and leave them for dead. Again. Mal did explain why he wanted to steal the Lassiter and jokingly blamed Inara for spurring him on. The crew, trusting Mal's secret plan to double-cross the con artist, reluctantly agreed, but not before Zoë punched Saffron in the jaw.

With a basic plan in mind, the *Serenity* crew flew to Bellerophon and were amazed by what they saw. Each private estate was a floating island that hovered above a crystal blue ocean. Each was guarded by its own private police force. Mal and Saffron would infiltrate Haymer's estate, while Wash, Jayne, and Kaylee hacked into the estate's automated trash bin into which Mal and Saffron were to deposit the Lassiter. While Saffron and Mal infiltrated Durran's estate to steal the Lassiter and deposit it into the automated trash bin, Wash, Kaylee, and Jayne performed their duties.

Wash positioned the ship beneath Haymer's trash bin, which allowed Jayne to grab the control unit and Kaylee to reprogram it. Unfortunately, the wind was so strong that this part of the job proved to be more difficult than expected. During Jayne's attempt to retrieve the control panel, he felt a jolt and was shocked unconscious. Shepherd Book, who'd been standing watch, lugged Jayne's unconscious body back inside. With the clock working against them, Zoë stepped into Jayne's position outside the ship. The First Mate barely managed to plug in the hacked control board, but was able to finish the job right before an automated ship picked up the trash unit and delivered it to its new destination.

To enter Haymer's secure estate, Mal and Saffron posed as florists and slipped inside without being suspected of foul play. Saffron led Mal to a room deep inside the property where the Lassiter was prominently displayed. Before they had a chance to steal the laser pistol, Durran Haymer entered the room and caught them in the act. Instead of calling for backup, however, Haymer embraced Saffron as his missing wife, 'Yolanda'. According to Haymer, Yo-Saf-Bridge had vanished six years earlier, the only clue to her disappearance being the body of Heinrich, a programmer. Without missing a beat, Saffron spun a tale about her kidnappers—a tale Mal knew was a lie. Haymer seemed to accept the story at face value, and offered Mal a reward for 'Yolanda's' rescue.

Confused but not surprised, Mal tried to leave, but Saffron was insistent he receive his reward. As soon as Durran left the room to retrieve the Captain's prize, Saffron and Mal fiddled with the display case to release the mounted pistol. Mal, making small talk, asked the con artist if Durran Haymer was her real husband, a question that got under her skin. Yo-Saf-Bridge responded by pulling a gun on Mal—just as Haymer returned. Saffron and Mal scuffled, and the Captain quickly pocketed her gun while Haymer watched. Caught in the act, Saffron was truthful to Haymer, believing she'd had the upper hand. Mal, on the other hand, told Haymer the truth about why they'd returned: they'd come to steal the Lassiter.

During their awkward conversation, Mal dropped the pistol down a garbage chute, just as the crew had planned. When Saffron found out Haymer had called the Feds, she scrambled and tried to seduce him, but the Alliance officer wasn't buying it. True to her mercurial nature, Saffron tried to seduce Durran, getting close enough to knock him unconscious. With Durran Haymer temporarily disabled, Mal and Saffron slipped away in Shuttle Two, barely escaping the freshly arrived police force. With their part of the plan completed, Mal and Saffron flew to Isis Canyon to rendezvous with *Serenity* and the redirected trash bin.

So far the *Serenity* crew's plan had unfolded exactly as they'd all hoped. Though Jayne needed medical care, Mal and Saffron were free and clear, and flew into the desert. Saffron, never one to pass up an opportunity for a double-cross, finally made her move. Mal wondered aloud when she'd conspire against him and taunted her. Right on cue, Saffron lifted Mal's favorite gun from his holster and pointed his precious Liberty Hammer back at him.

Meanwhile, the *Serenity* crew struggled to maintain control of *Serenity*; Saffron had managed to sabotage the ship's alternators, forcing Wash to land prematurely. Knowing *Serenity* was far behind, Saffron forced Mal to take off all his clothes and stranded him naked in the hot desert.

With the Captain and crew out of the way, Saffron piloted Shuttle Two to the stolen trash bin containing the Lassiter. Jumping inside, the con artist picked through every piece of garbage, but failed to find the priceless antique. Moments later, Inara interrupted Saffron's search. The Companion, standing above her, shot the Lassiter, but it fizzled out.

Then, Inara told Saffron she was 'in' on the plan all along; the crew knew Saffron would double-cross them, and sent Inara to wait at the drop point to gain the upper hand. Before Saffron could escape the crew's clever trap, Inara closed the trash bin's lid, trapping the thief inside. With the local police hot on their tail, Saffron would no doubt be arrested, as *Serenity* safely sailed away with the priceless artifact.

Much to their surprise, the *Serenity* crew won twice that day. First, they managed to steal a priceless artifact from an Alliance loyalist, a bioweapons expert who was rich through ill-gotten means. What's more, they managed to double-cross Saffron and ensure her arrest. The only wrinkle was Jayne's injury—but that was a small price to pay for a successful heist.

After Jayne came to in the infirmary, the mercenary realized he couldn't move his arms or legs. Worried, Jayne tried to ask the Doctor what happened, but Simon had medically paralyzed him, and his speech was slurred. Instead, Simon was the one asking the questions. "How much did the Alliance offer Jayne for their capture?" Simon asked. Simon already knew the truth about what Jayne had done on Ariel and had found out from an unusual source: his sister, River. Simon, following their escape, began to believe River's oddly prophetic ramblings. River had read Jayne's mind, and realized he was responsible for their betrayal. Simon surprised Jayne, however, and promised to uphold his doctor's oath and not harm him. He suggested that from now on they trust each other.

River, however, gave Jayne an ominous warning that she could kill him with her brain.

With the job done, the *Serenity* crew hoped for a bright future paid for by the sale of the Lassiter. The antique weapon from Earth-That-Was proved to be difficult to sell, however, because of its uniqueness. Mal understood he'd have to find a buyer with credits and no love for the Alliance. Thus far, he'd dealt primarily with small-time smugglers and middlemen—except for Adelai Niska, of course. To fence the pistol, Mal wanted to explore his options, but decided to visit Li Shen's Space Bazaar in the Red Sun System for supplies and a little R&R.

PACKAGES AND LAST REQUESTS

The space station moved slowly, attracting tourists and buyers throughout the Border Planets and rim. After docking, the *Serenity* crew wandered the sprawling facility. Simon and Kaylee visited a sideshow carnival, and viewed an attraction billed as 'proof of alien life'—which turned out to be a mutated bovine fetus. Once the crew had their fun, they collected their mail from Amnon, the postmaster. Jayne received an orange-striped hat and a letter from his mother, while Mal picked up a larger package, a crate addressed to him and Zoë containing the body of Private Tracey Smith of the 57th Overlanders and a digitally recorded message.

Back on *Serenity*, Mal and Zoë were surprised to find the body in such good condition along with a message containing Tracey Smith's last request. The former private, who'd made some bad choices, had assumed he might die and made his final arrangements ahead of time. Tracey trusted Mal and Zoë, and asked his superiors to bring his body home to St. Albans in the Red Sun System.

The delivery of Tracey Smith's corpse had a funny way of affecting the crew. Jayne mused about death with Shepherd Book and confessed that the sight of a body he didn't kill motivated him to 'do stuff.' Book consoled Jayne, telling him that the urge to live was a natural reaction. River, on the other hand, entered the cargo bay and laid down on the casket. The crew's peaceful moment was temporary, however, for the Alliance was hot on their heels. A small Alliance Short Range Enforcement Vessel or A.S.R.E.V., piloted by Lieutenant Womack, shot at *Serenity* and barely missed its target.

Womack hailed the ship and issued his demand: to board *Serenity*. At first Mal assumed the Feds had caught up with them because they wanted the Lassiter they stole from Durran Haymer. Womack, however, didn't know they had the antique pistol; the Lieutenant was after Tracey's coffin. Once Mal realized what Womack was *really* after he stalled for time, giving the crew the chance to investigate the crate they'd picked up at Li Shen's Space Bazaar. Finding nothing inside, Mal asked Simon to perform an autopsy on Smith's body, but as soon as he made the first cut the 'corpse' jumped up off the operating table. Tracey Smith was very much alive.

Confused and bewildered, the former private saw his own blood and instinctively grabbed the Doctor's scalpel. Just as Smith lunged to stab Simon, Mal pinned him to the ground and ordered him to calm down. As soon as he did, Smith explained what had happened. Like Mal and Monty, Tracey Smith had also become a smuggler after the War, only the former private opted to deal with highly illegal, dangerous goods: lab-grown internal organs called blastomeres. Unlike other types of contraband that could be stowed beneath panels in a crate, blastomeres needed to be implanted into a host.

WET CONTRABAND

So he could carry the blastomeres, a
doctor had removed Tracey Smith's original organs, and filled his torso with the experimental, lab-grown versions. There were valued at a million credits or more. Unstable and highly illegal, the blastomeres taxed the young man's system, increasing his temperature and heart rate. Two weeks previously, Tracey was due for an appointment to retrieve the organs at a clinic on Ariel, but another buyer offered three times his typical payment. The original buyer, upon discovering this betrayal, killed Tracey Smith's new client before pursuing the young man. The client wanted their stolen blastomeres back—which was partly why Smith staged his own death and shipped his body to Li Shen's Space Bazaar. The Tracey knew Mal and Zoë would protect one of their own.

Undeterred, Womack fired two more warning shots at *Serenity*, forcing Wash to fly low. The pilot dropped into a narrow valley, hoping to elude Womack in a snowy cave, but the A.S.R.E.V. was better armed. Womack unloaded high-yield mag-drops to flush them out of their hiding place; the concussive explosives shook the cave. It was only a matter of time before the Alliance officer caught up with them.

While Wash concentrated on evading Womack, the rest of the *Serenity* crew cobbled together a plan. Book used his resources and investigated Womack's background. After realizing the lieutenant may not be operating under Alliance jurisdiction, the preacher suggested they allow Womack to board the ship. Kaylee, however, was drawn to Tracey's charm and flirted with him, not realizing he wasn't trustworthy. Smith had overheard Book's comments to Mal and wrongly assumed the crew was turning on him. Desperate to stay alive, no matter the cost, Smith had brought more than blastomeres on board. He had delivered heaps of trouble, right on Mal's doorstep.

At that point, Mal was disgusted by what had become of Tracey Smith: he had manipulated his crew, forced them to deal with his mess, and was dangerously unstable. Mal, always one to keep a clear head, ordered Wash to allow the Feds on board. Tracey didn't trust Mal; he grabbed a gun and tried to

shoot him, but the bullet ricocheted and grazed Wash across the temple. Before he could fire another shot at the pilot, Zoë returned fire, shooting Tracey in the chest. Wounded and desperate, Tracey grabbed Kaylee, took her hostage, and headed for the cargo bay.

The *Serenity* crew followed Tracey Smith to the cargo bay. During a tense conversation with Mal, Wash finished his call to Lt. Womack, who immediately ceased fire. Tracey acknowledged the peaceful moment, put a gun to Kaylee's head, and told the Captain he had murdered him. Jayne responded by cocking his gun. One way or the other, Tracey Smith would die. Panicked, Tracey spun around to see the shooter, giving Kaylee the chance to wrestle free from his grip. Once Kaylee was clear, the Captain shot his former subordinate in the chest. Then, he spoke the truth: Tracey Smith killed himself.

The *Serenity* crew solemnly fulfilled Tracey Smith's last request, and returned the body of the fallen Independent to his family home on St. Albans. Though Smith fell on hard times after the War, his parents never knew what trouble he'd gotten himself into. To them, the young man was a son, a veteran of the Unification War, and a great loss.

ABOVE: **Tracey's plan ends in his tragic demise.**

> "*Rance Burgess is just a man…and I won't let any man take what's mine.*"
> *Nandi*

FAVOR FOR AN OLD FRIEND

Occasionally the Serenity crew set aside **their need to get paid to fulfill favors for old friends. After a former Companion called Nandi asked Inara Serra for help, the crew flew to Deadwood at the edge of space between the Blue Sun System and the Border.**

Unlike Inara, who remained a Registered Companion, Nandi had abandoned her life to open a whorehouse in the rim called the Heart of Gold. Though the Companion offered to pay Mal for his help, he refused Inara's credits and explained their mission to the crew: protect Nandi and her employees from a godly bully named Rance Burgess. Rance, who'd sidled up to the Alliance, believed he had impregnated Petaline, one of Nandi's girls, and wanted her soon-to-be-born child.

At first Jayne Cobb objected to volunteering, but Mal reminded him who they would be protecting: whores. The prostitutes weren't Registered Companions and didn't know how to fight, how to use their feminine wiles, how to wield the power they possessed. Often, whores were drugged, beaten, or worse—but not these girls. Nandi rescued the staff from the Heart of Gold's former unsavory owner, creating a kind of close-knit family of her own.

To prepare for their encounter with Rance Burgess, the *Serenity* crew landed on Deadwood and met with Nandi and her staff. While Simon examined a very pregnant Petaline, Mal and Zoë got the lowdown from Nandi, who explained the type of fire-and-brimstone man Burgess was. Curious, Mal took Inara into town later that same night to attend a Balinese shadow puppet show that told the story of Earth-That-Was.

Burgess, arrogant to a fault, showed off his laser pistol to display his power and godly 'virtue'. The Deadwood native claimed the whorehouse was a blight on their society (even though he'd used the services himself) and gathered his strength to wipe out Nandi and her girls. Mal, having confirmed that Burgess was every bit the villain Nandi claimed, left. Shortly afterwards Burgess confirmed he was the father of Petaline's baby.

Mal and Inara returned to the Heart of Gold with sobering news. After sizing up the odds, the Captain decided the *Serenity* crew would not participate in the upcoming battle. One skirmish wouldn't be enough to dissuade Burgess from pursuing his goal. Worse, the hypocrite was so full of God-fueled righteousness he'd never back down. Nandi understood the Captain's devotion to his crew, and expected him to leave. Instead Mal clarified his position and told the former Companion they should evacuate the Heart of Gold. Nandi refused. Mal admired her, and in the end refused to abandon Nandi and her staff.

THIS PAGE: **Nandi had set up a profitable and safe place for her girls to work, and she wasn't about to let anyone tear it down.**

The next day the *Serenity* crew reviewed the Heart of Gold's defenses, unaware that one of the girls, Chari, spied for Burgess and ran to tell him about the *Serenity* crew and their plans. During their preparations, Zoë and Wash talked about the possibility of having a baby. Wash was more than a little nervous about bringing a baby into their hectic lives, while Zoë said she felt it was worth the risk. The remaining crewmembers, Simon, River, and Inara, watched over Petaline, who was hours away from giving birth.

With the rest of the crew occupied, Nandi and Mal shared a private moment alone. After showing off her prized collection of guns, the former Companion asked about the Captain's relationship with Inara Serra, sensing their connection. Then, Nandi offered information Mal wasn't aware of. On Sihnon, at House Madrassa, Inara had pledged to become House Priestess. Though her position at House Madrassa was secure, the Companion suddenly abandoned her home, citing her desire to visit other Alliance-occupied worlds.

Nandi had left House Madrassa before Inara did; she wasn't as well-suited to the rigorous training and rules a Registered Companion was expected to follow. She, too, left the Companion House, but unlike Inara she wanted to build a different kind of life for herself far away from the Central Planets. After taking over the Heart of Gold from its previous owner, Nandi cleaned it up and created a better environment for her staff to work in. As the two chatted, Mal couldn't help but feel attracted to her. Despite Nandi's reminder that she wasn't Inara, the pair became intimate, and spent the night together.

At dawn the next morning, Mal readied himself for battle. Leaving the comfort of Nandi's bed, the Captain crossed paths with Inara and was completely caught by surprise. Mal awkwardly attempted to soothe the Companion's feelings, but she deftly silenced him and thanked him for comforting her friend. Despite her calm demeanor, Inara was incredibly upset and collapsed to the ground in tears as soon as she was alone.

Both the Captain and the Companion had feelings for one another, but they had a hard time showing them for different reasons. Mal, hardened by the Unification War, hated what Inara did for a living, who she worked for, and what the Alliance represented. Inara, in many ways, felt the same. Mal was a petty thief, a smuggler, a man so broken he'd never win against the Alliance—or could he? Inara did not have time to untangle her feelings, however. There was a favor to be performed, a battle to be fought, a baby to be born.

Right after breakfast, the Captain gave a few suggestions about Burgess' impending attack: to shoot the rider and not the horse. A dead horse could be used as cover, but a panicked animal was harder to control. While the fighters manned the front lines, Nandi quickly checked up on Petaline, who'd gone into labor. Inara was helping the young girl with her breathing exercises, and exchanged a pain-filled look with her friend. Like Mal, Inara's feelings were stronger than she cared to admit. Nandi tried to discuss the situation with Mal, but she didn't have a chance: the fight was about to begin.

THIS SPREAD: The situation culminates in a vicious siege and gunfight, with tragic results.

FIGHT FOR A GOLDEN HEART

Burgess and his men launched their attack **on two fronts: the Heart of Gold and *Serenity* herself. Worse, the wealthy rancher had a hovercraft armed with a machine gun and deadly laser guns to boot. Jayne shot Kozick, the machine gunner, disabling the main weapon, while Book dealt with a different threat: fire caused by the laser guns. The preacher worked a specialized hose Kaylee had rigged up to douse the fires; the pressure from the water not only put out the fires, it could take a man off his horse without killing him.**

While Burgess concentrated his firepower on the whorehouse, a small group of his men ambushed Wash and Kaylee back on *Serenity*, which removed the possibility of air support. Wash, who knew *Serenity* far better than the attackers did, drew the men into a remote hallway near the engine room, while Kaylee did the same near the cockpit. Once inside their rooms, both crewmembers locked their doors that comically trapped them at opposite ends of the ship. With Wash stuck in the engine room and Kaylee in the bridge, they were unable to provide the air support Mal was counting on.

During the commotion, Petaline gave birth to a boy. Chari, the traitor who informed Rance Burgess of the crew's plans, unlocked a door and welcomed Burgess inside. Wasting no time, Burgess stormed into the delivery room and stole the child. Petaline screamed in anguish, alarming Nandi and Inara who stopped Burgess from leaving the whorehouse. While Nandi faced Burgess, Inara slipped behind him and put a knife to his throat. His life on the line, Burgess surrendered the child to one of Nandi's girls. Burgess was a mite slippery, however, and broke free from Inara's grip. Before he escaped, the villain shot and killed Nandi. It was only a matter of time before Burgess recovered his son.

After discovering Nandi's body, Mal was so filled with rage he mounted a horse and galloped after Burgess' fleeing hovercraft. After catching up to the hovercraft, the Captain leapt from his horse to the moving vehicle and yanked Burgess out of the driver's seat. Once captured, Mal dragged the villain back to the Heart of Gold and forced him to his knees in front of Petaline and the newborn babe. The young mother introduced her son, Jonah, to his father, and then executed him. Taking charge, Petaline ordered Burgess' men to leave along with Chari, whose betrayal cut so deep she was no longer welcome at the ranch.

Before the *Serenity* crew broke atmo, they attended a funeral for Nandi. Lucy sung 'Amazing Grace', an old, beautiful song from Earth-That-Was to mark the former Companion's passing. The death of Nandi affected Mal, forcing him to rethink how he was treating Inara. He tried to broach the subject of their relationship, and believed Inara understood his meaning. Inara reflected on the life and home Nandi created for herself, the family she was bound to, the ties that kept them close. Then, before admitting the truth about how she felt, Inara shocked the Captain and told him she was leaving *Serenity*, and broke his heart.

A SEA OF THOUGHTS AND FEELINGS

Sailing past Deadwood into the Black
toward New Melbourne in the Red Sun System, the
Serenity crewmembers broke from their normal
routine to enjoy one another's company. River,
the lone crewmember who still felt out of place,
wandered the ship, observing the rest of the crew.
Simon shared a funny anecdote with Kaylee about
medical school and the evils of too much sake. During
the conversation, River imagined Simon 'looking' at
her, telling her he'd be back on Osiris in Capitol City
if it wasn't for her.

As she walked through *Serenity*'s halls, River encountered each
crewmember 'telling' her their thoughts and feelings. Jayne
confessed to Mal what had happened on Ariel, and Shepherd
Book said he didn't care if she was innocent or not. Drunk
on emotion, River paused to 'feel' Zoë and Wash enjoying a
moment of marital bliss while, in sharp contrast, Mal and Inara
dealt with their unspoken feelings for one another.

Overwhelmed with strange thoughts and powerful feelings,
River fled to the unoccupied cargo bay, to catch a break from
'reading' the crew. There, after seeing herself on a leaf-strewn
deck, River spotted a tree branch and picked it up. After doing
so, her vision shattered, forcing her back to reality. When
she regained her perspective, River realized the tree branch
she'd grabbed wasn't a harmless object after all, it was one of
Jayne's pistols. She was no longer alone, either. The crew had
surrounded her and were urging her to drop the gun. Confused
and bewildered, River froze until Mal took the gun. The
Captain quickly inspected it and, after discovering it was loaded
and ready to fire, he scolded her for handling a loaded weapon.
Scared and distressed, River ran back to her room, claiming it
was getting very, very crowded.

The incident worried the crew and forced them to face the
possibility of leaving River Tam and her brother behind. The idea
of River handling a gun concerned everyone, especially Zoë. After
wondering aloud whether River had experience with a pistol,
Kaylee confessed what had happened back on Niska's Skyplex.
Kaylee relayed how River saved her life, and how she easily killed
each opponent with a single shot with her eyes closed. Upon
hearing this news, the crew speculated as to the nature of River's
abilities. Was she a reader? Psychic? Though Simon objected
to their claims, the crew wondered if River would put them in
harm's way.

THIS PAGE: Here we catch a glimpse of what River sees with her
troubled mind, and the danger and confusion that can come from it.

ANOTHER PAIR OF EARS

Serenity's crewmembers believed they were having a private conversation, but they were not alone. River Tam had returned to the cargo bay, and was listening to them. Another person, however, was also eavesdropping: a bounty hunter named Jubal Early, who'd been hired by the Alliance to capture River and Simon. While the crew talked, Early breached *Serenity*'s hull and waited for an opportune moment to slip inside.

River Tam's presence on board continued to be disruptive, but the decision to remove her and her brother was ultimately up to the Captain. Mal postponed the matter, saying that the decision to abandon them was a serious one, and told them he'd sleep on it. Taking a break from the tension, Kaylee and Simon checked up on River. The two shared their regrets: Kaylee was sorry she revealed the truth about River's abilities, and Simon felt bad because he couldn't successfully treat her. There were too many unknowns, too many questions, too many possibilities.

After the crew fell asleep in their quarters, Jubal Early made his move. First, he ambushed the Captain, knocked him unconscious, shoved his body into his cabin and locked the door. Then he secured Wash, Zoë, and Jayne in their quarters. With half the crew out of commission, Early headed to the engine room to frighten Kaylee. Afraid of the bounty hunter's violent threats, she surrendered and allowed herself to be tied up. Three crewmembers, Simon, River, and Book, were left. Early dealt with the preacher first by kicking him in the head and locking him up.

Alarmed, Simon Tam rushed to check up on his sister—only to come face to face with Jubal Early. The bounty hunter referred to Simon by name and demanded River Tam's location. Simon resisted until Early reiterated his threats to kill him and rape Kaylee if he refused. Reluctantly, Simon agreed to help. The alternative wasn't acceptable, so he had no choice but to play along.

The Doctor 'helped' Early tour the ship to find River. First, they inspected the cargo bay, then moved on to the shuttles. Inara emerged from Shuttle One, and tried to reason with Early. For intervening, Early smacked her across the face and then locked the Companion in her shuttle. At that point, the only place the bounty hunter hadn't searched was the bridge. Still on the loose, River spoke to Early over the ship's comms. Early responded by threatening Simon again, telling River he'd murder her brother if she didn't come forward.

AT ONE WITH *SERENITY*

Stalling for time, River told Jubal

Early how she felt unwanted on the ship, but couldn't leave. Instead, she melted away, and 'merged' with *Serenity*, pretending to meld with the ship. The bounty hunter was dubious of her claims, especially after River fell silent. Unbeknownst to Early, River had the upper hand. When she wasn't addressing Early, she was talking via the intercom to the other crewmembers who were slowly coming to. First, River talked to Kaylee, reassuring her and asking for her help. After the mechanic freed herself, River asked her to unlock the other cabin doors to release the rest of the crew.

Meanwhile, River continued to confuse Jubal Early by revealing truths about the bounty hunter and his fragmented mind, slowly convincing him that she had found a way to become part of *Serenity*. While Early was distracted, River bought precious time and informed the *Serenity* crewmembers of her plan, one that didn't require guns. It took Jubal Early a long time to piece together where his mark was: River Tam had managed to sneak onto his ship and was peering back at him through the cockpit window.

Upset by this new development, Early wasn't sure what to do. River, on the other hand, surprised him by surrendering herself. She told Early she'd leave with him, and admitted she was as dangerous as he was.

Simon, who couldn't bear the thought of being separated from River, refused to let Early escape. He tried to overpower Early, but the bounty hunter was a better fighter and shot the Doctor in his upper thigh. Convinced River Tam would leave with him, Early left the Doctor behind in the cockpit, and trekked back to his ship. Before he left *Serenity*, however, Mal ambushed the bounty hunter and shoved him into the blackness of space. Then the Captain welcomed River Tam with open arms as she floated back to *Serenity* after Early was safely gone. This time, Simon didn't have to rescue her. This time, she saved herself—which was her plan all along.

The crisis brought the *Serenity* crew together in unexpected ways. Zoë helped Simon remove the bullet from his leg, Jayne gave Book a hard time, and Kaylee played jacks with River. River's defeat of Jubal Early had somehow managed to reassure the crew that she was not as unstable as they'd believed. Their lives having been saved by River's quick thinking, Mal opted to keep both her and her brother on board, not realizing Early survived.

By this point the *Serenity* crew had flown together for many months. They were family, friends, lovers...and were about to be separated. Inara Serra had told Mal she wanted to leave, but the Captain prolonged her request as much as possible, trying to find the means to tell her how he felt, to convince her to stay. Book, on the other hand, wanted to become a bigger part of the crew, and tried his hand at a little crime—a decision he'd later regret.

A TAINTED FLOCK

The Serenity crew had flown to Constance **in the Kalidasa System to rip off another bank. This time, Shepherd Book provided the distraction the crew needed: he gave a sermon to the faithful while Mal, Zoë, and Jayne dealt with a local gang run by a man named Ott. Ott had gotten word of Mal's plans, and plotted to intercept the crew and swipe their loot.**

Ott, a fierce individual, was well-armed and had the advantage. He confronted the *Serenity* crew during the heist and demanded the payload and the Captain's Liberty Hammer. Though Mal was prepared to walk away from the money to save his crew, he was not about to give up his favorite gun. The pistol was one he'd used in the Unification War, and it had special meaning.

Feigning surrender, the Captain dropped his gun but then kicked it into Ott's face so hard a few of his teeth fell out. The gang leader told his crew to open fire and managed to retrieve the money and retreat with it. Mal, Zoë, and Jayne tried to pursue them, but Ott had anticipated their every move. The townsfolk heard the commotion and left their pews to fetch their guns—abandoning Shepherd Book. Before Ott broke atmo, he lied to the townspeople and told them the source of the gunfire: the *Serenity* crew had ripped off the bank.

Unaware that Ott had their money, the town wanted to rain down justice on Mal, Zoë, and Jayne—but they never got the chance. As soon as he heard bullets flying, Book grabbed a transport, intercepted the crewmembers, and then drove off to find *Serenity*. With the townsfolk hot on their tail, Mal contacted Wash and told them they needed to make a quick getaway. Reviewing their options, Wash and Kaylee performed a maneuver to knock over a water tower; the force of the water stunned the townsfolk but didn't kill them. This allowed Mal and the rest of the crew to make a clean getaway.

THIS SPREAD: One by one, Early disabled the crew until only he and River were left, each trying to outwit the other.

OPERATION: RECAPTURE RIVER

The Operative, one of the Alliance's best and most capable special agents, flew to a secure Alliance facility to talk to Doctor Mathias and review the footage of River Tam's escape in the Records Room.

While retracing Simon Tam's steps, the Operative learned he'd infiltrated the facility by posing as an inspector who was interested in a status update. Doctor Mathias, eager to talk about his work, chattered about River's prowess, never once suspecting Simon was there to rescue his captive. Simon listened to the doctor until the time was right, and then slammed a baton into the ground. The top popped off, flew over their heads, and emitted a circle of blue light that washed over the room's occupants and knocked out the Academy workers.

With the first part of his plan complete, Simon woke River up and took off his officer's uniform. Disguised as an orderly, Simon simply had to find the way out—before the Alliance caught up with them. The siblings heard movement. Someone was coming. River cryptically noted the Feds were aware of his presence, and climbed up and over some lab equipment to reach the top of the corridor. Graceful and limber, River braced her legs in a perfect split against the walls, grabbing on to a sprinkler head for extra support to avoid detection by the doctors milling about in the hallway. Luckily for Simon, the doctors never noticed the lone orderly, and didn't suspect their prized pupil was seconds away from escaping.

As soon as the doctors passed by, the siblings climbed into a ventilation shaft and moved toward a window. After slipping through, Simon shut the pane behind him and wedged his baton into the handle, preventing the facility's agents from following them. The pair were almost at the rendezvous point when the staff caught up with them. Security fired at Simon and River Tam, but their lasers were not effective against the glass. Simon and River climbed up on a small platform that had been lowered down to them, and were quickly hauled up ten storeys to a waiting ship. The doctor from Osiris had done the impossible: he had managed to break into a secure Alliance facility to rescue his sister without getting captured or killed.

The Operative chastised Doctor Mathias and accused him of being sloppy. Prideful to a fault, the doctor had allowed key members of Parliament to inspect his work on River, not realizing the ramifications of putting them in the same room as a psychic: River had gleaned secrets from their minds, information that could bring down the Alliance if it fell into the wrong hands. Doctor Mathias disagreed, theorizing that the knowledge River carried was buried underneath layers of her subconscious.

To the Alliance, however, Mathias' sloppiness was a crime that could not go unpunished. The Operative drew his sword and killed the doctor's bodyguards. Mathias turned to flee, but didn't get far—the Operative hit him on a pressure point and paralyzed him instantly. Then the agent knelt beside his upright sword, planted hilt-first on the ground, and waited for the doctor to fall on the tip, giving Mathias what he called a 'good death'.

BELOW: The Operative provides the good doctor with a 'good death'.

RIVER TAM SESSIONS

The Anglo-Sino Alliance experimented on its most talented subjects, creating an elite group of sleeper agents who'd be activated with a trigger word or phrase, using drugs like delcium to manipulate a victim's subconscious. Under the guise of an Academy, the government accepted 'willing' volunteers, and then slowly forced them to obey their every command using subliminal messages while they slept.

As part of these experiments, the Alliance recorded their progress to continually update Parliament. To date, four such sessions recorded by Doctor Mathias have surfaced: R. Tam Sessions No. 1, 22, 165, and parts 1 and 2 of 416.

The sessions revealed River Tam's transformation from a gifted, intuitive, fourteen-year-old student, to an unstable experimental subject, to a deadly psychic assassin. In one session, it was clear River Tam had suffered a psychotic break; she hysterically babbled about the mattress she'd cut up and the 'pea' (Miranda) that'd been affecting her mind. In another, River followed Doctor Mathias' orders and killed her interviewer, never fully understanding why.

Meanwhile, the Serenity crew did what they always did: a little crime. They expected the Alliance would continue pursuing Simon and River, and kept moving to avoid being captured. Still, their crew was smaller than it had been in the past several months. Shepherd Derrial Book had left *Serenity* to live on Haven in the Blue Sun System, and Inara Serra decided to work at a remote Companion Training House high in the mountains with her dear friend Sheydra. The rest of the crew stuck to the Border Planets, knocking off the occasional bank or smuggling cargo.

Mal and the crew did have some luck. They managed to sell the Lassiter and used the proceeds of the sale to renovate sections of the ship, but credits never last and the Captain had a reputation. He'd been Bound by Law five times for smuggling and tax evasion, which clearly put him in the category of petty thief as Inara had once claimed. Worse, the Firefly-class model was an older ship that could only be repaired provided Kaylee had the parts to fix her. *Serenity* needed a mechanic's touch, but there was no time and no way to work on her. Bound for a desert on Lilac, the crew planned to rip off another bank for their contacts Fanty and Mingo Rample.

Like so many of their jobs, Mal enjoyed sticking it to the Feds; the specifics of the crew's new heist targeted the Alliance where it'd hurt. The government couldn't possibly reach every planet and moon on the 'verse, so it often employed backwater outfits to do its dirty work for them. That said, an Alliance-funded security company would likely be too embarrassed to report the theft of their payroll.

The job was easy, but *Serenity* was in worse shape than the crew thought. The stress of re-entering Lilac's atmosphere caused the primary buffer panel to come loose. Though Kaylee had double-checked the entry couplings, the panel fell off during a rough landing in a desert gulch. Pressing forward, Mal ordered River to come along because he thought she was a Reader. The Captain had seen and heard too many things to believe otherwise, and was convinced she'd be useful.

Though Simon protested, River, Zoë, Jayne, and Mal drove out to the Trading Station on the Mule. The Captain encountered a little resistance, but nothing they couldn't handle. He'd found a trade agent who led them straight to the vault and an armed guard. Turned out the vault wasn't something the crew had seen before. It was Alliance tech, the kind of safe they'd expect to see in the Core. Sure, they needed a password, but after Jayne fired his gun the guard was happy to cooperate.

While Mal, Zoë, and Jayne robbed the bank, River was on the lookout for Feds or rival crews. Though the job was easy, River not only sensed trouble, she'd managed to read the mind of a local 'brave hero', too. Then she found something else. Reavers were a-coming their way. Looking to protect the town and his crew,

Mal yelled at the guard to lock up the townsfolk in the vault and stay down there provided they had air to breathe. Next, the crew hopped on the Mule with the loot as fast as they could—but couldn't leave. Not yet. One of the townsfolk grabbed the back of the Mule and begged Mal to take him along, but the Captain was resolute. The Reaver ship, a predatory mess of parts and war paint, roared over their heads. The man wouldn't budge, however, and the Captain had no choice but to kick the young man off the Mule and watch as four Reavers grabbed him. Mal shot him twice in the chest as an act of mercy, knowing what the Reavers do to their victims.

Unfortunately, the *Serenity* crewmembers weren't free of the Reavers just yet. The Reaver skiff doggedly pursued them as they fled. Jayne shot at the ship, wondering why the Reavers hadn't blown them to bits. River supplied a terrifying answer: the Reavers wanted to eat them alive. Their only chance was a thrillin' rescue. Zoë radioed Wash, and told him they'd been hit by Reavers. Wash scrambled, put *Serenity* back in the air and moved to intercept them. The Reavers, however, had a few nasty tricks up their sleeves. During their pursuit, they shot a harpoon, penetrated Jayne's leg, and started to reel his body toward them; Jayne flew off the back of the Mule, and hung on to it for dear life. The Captain reacted quickly, aimed his Liberty Hammer at the rope, and fired

three times. The first two shots missed, but the last one split the rope in two. The Mule pitched forward, and Mal hauled Jayne back inside.

With moments to spare, Wash told Zoë to head for the flats and swing around. Simon opened the bay doors to help Wash perform a special maneuver called a Barn Swallow. After swooping up the passengers, cargo, and Mule inside, Wash punched the accelerator—but he couldn't get the altitude he needed. *Serenity* slammed into the Reaver ship; the impact tore it apart and dumped flaming wreckage down onto the planet's surface. Worse, unbeknownst to the crew, a lone Reaver snuck into the cargo bay. Before Simon could react, he shut the cargo bay doors and put out the Mule's engine fire with spurts of carbon dioxide.

Wash's maneuver wasn't perfect; the Mule had crashed into the ship and started a fire. What's more, everyone but River had been thrown from the damaged Mule. As Kaylee wondered aloud if Simon was all right, the Reaver lunged at the Captain—and was shot simultaneously by Mal, Zoë, and Jayne.

THIS PAGE: **Even by the *Serenity*'s crew's standards, this was a real skin-of-their-teeth escape.**

BEAUMONDE

With the loot burning a hole in their hull, **the *Serenity* crew flew back to Beaumonde to meet with Fanty and Mingo. Though they had survived the Reaver attack, Mal's bristly attitude pushed the crewmembers away. Simon decided it was finally time for him and River to leave *Serenity*, and Zoë voiced her objections to Mal's brutal decision to leave the young man behind for the Reavers. Though Mal did shoot the victim before the Reavers tortured him, his behavior frustrated the First Mate. Didn't they always pledge to leave no man behind?**

True to his word, both Simon and River left the ship as soon as they arrived on Beaumonde in the Kalidasa System—much to Kaylee's disappointment.

After an awkward send off, the five remaining *Serenity* crewmembers—Mal, Zoë, Wash, Kaylee, and Jayne—visited a bar called the Maidenhead to wait for their contact. Kaylee was noticeably upset about Simon's departure, and was angry at the Captain's harsh mannerisms. She told Mal off, and didn't let his cutting remarks get under her skin. Instead, she pointed out that he was a hypocrite. The Captain had no right to tell Kaylee that Simon didn't stay simply because he didn't want her badly enough; Mal had pushed Inara away because of the way he treated her. Then, the mechanic stormed off.

After Kaylee left, Mal sent Zoë and Wash off to have a romantic meal while he and Jayne met with the twins, Fanty and Mingo Rample, to discuss payment. To avoid the eyes of the Alliance, the twins paid a dancing girl to perform in front of the security feed and block the camera. Though Mal was ready to close the deal, the Rample brothers wouldn't accept their payment and tried to renegotiate; they had agreed to receive 25% of the take, but upped their portion of the proceeds to 40%.

FRUITY OATY MESSAGES

Mal and Jayne were so embroiled in their conversation with the Rample brothers they didn't notice River Tam entering the bar. Jayne was the first to spot her; the mercenary tried to alert Mal, but he ignored her presence. River was acting a mite strange. She was drawn to an animated commercial for Fruity Oaty Bars playing on the vid screen, and stared at the advertisement that promised to "Make a man of a mouse, make you bust out your blouse." Then, before the jingle ended, River muttered a single word—Miranda—and launched a surprise attack on the unsuspecting patrons of the Maidenhead bar.

Unprovoked, River assaulted two men who'd been quietly sipping their drinks, and then quickly moved on to the next table. She whirled in a blur of precise movements, easily taking out one patron after the other. Facing four assailants, she dodged and kicked her opponents. By now a full-blown brawl had started in the bar.

Jayne, who enjoyed a ruckus, was anxious to get into the fight, but Mal didn't want to have anything to do with River or her brother, Simon. Mal passed the Rample brothers their share of the take under the table and told them to leave—but they wouldn't take orders from the Captain. Meanwhile, Jayne entered the fray.

When he tried to disable River by grabbing her from behind, she quickly incapacitated him as if he was a total stranger. To end the attack, Mal retrieved his Liberty Hammer and moved to shoot River, but she had found a gun of her own. Before either of them fired, Simon entered the bar and issued a command in Russian: "Это курам насмех (Eto kuram nasmekh)."

The words had a powerful, instant effect on River: she dropped unconscious to the ground. Leaving the carnage behind, the crew returned to *Serenity* with Simon and River to suss out what'd just happened. Simon explained that he'd discovered why the Alliance had been experimenting on River: the government wanted to use her as a sleeper agent to assassinate their targets.

Once activated, River would carry out commands planted in her subconscious, unaware of what she was saying or doing. Then, when the Alliance wanted to disable her, they'd 'wake her up' by speaking a catchphrase—the Russian command Simon had recited in the bar. The phrase was the only way, short of killing her, to ensure she'd stop acting on the Alliance's ingrained orders.

Mal was furious at this revelation, and the fact they'd been harboring a bigger danger than he had initially feared. Yet despite his doubts the Captain allowed Simon and River to remain on board *Serenity* as members of the crew. Not knowing where to turn next, Wash suggested they talk to Mr. Universe for more information.

THIS PAGE: A subliminal message in an advert 'triggers' River.

BROADCASTS ON A MOON

Desperate for answers, the Serenity crew contacted Mr. Universe, a technologist who lived in an isolated, sprawling communications complex on a tiny metallic moon shrouded by an opaque ion cloud. Mr. Universe was a genius when it came to technology but awkward with people. The tech junkie lived alone with his robotic wife, Lenore, scanning the broadwaves for information.

After agreeing to help, Mr. Universe accessed the Maidenhead's security footage and watched what happened. Analyzing the data, he discovered that a subliminal message had been buried in the Fruity Oaty Bar commercial River had watched before she started attacking the bar's patrons. What's more, he'd seen the embedded signal before, too. Mr. Universe explained that the Alliance had been broadcasting that signal for several weeks. The footage revealed something else as well: for the first time the Captain noticed that River whispered the word Miranda.

With this information, the *Serenity* crew understood the danger they were in. They'd been chased by the Alliance before, but not like this. Whoever was after them was closing in on their location.

Fast.

THIS PAGE: Mr. Universe helped Mal understand what happened to River, and how the Alliance was involved.

NOWHERE TO RUN

Shortly after arriving on Haven, Mal received a wave from Inara Serra on board *Serenity*. They exchanged pleasantries, which wasn't like them at all, and discussed the possibility of a job. Inara was having some trouble with the locals, but since she wasn't acting like her usual self, Mal suspected they were walking into a trap. Inara was in trouble, and despite their differences the Captain wouldn't abandon her in her moment of need.

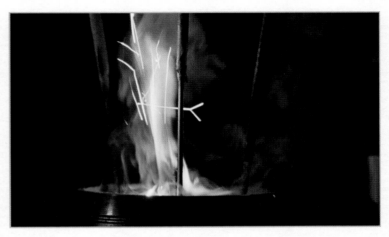

Mal, posing as a pilgrim, entered the Companion Training House to check up on Inara. Once inside, he met the Operative for the first time. Not only did he manipulate Inara to get into the Companion House, the Alliance agent proposed a deal: let River Tam go and the Captain and crew could be on their way. Mal, stubborn to a fault, wouldn't negotiate with the special agent. Anticipating the Operative's threats, Mal showed him the one piece of equipment the Alliance could lock onto: *Serenity*'s pulse beacon. If a warship happened to target it, then the Operative would be blown sky high along with the rest of them.

The Operative wasn't fazed by Mal's threat. Speaking calmly and carefully, the agent continued to appeal to the Captain's self-interest. Mal, thinking he had the upper hand, shot the agent—but the bullets were deflected by his body armor. When the Captain moved

to punch him, it was clear the Alliance loyalist was better trained than he was. Moving with precision, the Operative spun, kicking Mal in the head and dropping him to the ground. Then the agent opened a case and withdrew his sword.

Inara knew the Operative planned to execute the Captain, and hoped he'd prolong the moment. The incense she lit to pray for Mal's soul was a slow-burning fuse attached to a flash bomb. When the fuse burned down, the explosive detonated, allowing Inara and the Captain to flee back to *Serenity* in a shuttle and break atmo before the Operative caught up with them. He did try to locate the nav sat, but was surprised to find there was a total of seven, not just the one he'd expected to find. The *Serenity* crew was used to being on the run, and the Alliance hadn't figured out how to capture them.

Yet.

A BLACK ROCK

Though the threat of the Alliance loomed large, the *Serenity* crew enjoyed a brief reunion with Inara, before discussing what happened back at the Companion Training House. Inara shared that the Operative was a true believer devoted to his cause: capturing River. While the crew puzzled over this new information and River Tam's cryptic use of the name Miranda, River knocked Jayne out and headed straight for the bridge. Possessed by an invisible force, River stunned her own brother to find the planet Miranda on the ship's console. River had to know what her vision of Miranda meant; the secret was killing her slowly, eating away at her subconscious and her sanity bit by bit.

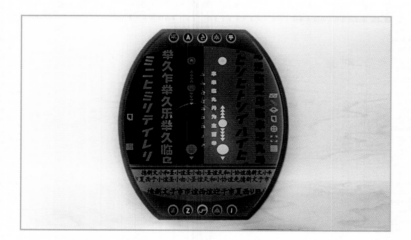

Miranda referred to a planet in the Blue Sun System tucked behind its second star, Burnham, located in the furthest sector of that remote quadrant. Years before the Unification War, the Alliance had put out a bulletin asking for volunteer settlers. Something, however, didn't take. The terraforming process went awry and poisoned the world and all her people.

Most folk believed Miranda was a 'black rock', an uninhabitable world, like Shadow, and had been erased from the Cortex. Its history was lost, forgotten, and the planet had never been referred to again...until River learned the name during her training at the Academy. As the Operative feared, Doctor Mathias had allowed key members of Alliance Parliament to review River's progress. During one of their tours, River had telepathically connected with her captors' minds, and gleaned the planet's name from their thoughts.

The *Serenity* crew suspected that Miranda possessed secrets the Alliance wanted to keep, but they knew the dangers of investigating it further: Miranda's remote location would force them to fly through Reaver territory. According to Zoë, a massive fleet of a hundred Reaver ships had gathered in the Blue Sun System; flying into their territory would be suicide.

Needing answers, the crew flew back to Haven, hoping Shepherd Book would help them find a place to hide until they could figure out their next steps.

LEFT: A chilling sight for the *Serenity* crew.

WORLDS ON FIRE

Wash was the first to notice that something **was very, very wrong on Haven. The pilot noticed on his monitors that the mining colony had been hit by the Alliance. Men, women, and children had been cut down like wheat in a field.**

Horrified by this turn of events, the *Serenity* crew landed on Haven and searched for survivors. The Captain ran to find Shepherd Book, who'd managed to shoot down the Alliance Vessel A.V. *Sparrow* that had attacked the colony. Book had been seriously wounded in the fight. Gasping for breath, he told Mal to find his faith, and then died in his arms.

Not long afterward, the *Serenity* crew realized in horror that the Alliance didn't just destroy the mining outpost on Haven. The Operative had ordered a deadly attack on all their allies and anyone who lent the crew a hand or place to hide: the Sanchez brothers; Li Shen; even Fanty and Mingo Rumple.

THIS PAGE: **The relentless purpose of the Operative is revealed in his brutal actions.**

"I don't care what you believe! Just...believe it. Whatever you have to..."
The last words of Shepherd Derrial Book

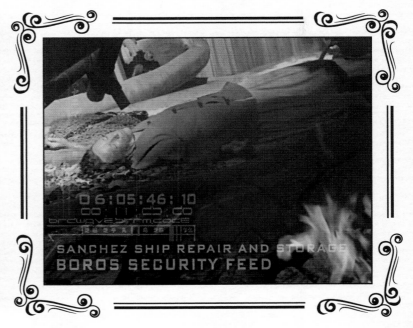

SANCHEZ SHIP REPAIR AND STORAGE
BOROS SECURITY FEED

Upon hearing this news, Mal made a hard decision. Before the crew had a chance to grieve, the Captain ordered them to turn *Serenity* into a Reaver ship. He told them to string up the bodies of dead settlers to the prow, to muck with the reactor, to paint the hull. The crew, devastated by the losses they had suffered, argued with the Captain—but their words had no effect. Mal aimed to live, and that meant he'd shoot anyone who stood in his way.

Mal wanted to know why the Operative went to such extreme lengths. What was the Alliance so desperate to hide? To find answers, the Captain felt forced to go where no one else would: through Reaver territory to find Miranda.

After the crew had finished carrying out his orders, even Mal didn't recognize *Serenity*. Lucky for them, the disguise was effective. When they reached Reaver territory, the *Serenity* floated past dozens of Reaver ships, noticed but unharmed.

DEVASTATING SECRETS

After landing on Miranda, the Serenity crew was shocked to find the planet wasn't the black rock they thought it was. Instead, they found gleaming high-tech cities manufactured from metal and glass stretching as far as the eye could see. The air was breathable, too, and weeds had grown into the cracks—signs the planet was habitable after all. Soon, though, they realized how eerie the world was. Where were all the people? How could this vast metropolis built to rival Ariel City in the Core remain empty?

Suddenly, inexplicably, the *Serenity* crew understood why Miranda was quiet: all the occupants had died from mysterious causes. The vehicles and buildings were filled with decomposed bodies that showed no signs of discoloration, disease, or violence. Curiously, a few of the bodies were unnaturally thin, as if they'd died of starvation—which didn't make any sense. To the crew, it seemed as if the people simply fell asleep and didn't wake up. River begged them to. River heard the voices of the dead. And only River felt the victims' pain. This was the secret that drove her mad.

To uncover the reason for the devastation, the *Serenity* crew followed a beacon's weak signal and found a holographic message recorded by Doctor Caron. She explained that they'd added a chemical called G-23 Paxilon Hydrochlorate to the air processors, which affected thirty million people. The Alliance hoped the Pax would artificially manufacture the first peaceful population by quelling dissent and violence. The chemical, however, affected the population in ways they did not expect. Most people surrendered their will and became lethargic, wasting away despite having access to food and medicine. They simply stopped moving and eating—and eventually died.

THIS PAGE: **What the crew found on the planet Miranda was the empty remains of a once bustling city.**

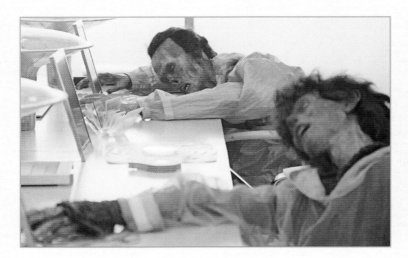

Approximately 30,000 settlers, one tenth of a percent of the population, experienced a different reaction to the drug. Instead of falling into a trance, the Pax made them mentally unstable, forcing a heightened aggressor response. They unwittingly tapped into their darkest, primal urges. The victims became the aggressors the Alliance feared; they mutilated, raped, and cannibalized the people of Miranda—including Doctor Caron and her team of researchers.

Following the end of Caron's message, the crew finally understood what secret the Anglo-Sino Alliance was desperate to protect: the government was responsible for the creation of the greatest threat spacefarers have ever known. With their use of the Pax, the Alliance had created Reavers. When the Pax-affected citizens were done attacking their homeworld, they abandoned Miranda and flew into space, spreading like a plague.

With the truth exposed after twelve years of silence, River finally felt a moment of relief—but Mal did not. The Pax represented everything wrong with the Alliance. They expected loyalty without cause, obedience without question, faith without justice. Worse, the government tried to improve upon people who didn't need to be controlled—and it had backfired on them. Yet they hadn't learned from their mistake. The Alliance still waged war with worlds on the Border and rim in the four systems, and dealt a brutal blow to the Independent Faction that opposed them during the Unification War.

Mal understood how dangerous the truth was, how it could be wielded like a weapon, how it couldn't remain buried forever; he saw himself as the man who'd bring down the Alliance one day. He feared they'd try new experiments with chemicals like the Pax again, and the only way to stop them was to share Doctor Caron's message with the rest of the 'verse.

After appealing to the *Serenity* crew, the Captain decided to leave Miranda behind and fly to the one person who could help them with their mission: Mr. Universe.

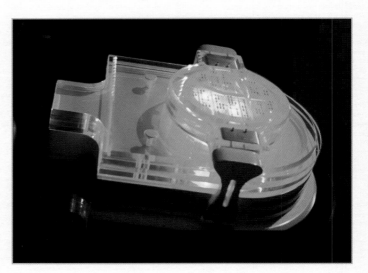

BROADWAVE TO THE 'VERSE

In the burst of unexpected clarity, River
Tam explained they were only 367,442 miles away from Mr. Universe's communication facility, and if the ship went to full burn they could be there in four hours. While this lucid statement surprised them, the *Serenity* crew still had to fly through an armada of Reaver ships and engage the Alliance. After seeing what the Operative had done to their contacts, the crew was certain the special agent would have reached Mr. Universe by that point.

Wash contacted Mr. Universe and was happy to find him alive. Not knowing that the Operative had beaten them to the facility along with a fleet of Alliance gunships, the crew shared the details of their plan to Mr. Universe to broadcast Doctor Caron's message. The recluse claimed he was all too happy to help. After Mr. Universe ended his transmission, however, the Operative fatally stabbed him and ordered his soldiers to burn the facility down. The *Serenity* crew was heading into yet another trap.

Mal, having fought with the Alliance for years, understood the Operative might be waiting to intercept them. If the Alliance did mount an offensive, the crew would be outmanned and outgunned. *Serenity* was primarily a transport ship, and one measly boat couldn't take on the entire fleet—but an armada of Reavers could. To draw their attention, Mal mounted a turret, fired at a Reaver ship and blew it up. The fiery wreckage spun into two smaller ships, destroying them on impact. The direct assault on the Reaver fleet worked as Mal intended: the Reavers were following *Serenity*, just as he'd planned. Provided they didn't catch up with *Serenity*, the Reaver fleet was a fearsome weapon against the Alliance, one that could keep the crew alive.

A few hours later, *Serenity* reached the ion cloud shrouding Mr. Universe's facility. The cloud scrambled their sensors—and the waiting Alliance fleet's as well. The Operative spotted *Serenity* entering the hazy atmosphere, but was shocked to see Reavers flying right behind them. Giving the order to attack, the special agent fought the Reavers in the *Dart*, but was forced to abandon his ship after it sustained heavy damage and fled to the lunar surface in an escape pod.

As the remainder of the Alliance fleet battled the Reaver armada, Wash maneuvered *Serenity* through the cloud, with a lone Reaver ship close behind. Flying into the moon's atmosphere, the Reaver skiff fired an electromagnetic pulse at *Serenity* and fried her circuits. The sudden power outage caused the Firefly-class ship to tumble down, down, down from the sky. To prevent a disaster, Wash restored emergency power before they hit the ground—but he couldn't stop *Serenity* from falling to the moon's surface.

Serenity crashed hard and skidded across a landing strip. While the force of the impact damaged the ship so severely she was no longer flyable, the crew survived the crash. Breathing a sigh of relief, Wash started to say, "I am a leaf on the wind. Watch how I——", but stopped short of finishing his mantra. The Reaver ship had pursued the *Serenity* crew all the way down to the surface, and shot a harpoon through *Serenity*'s cockpit, killing the pilot instantly.

Zoë rushed toward his body and tried to 'wake' him up, but Mal pulled her away just as another harpoon pierced the cockpit. With no time to mourn the loss of their beloved crewmember, the survivors fled the wreckage and holed up in a hallway with as many guns, grenades, and ammo as they could carry. The entire crew armed themselves including Kaylee, Simon, and Inara, who unwrapped her bow and arrow to join the coming fight. No one was safe. At least, not yet.

Maybe, not ever.

The *Serenity*'s crew put all of their lives at risk: while the Captain used Mr. Universe's equipment to transmit Doctor Caron's last report, the rest of the crew would hold off the Reavers for as long as they could.

THIS PAGE: **The death of a beloved crewmember.**

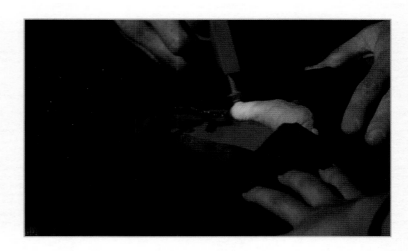

Jayne told the rest of the crew to create a wall by stacking storage crates scattered in the hallway. Then Zoë shared her piece of the battle plan. She and Jayne would be the crew's first defensive wave; once the Reavers broke through, Simon, Inara, and Kaylee would then start firing. Unfortunately, River was out of the fight, overwhelmed with fear and anxiety, drowning in the Reavers' blood-red rage.

Though they had some cover, the Reaver force quickly overwhelmed the *Serenity* crew, forcing them to fall back deeper into the facility. Worse, they'd taken on injuries, Simon's medical bag was missing, and they only had three full cartridges of ammo left. The Doctor had been shot by a stray bullet, Zoë had been slashed across her back, and Kaylee felt woozy—a side effect of the Reavers' poison-tipped darts. Down but not out, Jayne tossed his last grenade through the gap in the doors. The crew hid behind the partially closed blast doors, waiting to die.

Realizing that Simon might die without his medical bag, River stepped up to engage the Reavers. Setting aside her feelings, she told her injured brother that it was her turn to take care of him. Then she dived through the narrow opening and gracefully landed in a room filled with monsters. After slamming the control panel, River bobbed and weaved to avoid the Reavers, trying to rejoin the crew by leaping through the blast doors before they shut completely. Just before she could slip through, however, a Reaver grabbed River's ankle and dragged her toward him. As she fell backwards, River tossed Simon's medical kit back through the opening. She'd saved the crew, but now River had to rescue herself.

THIS PAGE: **At this most crucial moment the intense and destructive combat training River underwent came into its own.**

TRANSMITTING FOR HOPE

With the Serenity crew protecting him,
Mal wandered into the facility and discovered signs of the Operative's work. Mr. Universe had been killed, and the primary transmitter had been destroyed. Before he died, however, the reclusive techie had spent his last moments recording a message for Mal. As soon as Mal entered the room, Mr. Universe's robotic wife, Lenore, muttered his final words. "They can never stop the signal." Although the primary transmitter had been destroyed, there was a backup in the basement, just over the generator. But Mal was not alone: the Operative had landed safely and was following him deep into the facility.

Mal reached the backup transmitter but was frustrated to see that it was hard to get to. The equipment was mounted on a suspended platform that could only be accessed by swinging onto it from a chain. Unfortunately Mal had just worked out how to reach the transmitter when the Operative tackled him and kicked his Liberty Hammer away. Then, Mal returned the favor and threw a box of tools at the armored Operative to slow him down. The Captain grabbed an overhead beam, inched his way toward a heavy chain, and swung himself onto the platform.

After catching up with him, the Operative continued sparring with Mal and wounded him with his sword. Down, but not out, Mal headbutted the Operative and managed to pierce his ankle with a screwdriver. Stunned, the Operative slid to the ground, giving Mal the chance to withdraw the sword from his belly. Believing he'd won, the Captain moved to strike once more, but the Operative rolled out of the way and punched him in the stomach.

During their fight, the special agent tried to incapacitate Mal by hitting a pressure point on a specific nerve cluster. Luckily, the Operative's attack had no effect on the Captain because the former Sergeant had been hit by a piece of shrapnel during the Unification War and had the cluster moved during surgery. Seizing the moment, Mal disabled the Operative by hitting him in the neck, instantly paralyzing him. Then the Captain pinned his opponent against the railing with his own sword.

Unable to speak or move, the Operative was forced to watch the transmission. Now he, too, knew what the Alliance had done.

THIS PAGE: The truth behind the Alliance's inadvertent creation of the Reavers due to their attempt to create a docile population is broadcast to the whole galaxy.

CONSEQUENCES AND FUNERALS

After transmitting the truth about Miranda, Mal
returned to the *Serenity* crew, only to learn that River had sacrificed
herself to save them. Trapped on the other side of the blast doors,
the crew believed she was either dying or dead...which was why they
were shocked to learn she'd survived. Following Mal's return, the
blast doors opened to reveal a bloodied and breathless River standing
in a room full of dead Reavers. Then, as the *Serenity* crew held their
breath, Alliance soldiers blew a hole through the wall and swarmed
behind River. The troops did not attack, however. The Operative,
having seen the footage from Miranda, ordered them to stand down.
The special agent was no longer the Alliance's man; the Operative
had lost his faith in them. Forever.

WAKE FOR WASH

Hoban 'Wash' Washburne was an amicable pilot who had stayed friends with his peers and co-workers. Following his death, a trio of his former associates decided to honor Wash by christening a ship *Jetwash* during a 'floating out' ceremony. Leland, Trey, and Tagg purchased a Firefly-class ship, an 03 class, but struggled to find the right words to mark the occasion. What stories should they swap? The one about the *Reposita*? Or the story about the Reaver murder wedge?

After telling tall tales, Wash's friends grabbed a bottle of champagne to smash it over the bow. A pregnant Zoë told them Wash hated champagne, and swapped it with a cheap bottle of ngkapei (un-ga-pei) instead. He loved the Chinese liquor just as much as he loved flying and his friends.

Just like his soon-to-be-born daughter would, too.

Without a ship to speak of, the Operative stepped up to assist. He helped the crew bury their friends—Mr. Universe, Shepherd Book, and Hoban Washburne—and held a private ceremony in the desert. Then he hauled *Serenity* back to a repair yard on Persephone. As the crew finished its repairs, the Operative gave the Captain an update. Simon and River Tam were no longer being hunted by the Alliance. They did not, however, share any love for Malcolm J. Reynolds, and wouldn't forgive his attack on their reputation.

Before leaving, Mal warned the Operative that he'd kill him if he ever saw him again. The former special agent promised the Captain that he wouldn't.

ABOVE: **The Serenity crew gather to mourn their fallen friends.**

PAGING MALCOLM REYNOLDS

Though Mal broadcast the truth, not everyone believed that the Alliance was responsible for the deaths of thirty million loyal citizens. The broadwaves were filled with talking heads who argued the finer points of the broadcast, and even went so far as to suggest that the report was a hoax. Those who did believe Doctor Caron formed the New Resistance, a group of civilian activists who exercised their right to free speech.

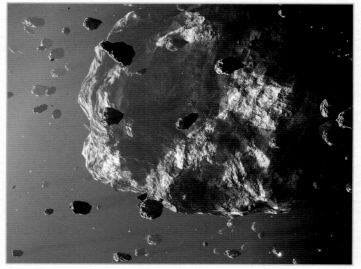

The Alliance understood the threat Malcolm Reynolds and his crew represented. Lt. Rodgers—the Parliament member River had 'read' back at the Academy—decided to put out a fresh bounty for their heads, just as the Operative had predicted. He was worried that River Tam had gleaned more than one secret from his mind. Would she act on her subconscious and hit the Alliance again and again? The Feds didn't have to wait long. Jubal Early, who'd been presumed dead, answered their call and confronted a senior official named Kalista. He told Kalista he wanted to finish the job he started and decided to employ new tactics. The bounty hunter would simply let someone else find Mal and the crew first.

The government wasn't the only force searching for Mal and his crew. The New Resistance also wanted to meet with them, but the crew was on the run—minus Jayne Cobb. The mercenary, who felt credits was more important than friendship, was done with the Tams and the Alliance. Plus, the money wasn't that great, either. The *Serenity* crew was happy enough without him, but they missed having an extra gun for the more dangerous jobs. Though Simon and Kaylee finally got together following their ordeal with the Reavers, as did Mal and Inara, they were broke, hungry, and needed fuel.

Babies, however, don't wait to be born at the right time,

and Zoë had a little girl, name of Emma Washburne. Unfortunately, something went wrong during delivery and Zoë suffered from internal bleeding; Simon could fix her, but he needed a hospital. Instead of flying back to the Core, however, the crew visited the Paquin Asteroid Mining Operation. They risked being arrested, but Zoë's life was on the line. After a trauma team greeted Zoë, the facility's doctor told them she needed surgery and wouldn't be able to leave for a minimum of five days.

During their visit, Mal was recognized as a wanted man and the miners called the Feds on them. Mal couldn't remember a time when he'd been forced to abandon Zoë and didn't want to leave her side, but his First Mate told him to go. She couldn't risk losing her newborn baby to the Alliance, and trusted she Mal and the *Serenity* crew to keep Emma safe.

Mal wasn't the only *Serenity* crewmember who was in trouble. Following the alert, Zoë was trapped in an Alliance facility, where Lt. Rodgers confronted her. Although he suspected the former Independent Corporal would never betray her friends, the Parliament member threatened to leave her stranded in the middle of nowhere at a desert prison camp. Zoë wouldn't budge—even if it meant she'd never see her daughter Emma again.

ON THE RUN AGAIN

After the crew escaped, they holed up in a ships' graveyard called the Goodrow Baron Dumping Grounds. There, River proposed a plan: she'd trade her knowledge for Zoë Alleyne Washburne's freedom. First, however, she had to unlock her mind to see if any secrets were still there. She told Simon to administer propofol and sodium thiopental to artificially induce a coma in which she would lose consciousness for twelve hours.

As luck would have it, the New Resistance did catch up with the *Serenity* crew. Jayne Cobb brought Bea Quiang and twelve other New Resistance fighters to meet with Mal in the Black. Jayne, always thinking with his wallet, had returned home to see his mama and found Bea Quiang and a suitcase full of credits waiting for him.

Though Bea was adamant they hadn't been followed, Jubal Early did pick up their trail. The bounty hunter slaughtered Bea's people and blew up their ship. Then Early approached *Serenity* and slipped inside when the crew was sleeping, just as he had done before.

Working his way through the crew, River sensed Early's presence while unconscious, but could not respond or stop Early from attacking her shipmates. The bounty hunter moved through *Serenity* with ease and disabled Simon, Mal, Jayne, Bea—but not Kaylee. She managed to whack his head with her wrench, then chained him to a chair. Hardened by their previous encounter, Kaylee threatened to torture Early with her tools.

Thankfully, River woke up just in time to tell the crew a terrible secret: the Alliance had manipulated other little girls, and experimented on them, too. With this fresh, valuable secret to trade, the crew planned to use it to free Zoë. Before they could do that, however, Mal had to break a promise. The Captain tracked down the former Operative on Theophrastus to ask for his help. Surprisingly, the man agreed.

Once the Operative was on board, *Serenity* broke atmo, and dropped Jubal Early along with the trash. The chained bounty hunter fell to the surface and landed in a tree, but was rescued by an old woman, a friend to the Alliance.

Early was in terrible shape, but could still breathe. To Kalista, the bounty hunter was an asset to the Alliance, the means to bring down Malcolm Reynolds once and for all.

ANOTHER RESCUE

The Serenity crew—Mal, Jayne, Inara Simon, Kaylee and River—plotted to break the other girls out of the Academy along with Bea from the New Resistance and the former Operative. The former Alliance loyalist told the crew what they'd need: a security clearance code that he could provide and a passenger shuttle. Bea offered to supply the ship. New Resistance outfits had been popping up all over the 'verse, which was good news to Mal.

The crew discovered the Academy was on Inara Serra's home planet Sihnon and was happy to learn the New Resistance also had a cell there. Once they acquired a passenger shuttle, Mal, Bea, Jayne, and River infiltrated the Alliance facility, but security was far lighter than they'd expected. In fact, the intel they'd received from the New Resistance was dead wrong, and they'd waltzed right into Kalista's trap. The crew quickly separated, giving the disgraced Operative an opportunity to face off against Kalista's assistant, Denon, while the remaining members explored the facility.

Unfortunately, River Tam encountered one of the doctors who'd experimented on her; the older man claimed they'd never got to finish their work. She was unfinished, imperfect, broken— unlike the other girls. While he talked, the doctor turned to a test subject, and River knew the truth: the Alliance hadn't stopped experimenting. The girl's head had been shaved, and her scalp was covered with the tell-tale scars of multiple brain surgeries. There was a good chance the victim had no idea who her own mother was.

The Academy doctor activated his test subject, who moved to attack River and the rest of the crew. Deadly and merciless, the unnamed experiment stabbed Mal in the neck and broke Jayne's arm. The Captain ordered Bea to escape and then fell unconscious, only to wake up moments later to see the test subject fighting with River. Mal had another trick up his sleeve, however; he activated a remote call button to summon a shuttle to their location. Then he turned to help River by tossing her a hypodermic needle filled with a tranquillizer. River caught it and plunged the needle into the test subject's chest, knocking her out cold.

Bea had managed to sneak out of the facility and ran to the Operative's side. The former special agent was bruised and broken, but alive. Though Denon was a skilled fighter, Kalista's assistant was no match for the Operative. He killed Denon by slicing his sword through his skull—an act that Kalista would never forgive. The senior officer confronted the Operative, right after Bea appeared, and asked him how he wanted to die. Before he could commit a ritual suicide, however, members of the New Resistance, who called themselves Browncoats, swarmed the area and killed all the Alliance loyalists at the scene.

After the skirmish, Mal, River, and Jayne exited the Academy with the unconscious test subject. Seeing this, the Browncoats stopped fighting and provided an armed escort to ensure the *Serenity* crew would make it back to their shuttle unharmed. Then, before taking off, the Captain took another hostage— Lt. Rodgers, who'd been wounded during the fight.

SET UP BY THE FEDS

After confronting Lt. Rogers, Bea realized how dangerous the Anglo-Sino Alliance was. The New Resistance, the hope for their future, was fake. The government had funded the rebels to root out dissenters. Though rebellion was on the horizon, this time the Alliance anticipated resistance, and funneled money, ammo, ships and supplies to help it grow—and learn its plans. The government knew everything: who the rebels were, what planets and moons were troublesome, where their hideouts and ships were located.

Worse, Lt. Rodgers had issued the command to destroy their outposts several hours earlier. All that was left of the New Resistance was a ragtag band of Browncoats on Sihnon. The officer believed they'd destroyed the resistance, and without a movement no one else would stand up to the Alliance. That wasn't good enough for Malcolm J. Reynolds. Not then, not ever.

Mal and the *Serenity* crew would never bow to the Alliance, and would *always* rebel. To prove how dangerous they were, the Captain sent in River Tam to extract the location of Zoë's desert prison from the lieutenant's mind.

RIGHT: Mal is not a captain who leaves anyone behind.

LOOKING AFTER THEIR PEOPLE

After figuring out where Zoë was being held, River assisted Simon in the infirmary. The rescued test subject didn't know who she was, let alone where. Her time at the Academy had devastated her psyche; the Alliance had all but removed her personality, her memories, everything that made her *her*. Alliance doctors had scooped out the girl's humanity to forge her into a living weapon without thinking about the consequences. Simon promised River he'd try to help her, because River thought of her as a sister, not just another scarred victim. If she could survive the horrors of the Academy, surely Simon could rescue one more test subject? Thanks to the Doctor's care and skilled MedAcad training, the girl awoke and told the crew her name was Iris, and her loyalties did not lie with the Alliance. She would one day seek revenge, with Bea's help.

While Simon concentrated on administering treatment to their patient, Mal and the *Serenity* crew plotted to rescue Zoë, with Bea offering to help. Mal had seen enough bloodshed for one day, and didn't want to be responsible for someone as inexperienced as Bea. The New Resistance fighter, however, told the Captain why she wanted to lend a hand. Her father, Li Quiang, fought under Mal's command during the Battle of Serenity Valley. Mal softened, and let her fight. Bea didn't have to say another word. The Captain knew what fighting the

Alliance with Sergeant Reynolds meant to her.

Anxious to rescue Zoë, the *Serenity* crew sailed toward the remote prison camp and prepared to fight. Zoë heard *Serenity* break atmo in the dead of night and, the minute she got outside the next morning, broke into a run. At first the guards thought she'd die in the desert—until they spotted the Mule. Mal, Bea, and the Operative accelerated toward Zoë, while Jayne provided cover fire from higher ground. Zoë managed to mount the Mule, but her escape wasn't certain; the prison guards swarmed the vehicle, forcing the crew to take 'em all out before they made it back to the ship.

Right before the Firefly-class ship broke atmo, the crew dumped Lt. Rodgers in the desert. Bound but not killed, the ranking member of Parliament was picked up by prison guards. The crew had left him alive to tell the Alliance just how dangerous Malcolm Reynolds could be.

Following Zoë's rescue, the crew had one more stop to make: Theophrastus, the Operative's home. After saying goodbye to Bea and Iris, however, Zoë followed the Operative. In her mind, it didn't matter how much the former agent helped them, the Operative was responsible for the death of her husband, Wash, Shepherd Book, and so many others. The former Corporal challenged the special agent to a duel, and managed to find the peace she was looking for.

Not everyone on Theophrastus was eager to say farewell. Kalista visited Jubal Early, and pledged the bounty hunter would have the means to complete his assignment. The senior officer, an Alliance test subject herself, commanded a squad of sisters just like her. Working with a medically-altered Jubal Early, the sleeper agents would bring their wayward sisters back into the fold.

A LITTLE THIEVING

With a baby on board, the Serenity crew picked their jobs a little more carefully than they had in the past. Mal targeted a poorly manned space station to ensure nobody got hurt. Things never go smooth for the crew, however, and during their heist a cruise liner sailed toward them. As soon as Mal saw the *Jade Dragon* rapidly approaching, the Captain told the crew to double-time their efforts to avoid complications and slipped away in Shuttle Two before encountering the passenger ship. River, who'd proven to be a decent pilot, held *Serenity* steady while the Captain docked. Then she flew away with no one the wiser. With the thievin' done, Mal congratulated the crew, only to learn the loot they'd stolen were rolls of toilet paper.

Mal was frustrated by this turn of events. Small jobs spelled hard times. He needed a bigger heist, something that could earn them enough credits to keep flying. He shared his worries with Inara, who'd settled in to the smuggler's life.

The former Companion tried to tell the Captain why she left the Companion House on Sihnon, but she couldn't find the words—at least, not yet. Inara had an idea, a way to help Mal, but she struggled to confide in Mal. Every time she spoke with her friends, like Guanyin back on Sihnon, Inara thought about confiding in the Captain. How much should she tell him? That she had rivals like Ceres? That Ceres had sidled up to the Alliance and was working for them out on the rim?

Before she sat the Captain down to share her troubles, Mal accepted a wave from Iris, who'd partnered up with Bea, back on Burnet in the Blue Sun System.

BELOW: Engines glowing, *Serenity* heads towards the sun.

NOT A LICK OF PEACE

The Serenity crew flew to Burnet to meet with Iris. During their conversation, they discovered that Bea had been missing for two days. Tapping into the Cortex, River learned that Bea's features had been picked up on a facial scan, and the rebel had been flagged for extradition. The Alliance had tagged Bea as a leader of the New Resistance, and sent an agent to pick her up. They hadn't finished stamping out every rebellious cell; the 'verse was too big to search in just a few weeks. Worse, the government was cracking down because a new group of terrorists—one they had not manufactured— threatened their rule: a splinter faction of the Independents called the Peacemakers. Unlike the rest of the Browncoats, the Peacemakers didn't lay down arms after the War ended. They kept on fighting and wreaking havoc, just as they'd done before.

Mal didn't want to have anything to do with the Alliance, but the crew convinced him to help Bea anyway. Retracing her steps, Iris took them to the Redemption House for Wayward Youths, Bea's last known location. She was to meet with a contact named Mericourt and had been instructed to go alone. Asking around, though, proved to be troublesome. The crew was quickly surrounded by half a dozen armed youths and was brought face to face with a woman calling herself Miss Thompson. Thompson explained that only trusted contacts could call her Mericourt, and the crew wasn't on that list.

After a quick tussle, the crew showed Mericourt they could hold their own, so she told her people to back down and gave them a chance to talk. The senior Browncoat was a Peacemaker, the head of an operation to train new members. The Peacemakers wanted to bring down the Alliance from the shadows. Instead of attacking them on the battlefield with soldiers, tanks, and ships, they'd use stealth to cripple the Alliance's infrastructure. With their forces populating the rim in dozens of such cells, they could carry out their missions without alerting the Alliance forces prominent in the Core. Though the Peacemakers were terrorists, Mal took a liking to them. He'd been in many battles and understood that winning wars meant innocents would die.

Mericourt pledged to help rescue Bea. Though she hadn't joined their outfit yet, Bea possessed enough knowledge to threaten her people. Directing Mal and the crew to the General Store for supplies, Miss Thompson provided them with a guide named Ophelia and sent them on their way.

At the General Store, Jayne Cobb received a package from his mama, an orange-striped sweater that matched his hat. Excited by his gift, the mercenary wrote her back, asking her to knit a smaller version for Emma. River wanted in on the fun, so she took off with Ophelia to find a gift for Zoë's daughter. Ophelia, pretending to be River's friend and tour guide, led her through back alleys into an abandoned storefront where Kalista and six sleeper agents were waiting to ambush her.

BROKEN SISTERHOOD

The senior officer mused about how easy it was to lead River into a trap. Initially, Kalista had collected the other girls to track down Bea, and never expected to run into Iris and River, too.

Believing she had the upper hand, Kalista repeated the Academy doctor's claim, that River was not complete, then gave the order to attack without the use of weapons. The officer didn't want to slice River up before delivering her to the Academy. Kalista embodied the spirit of an operative. She believed in the bonds of family, forged through shared human experimentation, and wanted to restore their unit to its full strength.

The attackers proved to be too much for River and overpowered her quickly. After tying River to a chair, Kalista claimed she was rescuing her and then told her wayward 'sister' about their plans. Ophelia had infiltrated the Peacemakers for a specific purpose: to stop them from attacking the Alliance in the Core.

Unfortunately for River, no one on board *Serenity* knew she was missing. They had bigger problems. The crew didn't trust Mericourt and sensed she was hiding something. After Mal hatched a new plan, Simon and Inara took a trip to the Alliance Planetary Offices (APO) where Bea was supposedly being held.

FANCY DISGUISES

Simon Tam, posing as a well-dressed **counsilor, approached a local functionary with the Companion Inara Serra dressed in her finest robes at his side. To prevent his capture, Simon wore special glasses to hide his eyes from retinal scanning equipment. Inara wasn't as worried, because her record as a Registered Companion was clean.**

To get inside the facility, Simon asked the official for the proper forms that would allow Inara to establish a Companion House on Burnet. The official was all too happy to oblige. Inara's presence impressed the government worker, who remarked she was the second Companion to visit him in the same week. The other Companion had red hair and only wanted a temporary docking permit, so it relieved the officer that a permanent installation would be built on his world. Inara suspected either her rival, Ceres, or the red-haired Saffron had paid him a visit, but she didn't want to upset Mal's plans to rescue Bea. She had so much to tell him, but had to wait until the time was right.

Once they had the right papers, Simon and Inara entered the APO to 'file' them with another official. Instead, Simon and Inara tracked down Bea's cell and avoided the administrative wing. The Companion picked the lock while

Simon stood watch, holding a tranquilizer just in case they encountered any trouble.

Shortly after freeing Bea, they encountered an Alliance officer and claimed they were lost. The officer was quick to notice the escaped prisoner and traded blows with Simon; the Doctor took a punch to the gut, and had the wind knocked out of him. Worse, he dropped the tranquilizer on the hard tiled floor, which broke the needle on impact.

The officer immediately called for backup, but his radio malfunctioned before he could get through. Inara seized the moment and delivered a spinning kick to the guard's jaw. Knocking the guard out cold gave the trio a small window of opportunity to escape. Making their way back down the hallway, the three exited into a stairwell and marched through the corridor. On their way out, the alarm sounded, alerting two guards at the end of the hall. Inara dropped a smoke bomb to cover their escape and urged them to run.

With the guards in pursuit, Simon, Inara, and Bea sprinted for the exit to rendezvous with Mal, who was parked outside in a hovercraft. Thanks to Inara's quick thinking, the guards were temporarily blinded and hadn't seen where they'd gone. After leaving the building, the trio hopped into the hovercraft—but despite all their careful plans, they'd been spotted. The Captain blazed down the city streets, followed by two guards on hover bikes. Mal shot 'em both down, which allowed them to get away clean.

THE TRUTH OF THINGS

Bea, frustrated by her ordeal, told Mal that she wasn't trying to join the Peacekeepers; she met with Mericourt to talk her down. The rebellious leader concentrated on bringing down prospecting ships called 'silverliners'. The miners, who weren't native to Burnet, set down on the planet's surface, stripped the soil of its riches, and then left. Their efforts hurt the native folk who could never leave, and damaged their ability to profit from iridium mining. The passenger ships were an unusual target, but one that mattered to Mericourt.

"I told you, Reynolds. Secession just ain't gonna cut it. We need to push the purple bellies out. Most folks here make their living prospecting the iridium, or by selling goods and services to them that do. It's a hard life, with low return for long hours, but they get by. And then they've got to deal with them." *Mericourt*

First things first, however. Before the Captain could confront Mericourt, he had to return to *Serenity*. Back at the ship, Mal, Simon, and Inara discovered that River wasn't River anymore. She and Ophelia had attacked the crewmembers who'd been left behind to capture Iris and bring her home. Iris resisted, and during their fight she taunted Ophelia, who let slip that they'd had a Companion's training so the girls could blend in, be more civilized. River had hit 'em hard, but acted like she didn't recognize Zoë or Emma. Kalista had done something to her, they were sure of it.

Mal called a meeting with Mericourt to discuss their options. The Captain would not abide hurting hundreds of innocent folk, and told her as much. However, the local resistance leader had spent a lot of time and energy infiltrating the spaceport, and Mal planned to use that intel to his advantage. Inara smartly pointed out that the Alliance facilitator had mentioned a registered Companion had put in a request for a temporary docking permit. She didn't think it was a coincidence, and neither did the rest of the group.

PREVENTING TAKEOFF

Just as Inara suspected, Kalista was preparing to leave Burnet and ordered the dock workers to load cargo onto her ship. The senior officer had taken no chances; she locked River in a jail cell with Iris and ordered Ceres, a registered Companion and Inara's rival, to stand guard. River, who'd been quiet for several hours, slowly came out of her catatonic state. Iris explained the triggered state was temporary, but there was something wrong with River's wiring. Her mind didn't work like the other sleeper agents' did. That, Ceres explained, was something they had to straighten out.

After discovering that Bea Quiang had escaped, Kalista met with Mal, who'd approached the ship. The Captain was not alone, however; the *Serenity* crew shared an open comm link with him, and had disguised themselves as dock workers. After getting into position, the crewmembers opened the crates to arm themselves with guns and grenades. Meanwhile, Mal met with Kalista inside her ship, claiming he had valuable intel on the Peacemakers.

The senior officer told Mal to confess what he knew, but the Captain wouldn't open up to her. He was being evasive for good reason: to buy the crew more time. Mal's cavalier attitude got under Kalista's skin, who asked him what prevented her from torturing the information out of him. He responded with one word: surprise! Timed perfectly, an explosion rocked the spacedock, setting Kalista's ship on fire. The blast was so powerful it also knocked Kalista to the ground, putting her in an awkward position. Mal, looming over the elite agent, landed a solid punch. The Captain thought he had the upper hand, but he really didn't. Kalista blocked every blow that followed, and gave Mal a sound thumping before offering to talk.

As the alarms blared, the *Serenity* crew split off into pairs to search for Iris and River. Bea and Simon stuck together, while Zoë and Inara split up. Luckily, Simon and Bea were the first to locate the prison cell. While Bea reunited with her friend Iris, Simon picked the lock to free them. River, who was starting to believe she was broken, was reluctant to leave. Wouldn't it be better if she was dead? Zoë joined up with them and talked River down. She was a fighter, and that was true. But River was also something else: a survivor.

HELL BREAKING LOOSE

Inara, who'd cleared the starboard side
of the upper deck, changed course and encountered a familiar face: Ceres. The Companion from House Madrassa taunted Inara; the Alliance compensated her so well, she didn't have to fly with a bunch of thieves. Inara hit back, telling the red-haired Companion that the crew stole because of their circumstances—but Ceres had another hurtful comeback. Ceres reminded Inara what happened at Fiddler's Green, a comment that uncharacteristically enraged her—because it was a secret she wanted to tell Mal on her terms. Ceres opened fire at Inara, but the Companion was too slow. Inara lunged for the Companion's wrist and grabbed it so hard Ceres was forced to drop her gun. Then, Inara punched Ceres across the face and threw her into the hard ground.

Following Inara's takedown of Ceres, the Companion rushed to rescue Mal from Kalista. The senior officer baited Mal, throwing him off-balance with the truth. Because of the broadcast he'd shared, the Alliance decided to crack down on dissent in the rim. Satisfied she'd beaten the Captain down both emotionally and physically, Kalista drew her sword to execute Mal. Before she could swing the longblade, however, Inara pistol-whipped the back of Kalista's head, knocking her out cold.

BELOW: Mal and Inara's destinies seem entwined, so much so that she saves him from being killed by Kalista.

ENDING AND BEGINNINGS

With the crew reunited, they climbed onto
the Mule, and tried to flee. Kalista's girls had other plans, however, and grabbed River and Iris off the transport. Mal told the crew not to worry, that they'd pick them up on the way, but then he noticed something else: Mericourt's kids were hanging out by a nearby silverliner. The Peacemaker cell leader didn't abandon her plan, she accelerated it. The crew circled back and picked up River and Iris, just as Mal ordered, but barely missed a series of devastating explosions. A bomb had been planted on the docked silverliners; one after the other they detonated, setting fire to the ships, killing their passengers. Mal barked at Mericourt over the open commlink, but it was no use. She wouldn't listen, and Mal was ready to escape in *Serenity*.

As soon as the Mule drove up the cargo bay ramp, Mal ordered Kaylee to take off. They'd lost a lot of souls that day, lives that didn't need to be taken just to prove a point.

Bruised and bleeding, Mal was tired of secrets, and confronted Inara to ask her what had happened at Fiddler's Green in the Georgia System. The world housed a secret Independent base, but harbored more refugees than soldiers. One day, the Alliance waltzed in and slaughtered every man, woman, and child. Turned out Inara was responsible for their deaths. Though House Madrassa had a strict confidentiality policy, Inara couldn't keep the secrets of an Independent supplier who serviced the base. Because of her actions, Inara was asked to leave the Companion House and never return. Angry beyond words, Mal left the room, leaving her to wonder if their young relationship still had a chance.

The *Serenity* crew barely managed to escape with their lives that day. Kalista had lured them into an elaborate trap, and when it was sprung it damaged their relationships with one another. Zoë didn't trust River anymore, and wouldn't let her come near her daughter, Emma. The awful part was that River didn't trust herself, either. A rift had also torn Mal and Inara apart, forcing them to realize they'd once fought on opposite sides of the War, each in their own way.

Though they had two new crewmembers, Iris and Bea, Mal had something else, too: determination. Mal didn't agree with Mericourt's methods, and he didn't want to rain hell down on his people, either. But the *Serenity* Captain had lost too much, and had seen too many battles. He saw the truth behind the Peacekeepers' aims.

His back against the wall, Malcolm J. Reynolds had two options left. He could surrender, or he could start another war with the Alliance. Only time will tell which path Malcolm Reynolds will choose.

To be continued...

book two

BROWNCOATS, THIEVES & PURPLE BELLIES

SERENITY'S CREW

MALCOLM J. REYNOLDS

Malcolm J. Reynolds was born on Shadow, one of the Border Planets, and grew up on a ranch. Though he might have enjoyed the quiet life of a moderately wealthy rancher, he gave up herding cattle to fight for the Independent Faction in a war that would determine the fate of the known 'verse. After leaving his family behind, Mal volunteered to put his life on the line for a cause he believed in: a free and independent life dictated by hard work and *not* the Anglo-Sino Alliance.

> ## "We've done the impossible, and that makes us mighty."
>
> *Cpt. Malcolm J. Reynolds*

A man of faith-fueled optimism, Mal joined the Independents as a private, and put his faith into the fight. Slowly but surely, Mal earned the rank of sergeant over the next few years. No matter how many soldiers he lost or how many battlefields he had to abandon, Mal never lost hope that one day his beloved Browncoats would win against the better armed and trained Alliance military—until the Battle of Serenity Valley. Despite his best efforts to gain higher ground and clear a path for air support, the craft did not engage. The battle—and the Unification War—was over. The Alliance had won on two fronts: they successfully unified all planets and moons in the 'verse under their rule, and they unwittingly destroyed Mal's faith in both God and humanity.

After the War, Mal sought peace of mind and convinced himself the only way to find it was on a Firefly-class ship he called *Serenity*. But Mal knew that he couldn't fly the known 'verse all by his lonesome, so he put together a like-minded crew to help him smuggle, salvage, and stay clear of the Alliance. For six years he took on odd jobs from middlemen like Bolles, Patience, and Badger, and eked out a living on his terms. However, his rough-and-tumble life took a turn for the worse after picking up Simon and River Tam on Persephone.

For the first time since the beginning of the Unification War, Mal finally had a cause to believe in. Despite his outward display of mistrust, Mal decided to help the Tams in his own way. The fine-mannered doctor had given up all he had to help his sister, one of the Alliance's little experiments; though Mal could have left the Tams behind, he kept them on board despite the danger they presented.

RIGHT: Mal's pistol prop was built around this Taurus 85 revolver.

BELOW: Exploded view of Mal's pistol, showing the Taurus 85 beneath.

RIGHT: Pistol's ammo clip.

RIGHT: Bullets modeled for Mal's pistol.

LEFT: Side shroud removed from prop.

BELOW: Civil War style jacket made from leather.

BELOW: Mal's costume contains frontiersman elements.

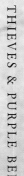

103

Over the next three years, Mal captained a crew of eight: Zoë, Wash, Jayne, Inara, Book, Kaylee, Simon and River. Together they flew from one end of the 'verse to another, until Mal couldn't run anymore. Since the end of the War, Mal had spent his days outrunning and outwitting the Alliance, but never confronting them. That changed after his encounter with the Operative, a true believer who never once questioned his actions on behalf of the Alliance. Following River's lead, Mal wound up fighting on the front lines in a new war to uncover the truth behind the Alliance's dirtiest secrets.

With this newfound sense of purpose, Mal has a new set of reasons to steer clear of the Alliance, while garnering the strength and people he needs to mount a rebellion. A man of many faces, Malcolm Reynolds is no stranger to the Alliance. To the government, he's a criminal. To his fellow Browncoats, a hero. And, to his beloved crew, their Captain.

RIGHT: Captain Malcolm Reynolds where he is most at home: on board his ship.

NATHAN FILLION

Malcolm J. Reynolds is portrayed by actor and producer Nathan Fillion.

The actor still remembers landing the part with enthusiasm. "I walked into [casting director] Amy Britt's office to have a meeting with Joss," Fillion says. "It was dimly lit and warm and cozy in there. I knew of Joss Whedon but had never met him, nor did I know what he looked like. There was this scroungy-looking fella in the corner. He had a purple sweater on with a hole in it on the left side of his chest and I thought 'Who's this guy and when do I meet Joss?' Halfway through the meeting, it dawned on me who *he* was," the actor laughs. "Joss told me a great deal about the show. I had so many questions and Joss had the answers. For whatever I asked, he had an entire universe planned. I was enthralled. We talked about the show, personal experiences, work ethics, how to keep things smooth on sets, and it became clear we had similar sensibilities. He said, 'Why don't you come back and audition for Malcolm Reynolds?' I said, 'Great,' and did just that."

Following his short stint on *Firefly*, the Canada-born Fillion has continued to lend his talents to voice acting for both animated shows and video games, as well as the Joss Whedon-directed *Dr. Horrible's Sing-Along Blog* TV series and *Much Ado About Nothing* movie. A fan favorite, Fillion also starred in one season of *Buffy The Vampire Slayer* (2003), *Castle* (2009-2016), and co-starred with Alan Tudyk in TV series *Con Man* (2015-2017).

Calm under pressure, Zoë Alleyne
Washburne doesn't like to waste her words. She was born on a spaceship, but other than that not much is known about her life before the Unification War. Like Mal, the battle took hold of her and wouldn't let go. A career soldier, Zoë fought in many battles alongside Sergeant Reynolds and earned the rank of corporal in the Independent Faction. Then, once the War ended, Zoë stuck to Mal's side. She continued to call him 'sir', for in her eyes Mal's actions during their long years of fighting the Alliance had earned him that title. Permanently.

"Big damn heroes, sir."

Zoë Alleyne Washburne

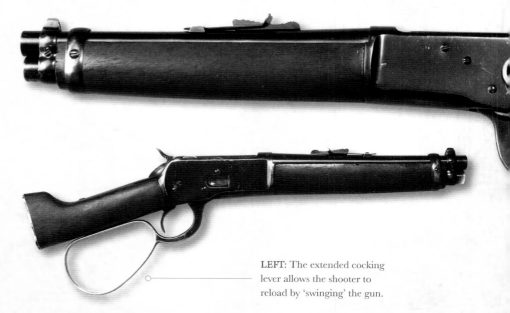

LEFT: The extended cocking lever allows the shooter to reload by 'swinging' the gun.

LEFT: Zoe's leather vest.

Zoe has always followed Mal's orders and half-baked crazy schemes...until she doesn't. She was *Serenity*'s first crewmember and slipped easily into the rank of first mate. When the Captain told her not to marry the ship's pilot she disobeyed and married Wash anyway. But when the Captain needs her steady gun hand and quiet determination, she stands by him just as she did in the War. 'Course, that won't stop her from standing up to the Captain when she has to; somebody needs to remind Mal to use a little common sense every now and again, and Zoë ain't afraid to speak her mind.

BELOW: Zoë's weapon is a 'Mare's Leg': a cut down Winchester rifle.

ABOVE: Bullets modeled for Zoë's pistol.

LEFT & RIGHT: The design inspirations for Zoë's outfit are similar to Mal's.

Zoë lost a piece of her heart when her beloved husband Wash died fighting them Reavers, but gained another after her daughter Emma was born. A family-minded woman, Zoë will fight for what's right and what's hers. Though she likes to keep things nice and simple, there's an air of mystery about her that may yet be explored.

Zoë wears a necklace made from the laces of her combat boots worn during the Unification War as a reminder of what she's been through and what she's lost. Her favorite weapon is Mare's Leg and, like Mal, she continues to wear her brown coat as a sign of her commitment to freedom.

RIGHT: Zoë is a fearsome warrior, forged alongside Mal in the fires of the Unification War.

LEFT: Wash and Zoe: partners in love, life and crime.

GINA TORRES

The quiet-yet-capable Zoë Alleyne Washburne is portrayed by actress, singer, and producer Gina Torres. A veteran of stage and screen, Torres starred in several genre television shows including *Hercules: The Legendary Journeys* (1997–1999), *Cleopatra 2525* (2000–2001), and *Angel* (2003) before slipping into the role of *Serenity*'s First Mate.

When asked about what drew her to *Firefly*, Torres replied: "I would say that even though there were several elements that were familiar, Joss had managed to create an incredibly unique world in the way he combined and juxtaposed those elements. So you had these challenged characters inhabiting a challenging world, and that makes for great storytelling AND NO ALIENS!"

Following the end of the show, the New York City-born Torres has continued to explore roles as a voice actress for beloved franchises such as *Star Wars*, *Justice League*, and *Transformers*, as well as acting in several TV shows, video games, and movies such as *Alias*, *Hannibal*, *24*, *Destiny*, and *Mr. Sophistication*.

HOBAN 'WASH' WASHBURNE

Hoban 'Wash' Washburne was born on an industrial planet he'd like to forget. As a child, he always wanted to see the stars, because the skies above were so polluted he couldn't see them. Turned out Wash was a natural at flying and making friends. In flight school, he crossed paths with Mr. Universe, a fellow student he caught cheating to stay at the top of the class. In exchange for his silence, Mr. Universe promised to lend Wash a hand whenever he needed it.

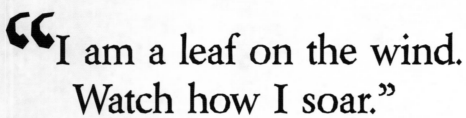

> **"I am a leaf on the wind. Watch how I soar."**
>
> *Hoban 'Wash' Washburne*

After Wash graduated from flight school he got mixed up in the Unification War, but he never told anyone which side he was on. Before, during, and after the War, Wash only cared about one thing: flying. He was so good at it his reputation often preceded him, ensuring he'd never have to worry about finding a job. That was good enough for Captain Reynolds, who needed a pilot who could dodge Alliance trouble, so he hired him despite his First Mate's objections.

Not long afterward, Zoë had a change of heart and fell in love with the anxious, tropical shirt-wearing, dinosaur-playing pilot. Defying the Captain's orders, Wash and Zoë married. Though Wash was happily married to his warrior woman, sometimes he felt that Zoë prioritized the Captain's needs over his. Tensions escalated, until Wash participated in a milk run on Ezra that quickly soured. Wash and Mal were kidnapped by a crime boss named Adelai Niska, but after some thrillin' heroics and a lot of luck, Wash finally understood why Zoë was loyal to Mal. She didn't love him in a romantic way; she owed him her life.

BELOW: Wash wears light colors to match his personality.

BELOW: Practical overalls leaving the arms free.

Unfortunately for Wash, all the fancy flying in the 'verse didn't save him from Reavers. Following an emergency landing on Mr. Universe's moon, Wash was relieved he didn't lose a single crewmember. Then, in the middle of reciting his favorite phrase, he was impaled by a giant harpoon and died instantly. He was remembered by Zoë, his daughter Emma, and several friends.

Unlike the rest of the *Serenity* crew, Wash didn't carry a gun and was nervous around the sight of blood. A pilot with a sense of humor, he could often be found in *Serenity*'s cockpit or collaborating with Kaylee, the ship's mechanic, when he wasn't enjoying a quiet moment or two with his wife.

ALAN TUDYK

Texas-born Alan Tudyk, who portrays Hoban 'Wash' Washburne, is a screen and voice actor who's performed for TV shows, video games, and films. A talented voice actor, he played the role of Heihei in *Moana* (2016), the robot K-2SO in *Rogue One: A Star Wars Story* (2016), and Alistair Krei in the TV series *Big Hero 6* (2017–2018).

Tudyk had this to say about his role: "A lot of who Wash is, Zoë is. I draw a lot of who the character is from that. He's a very loving husband, and she's just an intense lady. She's a killer. [Wash is] just: 'Fly the ship, we'll make some money, let's go on vacation!' He's that type of guy. He doesn't get too uptight about things, except when people start talkin' about killing. 'Why do we got to kill? Let's not do so much killing, please. Everybody relax.' He's that voice on the ship."

Tudyk also created, wrote, directed, and starred in a crowd-funded comedy series called *Con Man* (2015–2017), about a failed actor who toured science fiction conventions following the cancellation of his short-but-beloved show. *Con Man* was nominated for two Emmy awards and, following its debut on Vimeo, also aired on the SyFy channel.

JAYNE COBB

Jayne Cobb is a simple mercenary who speaks one language: money. When he doesn't, that's when he gets confused, because getting paid is often simpler than laying down arms.

Though he's the *Serenity*'s hired muscle and, in many ways, a necessary evil, Jayne is also a study of opposites on account of him being a hero to the people of Canton. Long before he encountered Mal and Zoë, Jayne and his best friend, Stitch Hessian, were attempting to rob Magistrate Higgins and get away clean with a pile of cash. Higgins was a shrewd man who did everything he could to stop the thieves, and even managed to damage their ship as they tried to escape with the loot. Unable to maneuver freely, the ship was hampered with too much weight, so Jayne pushed Stitch off to lighten the load. When that didn't work Jayne reluctantly dumped the bags of money overboard—right into the hands of needy workers.

> **"Let's be bad guys."**
>
> *Jayne Cobb*

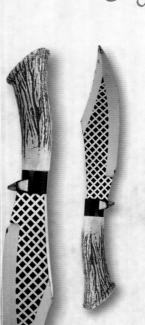

LEFT: Jayne's antler-handled knife.

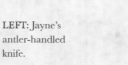

LEFT: Jayne's beloved hat.

BELOW: Jayne's outfits share a strong military aesthetic.

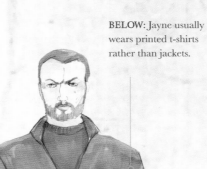

BELOW: Jayne usually wears printed t-shirts rather than jackets.

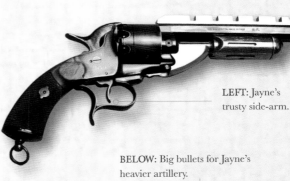

LEFT: Jayne's trusty side-arm.

BELOW: Big bullets for Jayne's heavier artillery.

BOOK TWO: BROWNCOATS, THIEVES & PURPLE BELLIES

Despite appearances, Jayne has a kind of code. He sends money home to his mother, Radiant Cobb, to help take care of his brother, Mattie. There's no telling if Radiant knows her son's a criminal; she sends him care packages from time to time, like an orange-striped hat and matching sweater. In addition to being a family-minded individual, Jayne also has a deep respect for Shepherd Book, and often lifted weights with him in his downtime. When he wasn't working out or harassing Simon Tam, whom he didn't like one bit, he spent time in his bunk cleaning his guns and maintaining his gear.

Though Jayne is the type to shoot first and ask questions later, he has saved the *Serenity* crew's lives on more than one occasion. When the occasion calls for it, he'll pitch in when he feels the moment is right, but has yet to overcome his biggest weakness—greed for credits.

RIGHT: Jayne might not be trustworthy, but there are few better when caught in a tight spot.

ADAM BALDWIN

Adam Baldwin is an Illinois native who first started acting in 1980 when he played a bully-turned-protector named Linderman in *My Bodyguard*. Since then, he's acted in dozens of movies, television shows, and video games including *Wyatt Earp* (1994), *Independence Day* (1996), *The X-Files* (2001–2002), *Stargate SG-1* (2004), *Angel* (2004) and *Chuck* (2007–2012). His most recent work includes *The Last Ship* (2014–2017), *Castle* (2012–2015), and the *Infinite Crisis* (2015) video game.

Despite his many credits, filling Jayne Cobb's shoes on *Firefly* was a dream come true. Baldwin has said that: "I've been fortunate to have had a few 'gigs of a lifetime', but this is my favorite so far. I realized it right away. I knew that this guy and group of people was something special. And I had learned from *Full Metal Jacket*, which I did when I was twenty-three, that you need to appreciate what you are doing while you are doing it, and not look back ten years later and wish you had appreciated it then. I actually did come to work every day looking to keep it special, positive, and fun. We were under the gun pretty much from the get go, and I think we all appreciated how fleeting it can be and how much of a risk you were taking with making television. That is why the work came out so well and at such a high level."

KAYWINNET LEE 'KAYLEE' FRYE

Kaywinnet Lee Frye, or Kaylee for short, is a genius in the engine room. A natural mechanic who hails from a Border Planet, Kaylee could 'talk' to *Serenity* the day she met her. See, Kaylee had been having sex with Bester, *Serenity*'s first mechanic, when Mal walked in on them to find out what was wrong with the ship. When Bester couldn't supply Mal with the answer, Kaylee corrected him and fixed *Serenity* right up. This impressed Mal, and after asking her parents for permission to fly, Kaylee left her simple home behind and joined his crew.

> **"I like to meet new people. They've got stories."**
>
> *Kaylee Frye*

ABOVE: The umbrella Kaylee twirls to entice passengers onboard.

Kaylee, like Wash, is not afraid to do a little crime, and has helped the crew by mucking with control panels, emergency beacons—even *Serenity*'s engine. Cheerful to a fault, she has always been impressed with high society, and was able to experience life as a socialite when she was invited to join Mal at a party on Persephone. Though she'd never admit it to anyone but Inara, Kaylee had a crush on Simon Tam from the moment she laid eyes on him. Thankfully, following months of effort and several awkward moments, they did wind up getting together after all.

Kaylee abhors violence and crime, and doesn't carry a gun. That doesn't mean she won't stand up for herself when she needs to, however. She feared for her life after a bounty hunter named Jubal Early secretly boarded *Serenity* and tied her up. Next time they met? Kaylee took control of her nightmares and knocked him right out with a wrench. It might not seem like it, but Kaylee's sunny, hope-filled disposition often keeps her going in a world where anything could happen to her, Simon, or *Serenity*.

BELOW: Practical
overalls for a mechanic.

BELOW: This costume
has an Asian twist.

BOOK TWO: BROWNCOATS, THIEVES & PURPLE BELLIES

119

LEFT: Kaylee's reprogrammer.

JEWEL STAITE

Jewel Staite, who plays Kaywinnet Lee 'Kaylee' Frye, was born in British Columbia, Canada, and has been acting since the age of six. In addition to her best-known roles as Kaylee on *Firefly* and Dr. Jennifer Keller on *Stargate SG-1* (2005–2009), Staite has also appeared on *Castle* (2016) and *Con Man* (2015) where she rejoined her former co-stars.

When asked about how she felt about Kaylee's connection to *Serenity*, Staite has said that: "I think Kaylee has always pictured *Serenity* as the tenth crewmember. It's very dear to her, it's her home, it's probably the only steady home she's ever really had, and I think that she's just so proud of it. Right from the very beginning, Joss said that he wanted Kaylee's affection for the ship to be really obvious, so there was a lot of patting of the walls and admiration for its engine. She's just so amazed by how it all works and the fact that she gets to work on it."

Following her recurring roles on TV shows like *The Killing* (2013–2014) and *State of Syn* (2013), Staite became Detective Penny Hart in a Canadian true crime show called *The Detectives* (2018–).

INARA SERRA

Born on the capitol planet Sihnon, **Inara Serra joined House Madrassa at the age of twelve and trained to be a Companion. A practicing Buddhist, Inara possesses many talents and is skilled in the arts of fencing, archery, seduction, calligraphy, and diplomacy.**

"You're alone in the woods. We all are."

Inara Serra

Inara supported Unification and, during the War, remained in House Madrassa to service clients. Though the Companion House has a strict "Don't ask, don't tell" policy, a member of the Independent Faction had confided in Inara and she, in turn, disclosed that information and the location of a secret Independent base called Fiddler's Green to the Alliance. Not only did the Alliance swarm the base, they slaughtered patients, soldiers, and refugees. Following this unforgivable break with tradition, the Companion was forced to leave House Madrassa and sought to continue her business elsewhere. Though she was able to legally maintain her position as a Companion, she had greatly damaged the reputation of her House.

BELOW: The designers took inspiration from many different cultures and historical periods.

Swept up in Mal's bitter fight with the Alliance, Inara rejoined the *Serenity* crew to fight alongside them. Following this, she did the one thing she thought she'd never do: abandon her lavish lifestyle, wardrobe and training to explore a relationship with Mal. Like many things on board *Serenity*, her happiness didn't last. After she was forced to tell Mal she was responsible for the worst recorded massacre of the Unification War, he stopped speaking to her.

Only time will tell if Inara and Mal will reconcile. Though she has recently adopted more pragmatic clothes, Inara is often recognized for the ornate ensemble she wears to mark her status as a Companion. She does carry a gun, called the Luger, but can also fight with a sword, bow and arrow, or words.

Inara decided to avoid resettling on Sihnon and opted to find a rough-and-tumble Captain with a ship where she'd be free to live and work as she pleased. After meeting Malcolm Reynolds, Inara negotiated with him to ensure she retained autonomy and could live freely in her own shuttle attached to *Serenity*. For many months, Inara was able to continue working as a Companion, and had unwittingly grown to like, even love, many of the crewmembers she encountered. She treated Kaylee, the ship's mechanic, like her sister, and the others as her friends. Mal, on the other hand, she fell in love with.

Inara's relationship with Mal has had many ups and downs. At first, she denied having feelings for him after he 'married' Saffron, but she could no longer keep them a secret after he slept with her friend, Nandi. Faced with the possibility of either abandoning her life as a Companion or divulging her greatest secret, Inara decided to return to a Companion House where she helped train young girls. As much as she tried, however, that didn't stop Mal from returning to rescue her from the Operative, an Alliance agent who (at the time) possessed true faith in the government.

BELOW: Flowing material and bright colors designed to draw the eye.

RIGHT: Inara's companion registry book.

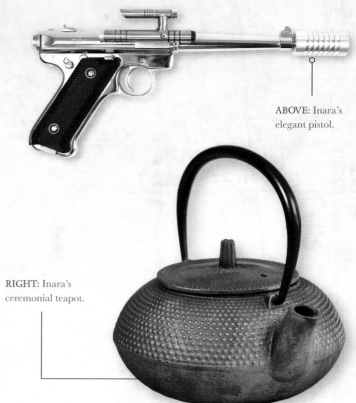

ABOVE: Inara's elegant pistol.

RIGHT: Inara's ceremonial teapot.

MORENA BACCARIN

Inara Serra is played by Morena Baccarin, a Brazilian-American actress who studied acting in New York City at Juilliard. She has worked in animation, video games, television, and movies in both lead and supporting roles. *Firefly* was Baccarin's first role for a television show. She once revealed how she learned from the other members of the cast.

"From Nathan, I learned you don't have to memorize anything until you get to the make-up room. I was always amazed. He would have pages and pages of dialogue, just read it once, and he would know the whole thing. He is a really hard worker and so am I. I was trained classically in theater where you are taught to be really disciplined. He did it with such pleasure, so I learned how to have fun with Nathan. Do your work to the best of your ability, but don't take it too seriously. It was a lesson to me in terms of the technical stuff and dealing with a camera in your face."

Some of her memorable performances following her appearance on *Firefly* include: Adria in *Stargate SG-1* (2006–2007), Anna in *V* (2009–2011), and Vanessa in *Deadpool* (2016) and *Deadpool 2* (2018).

SHEPHERD DERRIAL BOOK

The man the Serenity crew knew as **Derrial Book was born Henry Evans. After fleeing from his abusive father at a young age, Henry fell in with the kinds of criminals who could get him killed or arrested. For many years, Henry lived a life of crime—right up until he got arrested for mugging a couple in an alleyway. Now, for some unknown reason, the officer who tracked him down in a bar gave Henry a second chance. The Independent Faction needed scrappy volunteers, and the cop promised to wipe his record clean if he'd sign up to fight the Alliance.**

❝You don't fix faith. It fixes you.❞

Shepherd Derrial Book

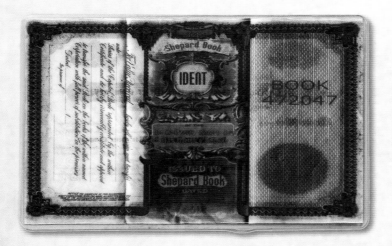

ABOVE: (Top) Book's ident papers.
(Bottom) Book's Bible with notations.

At first, Henry turned the officer down. But after a group of cops showed up at his door to arrest him, he had a change of heart. Unlike other volunteers who fought on the front lines, Henry was destined for deep cover operations. First, the Independent Faction replaced one of his eyes with a camera that transmitted data back to headquarters. Then Henry murdered an Alliance loyalist named Derrial Book, assumed his identity, and became a double agent—a fact that has never been revealed to the Alliance, even after the War was over. To most Alliance soldiers, Derrial Book was a war hero who tragically lost the lives of thousands by making an incalculable error while in command of the I.A.V. *Cortez*. Unbeknownst to them, Book orchestrated the greatest military loss in Alliance history, and was punished by being discharged from his post. Unfortunately, the Independent Faction never could overcome the well-armed Alliance, so many Browncoats don't know who Book is either.

After the War was over, Book found refuge at Southdown Abbey on Persephone, and became a shepherd. Book's faith granted him some peace, and when he was ready he decided to travel the 'verse for the first time in years. Though he could've picked another ship, Kaylee was right to tell him he'd choose *Serenity*. Like Mal, Book was also searching for something amongst the stars. As time passed, Book felt he was in danger of falling back into old, criminal habits, and decided to leave *Serenity* after spending nearly two years on board. Instead of returning to Persephone, he settled down on Haven and did the Lord's work in a mining colony.

As fate would have it, an Alliance operative ordered a deadly attack on the colony, to ensure Mal would have no place left to go. Book defended the colony and shot down the A.V. *Sparrow*, but suffered fatal wounds in the process. As he lay dying in Mal's arms, he spoke these words: "I don't care what you believe. Just believe it!"

BELOW: The grey shirt echoes Alliance colors.

RON GLASS

A devout Buddhist in real life, Glass says tackling Book's faith was intriguing from the start. "I did have some in-depth conversations with Joss in terms of suggesting that Book have more of a Buddhist persuasion in his Christianity. Joss explained to me that he wanted Inara to be the Buddhist in the group and Book to be more of a fundamentalist Christian guy. The wonderful thing was the commonality in terms of the two philosophies. What I was able to bring to the Christian part of it was the humanism and the humanistic point of view. It was the hook in terms of being able to make that adjustment. I wasn't born Buddhist, so I have some other traditions to pull from too.

"One of the things I was most delighted about as far as Book's character was concerned was that he was not a saint and he had not always been a preacher. Though rather mysterious, it was absolutely clear that he had had a very full life before he went off to the monastery and took on that responsibility. I loved the fact that he could save your soul, but he could also kick your ass. That's a really interesting combination to play."

IN MEMORIAM: RON GLASS (1945-2016)

To honor Ron's many contributions to stage and screen, I can think of no better way than to tell you a personal story about him. To me, Ron Glass was Detective Ron Harris on *Barney Miller* (1975–1982), a show I'd seen in re-runs as a kid. When I met him in 2005 at Gen Con: Indianapolis, he was kind, gracious, and incredibly humble despite being swarmed with fans. I couldn't help but tell him where I'd seen him before, and the minute I mentioned Barney Miller, Ron threw his head back and laughed. We chatted just long enough so he could greet his next fan, but he struck me as someone who was filled with appreciation for every role he'd played.

A few years later I met Mark Sheppard, who played Badger on *Firefly*. Mark was excited to promote his then-new role on *Battlestar Galactica*, in which he starred as Romo Lampkin, but took the time to talk about his memorable *Firefly* character. I mentioned Ron to him, to share how grateful I was to meet not one, but two *Firefly* actors, and Mark was gracious enough to tell me more about Ron. At the time, I didn't know Ron had appeared on *All in the Family* as Jack, the refrigerator repairman, in an episode entitled 'Everybody Tells The Truth' (1973).

In the episode, characters Archie, Mike, and Edith are arguing about why their refrigerator broke down; both Archie and Mike embellish their versions of the story. Not only do they lie, blaming Jack for the broken fridge, they both describe him using separate racist stereotypes of black men. Mark explained that to cope with the name-calling and bigotry in that scene, Ron grabbed a paring knife and slowly peeled an apple. This was not only preserved on film, that small act became such a powerful moment in television it hasn't been forgotten. In fact, Mark shared that the apple peeler was placed in Badger's office to honor Ron and his acting legacy.

I am certain, especially after hearing this story, that Ron Glass has touched many hearts and minds over the years, both through his roles and relationships.

May he always be remembered.

Monica Valentinelli, Author

MAURICE BROADDUS ON RON GLASS

I grew up with Ron Glass and have always felt like I've had a certain kinship with him. First, he was a fellow Hoosier. I didn't know it at the time when I first saw him in *Barney Miller*, where he played NYPD Detective Ron Harris. I was six years old when my family moved to this country. We first lived in small town Indiana in Franklin (before moving to big city Indiana in the form of Indianapolis). For Ron it was being born in Evansville…most folks would be challenged to find either place on a map. I remember laying in front of the television, looking up at Ron Glass. Always so debonair with his thick mustache and stylish suits, all 70s cool. He had a sardonic wit that I didn't always get, but I clearly remember my father laughing—which was always infectious.

And Ron was black.

Not an everyday occurrence in television back then. He became a familiar beacon for me. Always easy to spot in a cast photo, no matter what show he was on. Always with his gentle demeanor, his broad, easy smile, and razor-sharp jibes. It was such an encouragement seeing someone who looked like me pop up from time to time in the shows that I watched.

And I am a science-fiction-loving, spiritual person. I will never forget him as Shepherd Derrial Book on *Firefly* (especially since I've role-played that character so often in the *Firefly Role-Playing Game*). Book always carried himself with a deep abiding spirituality wrung from a life that had dealt its share of dirt. But the character's concern for others oozed from him in a way that ran deeper than just mere performance.

Ron Glass added grace, heart, soberness, and humor to his work. It was part of who he was. But it was his words as Shepherd Book that always charged my faith: "I don't care what you believe in, just believe in it."

Please see page 256 for Maurice Broaddus' biography.

SIMON TAM

Born to Gabriel and Regan Tam, Simon grew up alongside his gifted younger sister, River, on Osiris. The Tams were a wealthy family who had everything: credits, great jobs, bright futures. For many years, Simon pledged his loyalty to the Alliance, supported Unification, and studied hard at a MedAcad. Eventually his efforts were rewarded when he became a top-notch trauma surgeon. Simon was well on his way to becoming a Medical Elect when he began to realize that all was not well with his sister.

> ❝ **This must be what going mad feels like.** ❞
>
> *Simon Tam*

Convinced River's cryptic letters from the Academy she attended were a sign she was in trouble, Simon took it upon himself to investigate the situation further. Despite Simon's repeated warnings to his parents, he was unable to convince them that River was in danger. Simon was so desperate to save River, he went to a blackout zone to meet with Alliance informants. It was here where he was arrested. Though his father bailed him out, Simon was severely reprimanded for not only putting his career on the line but his family's social standing as well. Forced to choose between his comfortable life and saving his sister, Simon did what his conscience demanded and sacrificed everything he had to free her from the Academy. In response, the Alliance froze his assets and labeled both him and his sister as fugitives.

RIGHT: Simon's tools of the trade.

Simon left home and sunk every credit he had into rescuing River. Once freed, he worked with rebels to transport her as cargo, while she remained in a cryonic state. Then, when he was able to find a safe place for them to live, he planned to wake her up and help her recover. Though he managed to secure passage on board *Serenity*, Simon had been followed by a Federal agent named Lawrence Dobson. In his zeal to arrest the Tams, Dobson accidentally shot Kaylee in the stomach, forcing Simon to give Mal his own set of demands to ensure their safety.

Simon managed to elude capture that day and joined *Serenity* as the ship's doctor. Simon's primary patient for many months was his sister and, as caregiver, he was forced to set aside his personal feelings and hope of freedom until she was healed. Despite this, he began to have feelings for Kaylee and, following many awkward conversations, he found a way to win her heart.

LEFT: After a slow and rocky start, Simon and Kaylee's relationship became close.

SEAN MAHER

By the time Sean Maher played Dr. Simon Tam on *Firefly*, the actor had already starred in several television series, including *Ryan Caulfield: Year One* (1999), *Party of Five* (2000), and *The $treet* (2000–1). *Firefly* was his first science-fiction show. He credits Joss Whedon as the reason why he took the role. "Joss made my character and this universe so unique. That is the first thing I was attracted to when I read the pilot. It was like nothing I had read before. It was so unique and like a world of its own. Everything about it was so complete and well thought out, so that it was this altered world—there was no element that was missing. Everything about it…

"The characters were so rich and flawed. I was always drawn to the relationships between them and their dynamics because it was so fresh. Someone was asking me the other day about what archetype I would compare Simon to, and I really couldn't think of anything. In that regard, each character, Simon included, is a character of their own."

Maher, who hails from Pleasantville, New York, has continued to act post-*Firefly* in several TV shows and movies, including Joss Whedon's *Much Ado About Nothing* (2012) and *Con Man* (2015). One of his most recent projects is a psychological horror movie called *The Old Hag Syndrome* (2016).

RIVER TAM

River Tam is the youngest of two children **born to Gabriel and Regan Tam. Growing up on Osiris alongside her brother, Simon, River possessed extraordinary talents of the body and mind. To fulfill her great potential, River was accepted into a special Academy—without knowing the Alliance was luring 'volunteers' to be experimented upon within the confines of their facility.**

> ## "I can't sleep. There's too much screaming."
>
> *River Tam*

For many years, River was only vaguely aware she was not the only human experiment at the facility, for her mind had been physically altered by top-secret loyalists, including Dr. Mathias. River's amygdala had been stripped from her brain, and the surgeons repeated a series of surgical incisions in the hopes of creating a psychically gifted sleeper assassin they could control. Many of these experiments had been recorded in the 'R. Tam Sessions', which showed her progress and her ability to glean information from those around her.

By the time Simon rescued her from the Academy, River had become a teenager. Unfortunately, Simon did not possess the medical supplies required to help her recover, so he staged a heist at St. Lucy's Medical Hospital in Ariel City to gain a 3-D image of her brain and administer the right drugs. Despite Simon's careful treatment, River could only progress so far before she succumbed to her emotions. It wasn't until she had been triggered by the Alliance in the Maidenhead on Beaumonde that she began to realize what was causing her distress: the planet Miranda.

River tends to wear knee-high boots, a colorful, long sweater or shirt, and shorts. Though she doesn't carry a gun, River is an expert shot.

BELOW: The blades River wields with deadly effect.

Always on the run, River forced Mal's hand and used the ship's console to locate Miranda. After the *Serenity* crew discovered the gruesome secrets the Alliance had been desperate to keep, Mal took it upon himself to reveal the truth about Reavers to the entire 'verse. By doing so, however, the Captain had alerted new enemies, and unwittingly drawn the attention of Alliance Lieutenant Kalista, Iris, and her group of sleeper agents, who'd also been operated on. Though River gained acceptance on board *Serenity* and eventually became her pilot, she has struggled to reconcile her dark past with her future.

BELOW: Fruity Oaty Bar!

SUMMER GLAU

Ballerina and actress Summer Glau is the Texas-born native who plays River Tam. Like Nathan Fillion, Gina Torres, and Adam Baldwin, Glau had worked with Joss Whedon on *Angel* (2002) before joining the cast of *Firefly*. She once talked about how River connected with the fans by saying: "I'm constantly touched by the fans and the things that they've got for us or written to us. I get a lot of mail from people who suffer from depression or have schizophrenia or some kind of other mental illness and River has brought them comfort. I think the show as a whole teaches you about family and loving things unconditionally and being part of a team. River fights so hard to contribute to her family. Simon always said, 'River loves this ship. She just wants to stay here and be part of this.' If the series continued, you would have seen more of what you saw in the film, which is River defeating the demons and things that haunt her mind and being able to go back to the people that care about her—her new family on *Serenity*. I think that is why people love the story and want more of it. It's a story about love and loving something that doesn't make sense. Mal is always looking at River and asking himself why he is keeping this liability on board when she is not part of his family of crew, yet he can't walk away from her. I hope that's what people remember about our story and keep with them."

Glau's career has continued to flourish following *Firefly*, and she's had recurring roles on shows like *The 4400* (2005–7), *Terminator: The Sarah Connor Chronicles* (2008-9), *Dollhouse* (2009–10), *Arrow* (2013–14), *Con Man* (2015), and a guest appearance on *Castle* (2016).

FRIENDS & ALLIES

The characters in Firefly are all connected to the members of the *Serenity* crew in some way. Characters are either blood relatives or friends, war buddies or 'associates'. Most of the time, the crew's relationship to other characters is in some way complicated. Take Gabriel and Regan Tam, for example. Played by William Converse-Roberts and Isabella Hofmann, Simon and River's parents are comfortable in their position and their home. They are entrenched in their Alliance-funded lifestyle but are aware that the government has its problems. Gabriel, who bails Simon out of jail in a flashblack during 'Safe', warns his son to abandon his obsession to find River. To rescue her, Simon gives up everything he has, and this includes the rest of his family. Jayne, on the other hand, has a loving relationship with his mother Radiant Cobb—but he never sees her. Though the mercenary sends money back home when he can, his relationship with his family is strictly long-distance. Friendships like Nandi's, or Wash's old flight buddies Leland, Trey, and Tagg, are far less complicated. Sometimes, however, loyalty has a steep price.

"I won't let anyone take what's mine." *Nandi*

NANDI

Nandi was a former Companion who trained alongside Inara at House Madrassa on Sihnon, and remained a dear friend of Inara up until the day she died.

After leaving House Madrassa, Nandi flew to one of the farthest corners of the 'verse—the Blue Sun System. The former Companion settled down on Deadwood, claimed a patch of land, and built a brothel there called the Heart of Gold. The whorehouse became not only Nandi's home, but her girls' too. That's why, when Rance Burgess started causing trouble, Nandi called Inara and asked for her help.

Nandi had always defended what was hers, but knew she couldn't stop Burgess by herself. When the *Serenity* crew landed, her heart was filled with hope. When she met Malcolm Reynolds she fell head over heels for him. The night before the big showdown with Burgess, she slept with him, reminding Inara how she truly felt.

Nandi died the very next day, spurring Mal to seek revenge for her death. Not long afterward, Inara decided to leave *Serenity*, knowing the secrets she kept would one day catch up with her.

Nandi was played by Melinda Clarke. When asked about her role on *Firefly*, she said: "I always end up getting these characters who are madams or dominatrix. Ultimately, these women are not stupid; they're businesswomen and they're highly evolved in their way of thinking."

MR. UNIVERSE

Mr. Universe was friends with Wash in flight school. Then Mr. Universe went and did a stupid thing: he hacked the school records to alter his grades. Wash caught him in the act, but promised not to say anything. In exchange, Mr. Universe pledged to help him whenever he needed a technical hand.

One fateful day Wash did call, just as he'd done before. Believing he had the upper hand, Mr. Universe was excited to unravel the embedded message in the recording Wash had sent him. But by helping Wash he unwittingly attracted the attention of an Alliance agent known as the Operative.

Like Nandi, Mr. Universe stood by his convictions and understood the importance of what Mal, Wash, and his friends were hoping to accomplish. While he lived alone on a secluded moon with his wife, Lenore, free from the politics and dangers most people faced, the *Serenity* crew was in danger, and, to save their crewmembers they had to stand up to the Alliance. The trouble was, they needed Mr. Universe's equipment to do it.

Mr. Universe was killed by the Operative. Before he died, he programmed Lenore to tell Mal the location of a backup generator, hoping he'd survive long enough to stick it to the Feds.

Mr. Universe was played by David Krumholtz, and Lenore by Nectar Rose.

> **"You can't stop the signal, Mal."**
>
> *Mr. Universe*

"You protect the man you're with. You watch his back. Everybody knows that." *Stitch*

STITCH HESSIAN

There was a time when Stitch Hessian was Jayne's best friend, right up until money got between them. Stitch and Jayne were both mercenaries, and when the time was right they set their sights on Higgins' Moon. Unlike Ariel City, the moon only had one rich man to speak of—Magistrate Higgins. So they robbed the politician blind, not realizing he'd fight back.

Stitch and Jayne almost got away, until Higgins shot up their ship with an anti-aircraft gun. After that, the only way they could break atmo was by losing the weight that dragged them down, and much to Stitch's surprise Jayne dumped him first.

To teach Stitch a lesson, Magistrate Higgins held him captive and tortured him for years. When Jayne returned with the *Serenity* crew, he was released to seek revenge on his former partner and best friend. For all his suffering, Stitch died when he confronted Jayne in front of the entire town of Canton. Whether he was a tragic figure or a thief who made all the wrong decisions is up to the observer.

Stitch Hessian was played by Kevin Gage.

LEFT: Stitch Hessian learnt that his erstwhile companion Jayne did not take his bond of friendship as seriously as he did.

VETERANS OF WAR

Friendships aren't always formed at a school or on the job. Sometimes they form from necessity, or through the bonds of shared trauma, or the desire for freedom. Mal and Zoë, who both fought for the Independents in the Unification War, have a tight-knit relationship because of their time spent on the battlefield. The people they fought with also call them family or, in Bea Quiang's case, regard them as heroes. Some soldiers, like Mal's childhood best friend Finn, still suffer from the psychological and physical trials of war, while the Mericourt and the New Resistance have renewed the fight against the Alliance. Unfortunately, not every soldier has a place in this new 'verse. Veterans like Tracey Smith struggle to maintain life as a civilian, because they don't know who or what they're fighting for.

MONTY

Monty is a mustache-sportin', browncoat-wearin', giant of a man who fought with Mal and Zoë in the Unification War. He is a friend of the crew and, like Mal, decided to abandon the Alliance after the War ended and live life on his own terms. Monty bought himself a freighter and started collecting sundries and the like. When he had enough to open up shop, he contacted his fellow Browncoats and landed on a Podunk moon to sell them what he had.

One time, Monty got more than he bargained for when he met Bridget, a feisty redhead who he went and got himself hitched to. He didn't know Bridget was actually Saffron—not until Mal broke the news to him. It took him a minute, but after realizing Mal was telling the truth, he called Bridget a 'devil woman' and left her stranded. As Saffron pointed out, the war buddy bond is hard to crack—with good reason.

Monty's black market keeps him under the Alliance's radar. Normally he'd need a permit to sell and collect salvaged goods, maybe even two. By using his freighter as his 'store', he can fly away in a hurry if he needs to.

Monty was played by Franc Ross.

TRACEY SMITH

Private Tracey Smith reported to Mal and Zoë during the Unification War, and still referred to Mal as 'Sergeant' long after it was over. Both had saved his life many times over, but in the end they couldn't save him from himself.

After the War, Tracey fell on hard times. His family was from St. Albans, and he had trouble finding paid work. So, Tracey fell in with the worst crowd imaginable and sold his body in exchange for piles of credits…sort of. What he sold was his body's ability to incubate lab-grown organs called blastomeres. To do that he had to have his own organs surgically removed and replaced. Then, he just had to fly to the rendezvous point on Ariel to have them swapped out again.

Problem was, Tracey got stupid. Believing he could hold out for more credits, he pretended to be dead and relied on the bonds of friendship to get him through. That time, though, Tracey forgot that loyalty could be broken, and he did just that by bringing all kinds of trouble to Mal's door.

Mal wound up shooting Tracey to protect the crew, but did honor his last request. With heavy hearts the crew took his body home to St. Albans.

Tracey Smith was played by Jonathan Woodward.

VARMINTS & VILLAINS

As time passes, some members of the

Serenity crew move on. Though the crew had a mechanic named Bester, played by Dax Griffin, Kaylee proved to be better at the job than he did, so he was left behind. Book, Jayne, and Inara eventually leave the ship but, by doing so, lose the protection of the crew. Other times, the crew finds an unwitting ally or works with a favored middleman, like the Rample brothers played by Yan and Rafael Feldman. Sheriff Bourne is a friend the crew never thought they'd make, because he didn't arrest Mal after he found out who really stole the crates of Pescaline-D in 'The Train Job'. The Captain returned what was needed, and that was good enough for him. Most folk struggle to get by, and Sheriff Bourne, played by Gregg Henry, knew it.

Sir Warwick Harrow, a lord the crew encountered in 'Shindig', is another example. Played by Larry Drake, Sir Harrow was a nobleman Mal had to impress to smuggle his cattle from Persephone to Jiangyin. Though Mal was unsuccessful in his attempt to sell the herd, Harrow admired the Captain for the way he defended Inara, and even went so far as to back him up in his duel with Atherton Wing. Atherton, a socialite and bully played by Edward Atterton, had wanted to 'claim' Inara as his own, and Mal's misguided sense of honor thwarted his plans and scarred him for life.

Inara, too, has influence and power, rivals like Ceres, and many friends. After all, though she honored her agreement with Magistrate Higgins to accept his son, Fess, as her client in 'Jaynestown', he stood up to his bullying father. Fess Higgins, played by Zachary Kranzler, contacted Port Authority and told them to remove the digi-lock that prevented *Serenity* from taking off, which angered his father more than he cared to admit. Magistrate Higgins, played by Gregory Itzin, was forced to watch *Serenity*—and his chance for revenge—fly to freedom.

Though Magistrate Higgins was cruel, he wasn't a thief like Stitch Hessian or Ott. 'Course, the *Serenity* crew has encountered its fair share of the criminally-minded. In 'Safe', River ran afoul of the power-hungry Patron, played by Gary Werntz, and drew his ire. In episode 'Serenity' Mal tried to make a deal with Patience, who was played by Bonnie Bartlett, and wound up getting himself shot at on Whitefall. In 'Our Mrs. Reynolds' they were conned by Elder Gommen. Played by Bob Fimiani, Gommen had drawn upon the crew's sense of honor, and pretended to need their services. Then, Gommen conned Mal by 'gifting' him with a blushing bride, Saffron.

Sometimes the *Serenity* crew is two steps ahead of the trouble that follows in their wake. Often, however, they meet a man like Rance Burgess, and they're forced to either run or fight—even when they don't want to. Burgess, played by Fredric Lehne, preyed upon Nandi's girls and mounted an assault on the Heart of Gold because he was desperate for a son. Though he died by Petaline's hand, Burgess was nothing more than a common bully.

Most of the time, however, the *Serenity* crew has a run of bad luck—and that's caused by recurring villains who can't leave well enough alone.

BADGER

> ## "I'm above you. Better than. Businessman, see?"
>
> *Badger*

Badger hails from Dyton Colony, a settlement built on Dyton located in the Red Sun System. Dyton is a moon orbiting the planet Greenleaf and is part of the Border Planets.

Badger is a permanent fixture of the Eavesdown Docks on Persephone, and has an office that services thieves, smugglers, slavers, and the occasional Alliance representative. He is a local crime boss who has a gang of bodyguards, thieves, and enforcers at his beck and call. Occasionally he has a job that needs doing. When his gang can't do it, he contacts people like Malcolm Reynolds to illegally salvage cargo or transport cattle for him.

Though he wouldn't openly admit it, Badger has a love-hate relationship with Mal and the crew. Badger needs Mal, because he's not just another petty criminal—he's also a veteran of the Unification War who has conviction. Unfortunately, Mal's track record hasn't been great. The cargo Mal was supposed to steal for him was traceable; each bar of protein had a prominent Alliance stamp on it. Worse, an Alliance cruiser almost caught *Serenity*, and put out an alert for a Firefly-class ship. Then, after Badger gave Mal a second chance, he never got paid for the cattle they flew to Jiangyin. It was bad enough Sir Warwick Harrow didn't like Badger, but with no money or cattle to smooth things over, Badger was humped.

'Course, Badger is the type of criminal that will entertain any idea that could earn him some credits. Unlike Mal, Badger doesn't have convictions—he only cares about his survival. That's why, when the Alliance approached him to do a job, he took it and helped set a trap for Mal. Badger wasn't sure if Mal would squeak his way out of it, but that wasn't his problem. So long as he got paid and the Alliance didn't blame him if things went south, then he'd cooperate as much as he needed to.

Sheppard recalls his first scene on the *Serenity* interior. "That moment was about, wow, Badger gets that, Badger doesn't have this [a ship]. Badger thinks he owns it, because for some reason, he likes to think he can control Mal—financially, certainly. I think Badger just wants to be liked—that's his fatal flaw—but I don't know that Malcolm Reynolds likes him that much," Sheppard laughs.

Badger often dresses for his version of success. He's known for wearing a bowler hat, and he speaks with a Cockney accent. His character is played by Mark Sheppard.

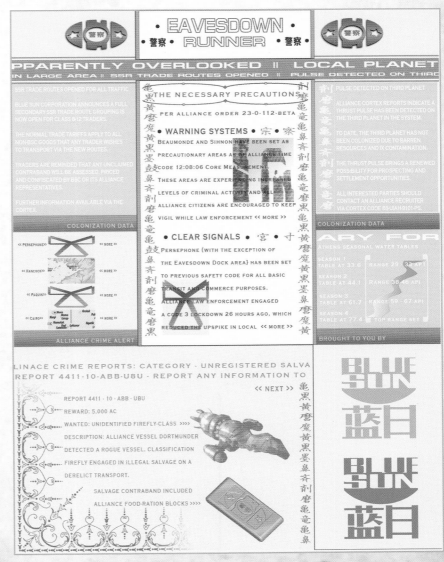

ADELAI NISKA

Niska is an organized-crime boss who lives on a space station referred to as Niska's Skyplex. He is a devotee of the psychotic warrior-poet Shan Yu, who uses torture to protect his reputation at all costs and often stoops to extortion and murder. As a crime boss, he operates openly and boldly, for the World Council doesn't treat his Skyplex as part of their jurisdiction. No one, not even Niska's own nephew, is granted leniency. If anyone crosses Niska, vengeance is guaranteed.

Niska offered Mal a simple job and, provided the Captain didn't ask too many questions, he'd pay him fairly. Mal, however, has a conscience and that got in the way of honoring his agreement to deliver crates of stolen Alliance cargo. The crates, which were filled with a drug called Pescaline-D, were worth thousands on the black market, and Niska wanted to re-sell them at exorbitant prices. Mal, however, didn't, and returned the medicine to the miners of Paradiso, who'd suffer without it. Though he tried to return Niska's money, the crime boss would not negotiate. Niska's reputation depended upon his lack of leniency, and he had more to lose than credits.

Following this, Niska watched and waited for Mal to return to Ezra. When Dalin spotted him, Niska kidnapped Mal and Wash, and his pet torturer mutilated Mal's body and tried to break his mind—just like he'd done so many times before. On this occasion, however, Mal not only survived the attack, he kept Wash's mind from shattering. Then, after Zoë negotiated Wash's release, Mal lost an ear and continued to be tortured until the *Serenity* crew was able to rescue him.

ABOVE: Adelai Niska is one of the most fearsome and brutal opponents Mal and his crew are forced to face—but needs must for smugglers in need of cash.

> **"I also have a reputation. Not so pleasant, I think you know."**
>
> *Adelai Niska*

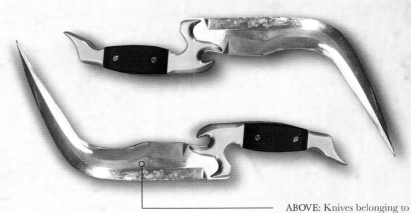

Unlike the Firefly regulars, Fairman didn't have to speak Chinese—instead he had a line in Czech: "There was a woman on set, one of the people behind the camera, and she was Czech. She wrote it out phonetically for me—'Cut off his ear'. I pretty much butchered it; as I recall, I made a motion with my hand."

ABOVE: Knives belonging to Niska's fearsome henchman, Crow, played by Andrew Bryniarski.

NISKA'S SKYPLEX

Niska's Skyplex is stationed in orbit above the planet Ezra, found in the Georgia System. This sprawling space station is Niska's base of operations and home to select staff that once included Viktor, the torturer, Crow, and Dalin. The Skyplex is well guarded, and a platoon of armed enforcers monitors the entrances and exits, and uses a fast-burn rocket shuttle to travel to and from the planet's surface. Though the Skyplex has multiple levels, the second is the largest and most important. Designed in the shape of a saucer, this area includes several corridors that connect the cargo hold, medical bay, cafeteria, and quarters to one another. Its main hallway also has a few pointed twists and turns, drawing visitors to Niska's private suites that are located toward the interior of the Skyplex.

YO-SAFF-BRIDGE

"I'd be a good wife."

Saffron

Saffron, Bridget and Yolanda are all names for a mysterious con artist and former Companion who spends her days finding suckers to marry and rob. She is a femme fatale whose antics range from stealing spaceships to cheating ex-husbands out of their most prized possessions.

Saffron's earliest known identity is Yolanda Haymer, the wife of Durran Haymer, an Alliance chemical expert who murdered cities full of refugees during the Unification War. Unhappy in her marriage, Yolanda seduced Heinrich, a security programmer, and then dumped his body before leaving Bellerophon. Following this, she assumed a new identity and used the skills she honed as a Companion to con new victims.

Sometime after leaving Durran, she became a Triumph Settler and threw her lot in with Elder Gommen. Gommen was an opportunist who teamed up with Saffron and a group of ship's thieves who ran a Carrion House. The con was simple: Gommen would ask a ship's captain for help, and to celebrate he'd get the crew drunk and 'marry' Saffron to one of the crewmembers. Then, once Saffron was stowed safely on board, she'd seduce victims and knock them unconscious with the Goodnight Kiss, a narcotic lipstick.

After disabling everyone on board *Serenity*, Saffron stole Shuttle One and flew to St. Albans. Mal was able to track the shuttle and confronted Saffron, who couldn't tell him the truth. The two eventually crossed paths again. That time, Saffron was 'Bridget', the devoted wife of Mal's old war buddy, Monty. When the truth was revealed, Saff-Bridge switched gears again, and tried to con Mal to help her steal the Lassiter—a priceless laser gun—from her first husband, Durran.

Fortunately, Mal anticipated Saffron would double-cross him and devised a plan to make sure she didn't. For all her schemes, Yo-Saff-Bridge couldn't resist returning to Bellerophon. She was arrested in Isis Canyon by local authorities.

Christina Hendricks, who plays Saffron, had a specific view of her character. "I decided that Saffron is so good at what she does, and she does it so often, that she almost has to convince herself. So I never tried to play the secret—I just tried to play what was happening at that moment, because I think she believes it and she was so convincing. I just tried to be honest about each one of those people that she was, each time. I loved all parts of her. I like the little moments where she might do an eye-roll or a smirk behind someone's back, and they don't know it's happening."

CARRION HOUSE

A Carrion House is a type of illegal salvage operation run by hijackers who target ships in the Black. In many cases, the targeted ships at that time are fully functional. First, Saffron deceives and disables the crew from responding. Then, the con artist heads straight for the cockpit to sabotage the flight controls and reprogram the ship's trajectory. This automated flight path guides the ship into an electromagnetic net, where it's trapped and unable to break free. If the ship is still occupied at that point, the passengers are electrocuted to death.

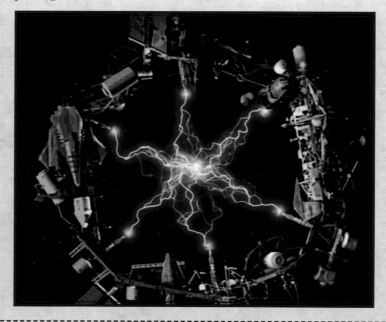

JUBAL EARLY

"The most difficult villain for me in *Firefly* was Jubal, and the most rewarding," Joss Whedon says. "That whole thing was the best experience I could ever have had. I had been trying to break the story, and it was about River, and her powers discovered, and, oh, the not-very-interesting stories we were going back and forth on. I called Tim in desperation and he said, 'Well, can't you just have Bobba Fett?' [Minier mispronounced Boba Fett, of *Star Wars* fame.] And I said, 'Who's Bobba Fett, first of all?' And, 'You call yourself a nerd?' And second of all, 'Thanks, bye'. Because it just clicked. And when I got to 'Objects in Space' I had this idea of this character, and I had the idea of River and what I had to do. I said, 'This will write itself'. And then I realized I was in…hell [laughs]. I had a couple of things that helped me. One of them was *The Minus Man*, which is a movie that I think has an extraordinary portrait of a serial killer, just the main character's comical observations.

"The other was…walking the set. I went one weekend, just walking the set doing everything River did and everything that Jubal did, climbing up on the ladders, standing on the railing. The physicality of the thing clued me into his *perception* of the physicality of the thing and ultimately what the episode was going to be about: the ecstasy of being, the idea of imprinting meaning on objects and that two people who really step out of the norm are very similar, but because what they bring emotionally is completely opposite, they ultimately are very different. That came from physically being there in the space, and once it unveiled itself, it was an extraordinary experience—but it was a long time coming."

Jubal Early is a sadistic bounty hunter hired by the Alliance to infiltrate *Serenity*, terrorize the crew, and return River to the Academy.

Determined to capture his quarry, Early talks to his victims and terrorizes them with threats of rape and abuse. He often lures his prey out of hiding by pretending to be a good man who doesn't want to hurt his victims—not unless he's forced to. Early is an animal abuser and skilled manipulator who has no sense of morality. Though he becomes obsessed with capturing a target, he feels no remorse and will continue to pursue victims if he fails the first or second time.

Early attempted to kidnap River by targeting *Serenity*. The bounty hunter's efforts were thwarted the first time and, despite Mal pushing him into the Black, he managed to survive. When the time was right, Early approached Kalista, a senior Alliance official, and pledged to kidnap River again only to be stopped, chained, and tossed from *Serenity*. He survived, thanks to a tree that broke his fall, and was saved by Kalista, who considered the bounty hunter one of her greatest assets.

Despite all of his many attempts, Early has yet to capture River. Only time will tell what the Alliance has planned for the bounty hunter, but thus far the *Serenity* crew remains elusive.

Jubal Early is a recurring villain in *Firefly* and is played by Richard Brooks. Inspired by Boba Fett from *Star Wars*, Early is a bounty hunter who flies a ship called *Coronis I*. The Confederate Civil War general, Jubal Anderson Early, may have inspired his name.

BELOW: Early's suit was designed to look airtight.

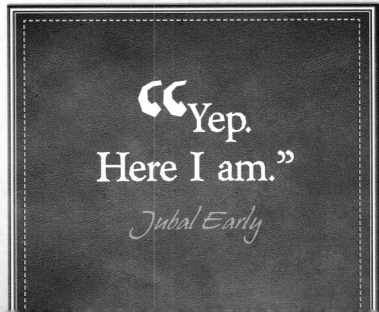

" Yep.
Here I am."

Jubal Early

THEM PESKY ALLIANCE FOLK

Most people who live, work and fight in the 'verse either dwell in the Core or are Alliance loyalists. In exchange for the freedom to do as they please, citizens are granted access to all that the government-sanctioned schools, hospitals, banks, and Companion Houses have on offer. Over time, many citizens have internalized the fact that part of their day-to-day job is to further the Alliance's propaganda. River's teacher, Dr. Mathias, and Dr. Caron all believed they were doing the right thing, because they see the evidence of what the Alliance has to offer. Rebelling against the government incurs a steep price that most people couldn't pay. Simon Tam, for example, sacrificed everything to rescue his sister: family, security, credits, career, and the ability to return home.

Though dirty cops like Lieutenant Womack and his goons Skunk and Fendris do exist, most people have become so immersed in the dream of a better life, they haven't bothered to examine who's providing that fantasy. Other loyalists, however, justify their horrific acts by becoming true believers. Kalista, the Alliance officer who is hell-bent on capturing River, thinks she's creating a 'family' of experimental subjects who share an unbreakable bond. The subject of free will has never occurred to her, and that is often the case with soldiers, officers and agents whose faith is seemingly unshakable. But, when the Alliance's careful machinations and web of lies are exposed, even its most loyal operatives begin to question who they've pledged their allegiance to.

THE TRUTH ABOUT REAVERS

The horrific events in 'Bushwacked' happen because Captain Harken, the captain of the I.A.V. *Dortmunder*, doesn't believe that Reavers exist. To many, Reavers are the bogeymen, a story made up to justify the crimes committed by thieves and murderers. Most Core citizens don't believe Reavers are real, until Mal transmits Doctor Caron's story to the wide known 'verse. The fact that Reavers do exist because they were created by the Alliance significantly altered what most people thought of the government. If the Alliance lied to them about Reavers, then what else did they cover up? Are the Border and the rim not as bad as they'd have them believe? And, if that was the case, was the Unification War a waste of time? These questions were explored in the *Serenity* comic 'Those Left Behind' to underline what happened after Mal revealed the truth to the 'verse.

Part of the reason why the Alliance remains the superior force in the 'verse is because of its wealth and resources. Some citizens idolize the rich and pretend that they earned their credits by working hard and staying quiet. This, however, is the worst lie of all, because the Alliance preys on people who think that loyalty can be bought. Durran Haymer is wealthy because he murdered towns full of people

during the Unification War, at the Alliance's behest, and then collected their valuables. Rance Burgess had access to a hovercraft and a laser pistol—rare sights in the rim—because he cozied up to the Alliance and gave them oversight on Deadwood. Magistrate Higgins was granted dominion over an entire moon, provided he kept supplying Canton mud to companies like the Blue Sun Corporation.

> ❝I'm going to show you a world without sin.❞
>
> *Cpt. Malcolm J. Reynolds*

REAVERS A COMIN':
Sketch of a Reaver ship.

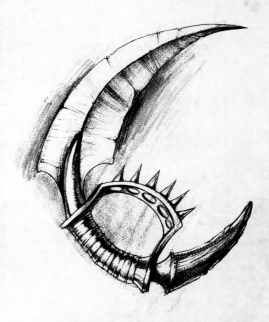

THE ALLIANCE FLEET

Like other neo-fascist governments, the Alliance's weight is prominent because the military's presence is felt and heard in every corner of the 'verse. The distinctive spaceships and cruisers they operate are only part of the Alliance's ability to remind everyday citizens who's truly in charge. Often, Parliament employs Federal agents, operatives, and specialists to do the Alliance's bidding, giving them permission to interrogate, bribe, burn, kidnap, murder, or torture if the situation calls for it.

ALLIANCE CRUISER

Massive, high-tech military vessels the size of a small city owned and operated by the Alliance. The Tohoku-class is noted for its size, population, and unusual shape. Five interconnected towers protrude from the U-shaped bottom of the cruiser to form this 'floating city'. In addition to their scientific, military, medical, engineering, recreational, and storage facilities, Alliance cruisers have the capacity to hold dozens of Alliance gunships and are fully equipped to survive extended trips in space. The I. A.V. *Cronenberg*, *Dortmunder*, and *Nakamura* are examples of Alliance cruisers.

ALLIANCE GUNSHIP

Small, heavily armed, short-range vessel engineered to support Alliance cruisers. A gunship is more maneuverable and faster than a cruiser, but it isn't powerful enough to take on a larger ship without assistance. Typically, Alliance gunships are flown in configurations of two or more, depending on the circumstance.

ALLIANCE SHORT-RANGE ENFORCEMENT VESSEL (A.S.R.E.V.)

Type of spaceship operated by official government representatives, usually Federal marshals, to track criminals and patrol specific regions of space. These ships are small, maneuverable, heavily armed, and can travel at high speeds. Munitions include missiles, hull-piercing bullets, and magnetic depth charges.

ALLIANCE POLICE SHUTTLE

Small, short-range vessel used by Alliance law enforcement stationed in or near municipalities found on a planet or moon. The police shuttle is designed to patrol the surface, is about the size of a hovercar, and can transport up to four people.

LAWRENCE DOBSON

Lawrence Dobson is a Federal agent with a plain face, the kind that isn't instantly recognizable or distinctive. As an agent, Dobson used his non-threatening appearance to his advantage, and followed Simon and River Tam to the Eavesdown Docks on Persephone. Booking passage to Boros, Dobson waited to make his move, and was exposed by Shepherd Book.

Dobson was shot in the eye and tossed out of the cargo bay on Whitefall, and the crew never expected him to survive. Not only did he live, the disgraced Federal agent became a hermit, slowly recovering and gathering his strength for many months until he was approached by the Hands of Blue.

After being given a second chance to redeem himself, Dobson was gifted with a cybernetic eye and used Badger to set a trap for the *Serenity* crew in a ship's graveyard. Convinced he'd finally capture River, Dobson made one fatal mistake: he underestimated Malcolm Reynolds. Mal killed him and managed to sneak away, leaving the Hands of Blue empty-handed once more.

Carlos Jacott portrays Lawrence Dobson in 'Serenity' and reappears in the *Serenity* comics.

> ❝I have a job to do. To uphold the law.❞
>
> *Dobson*

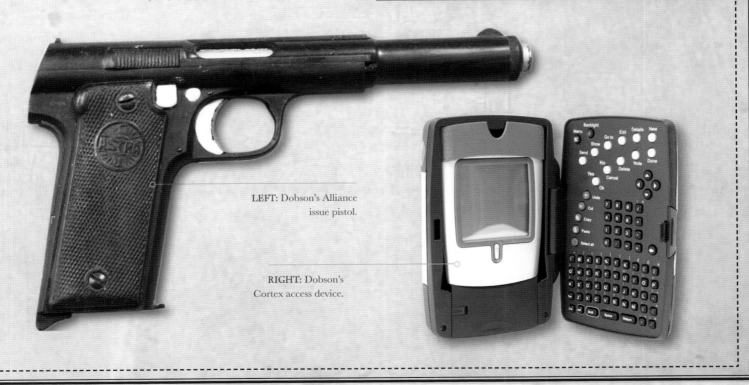

LEFT: Dobson's Alliance issue pistol.

RIGHT: Dobson's Cortex access device.

THE HANDS OF BLUE

The mysterious blue-gloved men, known only as the Hands of Blue, are not referred to by any human name. They are depicted as cold, merciless bureaucrats who wear impeccable suits and blue gloves. The Hands of Blue, however, are not human. They are more machine than man and are classified as cyborgs. It is unclear whether the Hands of Blue are by-products of the Academy or the Blue Sun Corporation. Regardless of their maker, the pair does Parliament's bidding and operates above, even outside, the law.

In their pursuit of River Tam at St. Lucy's Medical Center on Ariel, the Hands of Blue murdered Agent McGinnis and his entire staff with a sonic weapon that caused their eyes to bleed and their brains to liquefy. Following their failure to catch River, they recruited former Federal Agent Dobson on Whitefall and restored him to good standing. The Hands of Blue orchestrated the plan, forcing Mal, Jayne, and Zoë to deal with Dobson while they concentrated on *Serenity*. Despite their tireless efforts, the *Serenity* crew managed to prevent them from infiltrating the ship. The Hands of Blue were incinerated by *Serenity's* engine flare, and the cyborgs are believed to be dead.

Jeff Ricketts and Dennis Cockrum portrayed the Hands of Blue; their characters reappear in the *Serenity* comics. Jeff Ricketts talked about how they were characterized when he said: "I took the bureaucrat thing very seriously. When they're holding River for us, Federal Agent McGinnis is instructed not to speak to the prisoners. From my character's point of view, you just have a few orders: 'Get the prisoner, don't speak to her, hold her for us.' And McGinnis violates this one thing. Since I'm a very nit-picky bureaucrat, if you

do one little thing that I told you not to do, then we have to take out this instrument which makes you bleed from your eyes. So I'm very fastidious about the rules. It was Dennis Cochran, Blue-Gloved Man Number Two, who had to handle the instrument. Somehow he managed to endow it with a supernatural property."

> ## "We're looking for a girl. *This girl.*"
>
> *Hands of Blue*

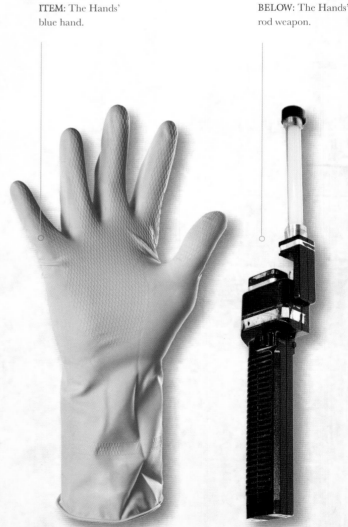

ITEM: The Hands' blue hand.

BELOW: The Hands' rod weapon.

THE OPERATIVE

The Operative is a secretive, methodical agent whose loyalty to the Alliance was once unmatched. Placed in charge of retrieving River Tam, the Operative had a fleet of soldiers at his beck and call. He began tracking River Tam's whereabouts by returning to the Academy to view the footage of her capture. Then, after speaking with Doctor Mathias, the Operative forced the scientist to fall on his sword, in what would be the first of many casualties.

Calm and collected, the Operative believed Mal was a sloppy amateur who couldn't possibly win against him. To corner the Captain, the Operative murdered many of his known contacts including Sanchez, Li Shen, and Shepherd Book. This, however, did not break Mal's spirit. It strengthened his resolve. After investigating the source of River's distress—Miranda—Mal visited Mr. Universe, only to find that the Operative had gotten there first.

Knowing Mal would return, the Operative hid and waited for the right moment to pursue him to a back-up unit. With a fleet of ships at his command and Reavers not far behind, the Operative believed he would win a fair fight against Mal—but he didn't. What's more, Mal did the one thing he thought would never happen: he broke his faith in the Alliance as soon as he had proof that they were, in fact, the 'evil empire' many claimed.

Following this, the Operative became Mal's secret ally. Though his name was never revealed, he helped the Captain by telling his men to stand down. Not everyone, however, forgave the Operative for the lives lost in pursuit of River. But when the situation called for it, Mal asked him for one last favor: help him mount an assault on the Academy on Theocrastus and put an end to the Alliance's experiments on young girls.

Chiwetel Ejiofor plays the Operative in *Serenity*. The elite agent is known for his calm demeanor, military tactics, impeccable appearance, and his expert use of a sword. His story continued in the *Serenity* comics, and ends with Zoë facing him one last time, to avenge Wash's death.

> **"Secrets are not my concern. Keeping them is."**
> *The Operative*

book three

WIDE KNOWN 'VERSE

BIG GORRAMN SKY
THE CORE, BORDER, AND RIM

"After the Earth was used up, we found a new solar system, and hundreds of new Earths were terraformed and colonized. The Central Planets formed the Alliance and decided all the planets had to join under their rule. There was some disagreement on that point. After the War, many of the Independents who had fought and lost drifted to the edges of the system, far from Alliance control. Out here, people struggled to get by with the most basic technologies; a ship would bring you work, a gun would help you keep it. A captain's goal was simple: find a crew, find a job, keep flying." *Shepherd Book*

Five hundred years into the future, after the Earth is no longer habitable, humanity finds a new home among the stars and calls it the 'verse. This vast sector of space contained hundreds of inhabitable moons and planets that, over time, were terraformed by the newly formed government, the Anglo-Sino Alliance. Over time, the 'verse began to take shape. The heart of the 'verse became the White Sun System, the seat of human civilization and a testament to human achievement. Following the establishment of two capitol planets, Londinium and Sihnon, the Alliance pushed further from the Core and encouraged settlement of worlds bordering the Central Planets in the Georgia and Red Sun systems. The last and newest region, known as the rim, contains the Kalidasa and Blue Sun systems.

Canon and Firefly: The *Firefly* TV show's setting was created and developed as each episode was filmed. Often, the locations were determined by availability, in addition to time and budget constraints during production. As such, *Firefly*'s canon has organic inconsistencies, in part because much of the setting details were fleshed out in print materials after the show aired. Add in an emphasis on character and story over facts, and differences tend to sneak in for the sake of a good old-fashioned yarn. As such, many of the details found in the *Firefly Encyclopedia* weight the show's scripts as the primary canonical source of information.

Each system in these three distinct regions of space, the Core, Border, and rim, is named after a star or protostar that provides a life-giving source of light. Each region has its own character and is distinguished by its proximity to the White Sun. Life on the Central Planets, which were the first to be settled, has flourished; billions of people benefit from cutting-edge technologies, access to a variety of food, clothing, and entertainment, and advances in medicine. The Border, on the other hand, was home to those who wanted a simpler way of life. The Alliance billed the Border as the new frontier and encouraged loyalists to help them rein in this region of space by granting them dominion over whole towns—even entire moons, like Higgins' Moon.

Everyday citizens needed some convincing, because the Border Planets lacked many comforts a shiny metropolis like Ariel City had to offer. The government gifted them with sanctioned supplies filled with Gen-Seed—genetically-modified seed engineered to grow in most soils. Though many settlers have remained loyal to the government, so many years have passed that the Border Planets became filled with free-thinkers and religious zealots, farmers and ranchers, petty thieves and poor folk struggling to find food.

The youngest and roughest area of the 'verse—the rim—is known for its lawlessness and the near-constant threat of Reaver attack. Located furthest from the Core, it's harder for the Alliance to maintain a tight grip on the smattering of towns and clustered cities in the Kalidasa and Blue Sun systems. Alliance loyalists in the rim tend to be power-hungry, ruthless, and easily swayed by a well-timed bribe. The rim is also home to one of the Alliance's worst-kept secrets, a planet called Miranda: the birthplace of the Reavers.

Though there are hundreds of habitable worlds in the Border and rim, billions of people live, work, and die in the Core. This grants the Alliance superior weight in numbers, supplying them with untold diehard loyalists, and unwitting citizens who'd be shocked to learn their government has a sinister side. As the most modern of the five systems, it's easy to understand why and how the Alliance won the Unification War.

THIS SPREAD: The planets of the 'verse are hugely varied, ranging from hi-tech urban environments to deserts.

NEXT SPREAD AND FOLLOWING PAGES: The systems and planets of the 'verse; planet images courtesy of Ben Mund.

White Sun　西方白虎　Qin Shi Hua[ng]

Bernadette
Nautilus
Spinrad

Londinium
Colchester
Balkerne

Sihnon
Airen
Xiaojie
Xiansheng

Liann Jiun
Tiantan
Fa

Gonghe
Xing Yun

Rubicon

Osiris
Epeuva
Tannhäuser

Santo
Tethys
New Luxor

Georgia　中心黄龙　Dae[...]

Ezra
Herschel

Regina
Alexandria

Boros
Ares
Turrent's Moon

Kerry

Ithaca
Priam
Perdido
Dunny

Prophet

Elphame
Summerhome
Fiddler's Green
Ithendra
Sweethome

Di Yu
Yama

Athens
Ahnooie
Argabuthon
Ormuzd
Whitefall

Arva[...]
Not[...]

Red Sun　南方朱雀

Jiangyin
Tongyi
Dangun
Rhilidore

New Melbourne
Maria
Destiny

M O T H E R L O D E

Greenleaf
Dyton
Agyar
Bryson's Rock

Harvest
Farraday
Higgins' Moon

St. Albans
Pi Gu

Anson's World
Spider
Varley
Steele

Jubilee
Covenant

Kalidasa　北方玄武

Sho-Je Downs
Miyazaki
Kuan Lo

Verbena
Lassek
Barrimend

Constance
Barrowclough
Disraeli

Glacier
Denali

Vishnu
Ganesha
Rama

Heaven
Urvasi
Menaka
Rambha
Tilattama

Angel
Zephyr

Delphi
Clio
Thalia
Calliope

New Kasmir

Whittier

Old Sol

Earth That Was
Luna

Mars
Phobos
Deimos

古老太阳

Blue Sun　东方青龙

Fury

Meridian
Burnet

New Canaan
Ugarit
Lilac

Muir
Arminius
Shepherd's Mission

Coldstone
Blackwood
Seventh Circle

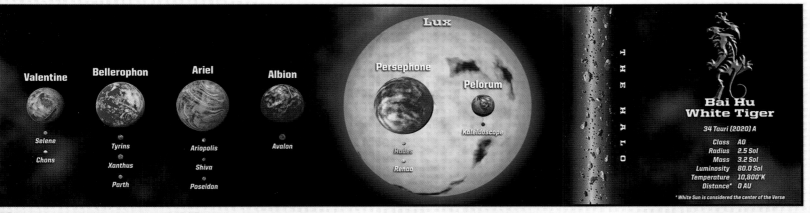

THE HALO

Lux

Valentine
- Selene
- Chons

Bellerophon
- Tyrins
- Xanthus
- Parth

Ariel
- Ariopolis
- Shiva
- Poseidon

Albion
- Avalon

Persephone
- Hades
- Renao

Pelorum
- Kaleidoscope

Bai Hu
White Tiger

34 Tauri (2020) A

Class	A0
Radius	2.5 Sol
Mass	3.2 Sol
Luminosity	80.0 Sol
Temperature	10,800°K
Distance*	0 AU

*White Sun is considered the center of the Verse

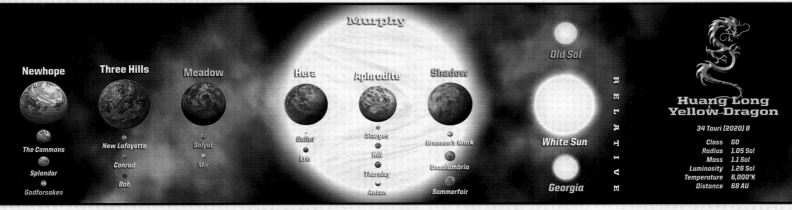

RELATIVE

Murphy

Newhope
- The Commons
- Splendor
- Godforsaken

Three Hills
- New Lafayette
- Conrad
- Bob

Meadow
- Salyut
- Mir

Hera
- Bullet
- Ezra

Aphrodite
- Sturges
- Hill
- Thornley
- Anton

Shadow
- Bronson's Mark
- Ossolambria
- Summerfair

Old Sol

White Sun

Georgia

Huang Long
Yellow Dragon

34 Tauri (2020) B

Class	G0
Radius	1.05 Sol
Mass	1.1 Sol
Luminosity	1.26 Sol
Temperature	6,000°K
Distance	68 AU

STAR SIZES

Himinbjørg

Heinlein

Moab
- Red Rock
- Masa

Brisingamen
- Freya
- Alberich
- Beowulf

Anvil
- Hammer

Triumph
- Mycroft

Paquin
- Shinbone
- Clawthorn

Lazarus
- Dora

Silverhold
- Beggar's Tin

Red Sun

Kalidasa

Blue Sun

Zhu Que
Red Phoenix

34 Tauri (2020) C

Class	G5
Radius	0.93 Sol
Mass	0.93 Sol
Luminosity	0.79 Sol
Temperature	5,610°K
Distance	68 AU

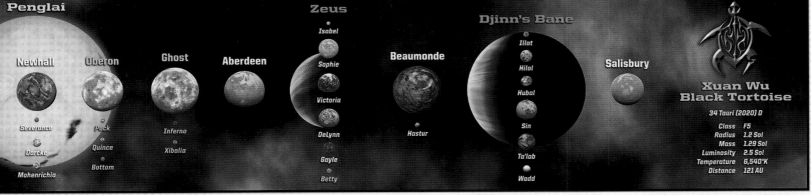

Penglai

Zeus

Djinn's Bane

Newhall
- Severance
- Darcke
- Mahenrichia

Oberon
- Pach
- Quince
- Bottom

Ghost
- Inferno
- Xibalia

Aberdeen

Zeus
- Isabel
- Sophie
- Victoria
- DeLynn
- Gayle
- Betty

Beaumonde
- Hastur

Djinn's Bane
- Illat
- Hilal
- Hubal
- Sin
- Ta'lab
- Wadd

Salisbury

Xuan Wu
Black Tortoise

34 Tauri (2020) D

Class	F5
Radius	1.2 Sol
Mass	1.29 Sol
Luminosity	2.5 Sol
Temperature	6,540°K
Distance	121 AU

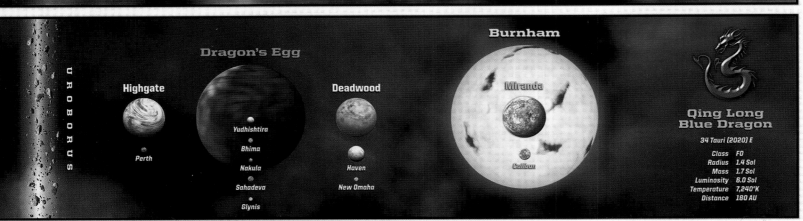

UROBORUS

Dragon's Egg

Burnham

Highgate
- Perth

Dragon's Egg
- Yudhishtira
- Bhima
- Nakula
- Sahadeva
- Glynis

Deadwood
- Haven
- New Omaha

Miranda
- Caliban

Qing Long
Blue Dragon

34 Tauri (2020) E

Class	F0
Radius	1.4 Sol
Mass	1.7 Sol
Luminosity	6.0 Sol
Temperature	7,240°K
Distance	180 AU

BOOK THREE: WIDE KNOWN 'VERSE

PUTTING THE 'S' IN SCIENCE FICTION

Television shows often weight decisions to tell a good damn story. Sometimes, in order to give the audience a sense of wonder and keep the camera focused on the characters, the 'science' in 'science fiction' is more sensational than real. In *Firefly*, the science fiction is present in the weapons and technology found in the Core, the spaceships that zoom overhead, and the terraforming of dead moons and planets to tame an inhabitable sector of space for humanity to thrive.

THE CORTEX

The Cortex is an Alliance owned-and-operated network used for communications, data storage, and broadcasting. Its signal strength spans hundreds of planets and moons and is intensified by orbital satellites positioned around the Central Planets. The Cortex is an integral part of society because of its ability to facilitate public and private messages called 'waves', sharing government or emergency-related alerts, data uploads and downloads, and customized searches.

Citizens in the technology-rich Central Planets log into the Cortex on personal devices, dedicated source boxes, public vidphones, Academy-owned consoles and so on. Elsewhere, Cortex access is limited to those who can afford the necessary equipment. This has led to a gap in information and data distribution, where the highest concentration of users are located in the Core. As such, the Alliance frequently uses Cortex bulletins and broadcasts to share propaganda designed to benefit its interests and keep Core citizens in the dark.

Ship pilots may access the Cortex via a console in the cockpit that is tied to the electrical system, or they might use a handheld device like the one Dobson used in the pilot episode, 'Serenity'.

LEFT: **Dobson's Cortex access device in its closed position.**

SERENITY'S FLIGHT PATH

The length of time that'd be required in 'real time' to fly from Miranda to Persephone is often shortened to accommodate the needs of the story. In the *Firefly* TV show, the crew's antics took place over a period of one-and-a-half to two years, before reaching Beaumonde in the movie *Serenity*.

The locations where *Serenity* lands tie into the setting and Mal's desire to avoid the Alliance. The ship's flight path is as follows and is presented in order of appearance, ending with Mal's transmission of Doctor Caron's recording on Mr. Universe's Moon.

Though ships often move at the speed of plot, sometimes the science is plausible. Michael Brotherton points out in his essay 'The Science of *Firefly*' (page 160) that the 'verse contains just enough believability for Whedon's vision to feel real.

DESTINATION	PLANET OR MOON	SYSTEM	REGION
Eavesdown Docks	Persephone	White Sun	Core (Edge)
Docks (never landed)	Boros	Georgia	Border
Canyon	Whitefall (Moon of Athens)	Georgia	Border
Watering Hole	Ezra	Georgia	Border
Niska's Skyplex	Ezra (in orbit)	Georgia	Border
Hancock	Regina	Georgia	Border
Paradiso	Regina	Georgia	Border
Derelict ship	The Black	Georgia	Border
I.A.V. *Cronenberg*	The Black	Georgia	Border
Bar	Santo	White Sun	Border
Eavesdown Docks	Persephone	White Sun	Core (Edge)
Drop Off	Jiangyin	Red Sun	Border
I.A.V. *Magellan*	The Black	Red Sun	Border
Patron's Town	Jiangyin	Red Sun	Border
Triumph Settlement	Triumph	Red Sun	Border
Chop House	The Black (on the other side of the Motherlode asteroid field)	Red Sun	Border
Shuttle Two (stolen)	St. Albans	Red Sun	Border
Canton Mudworks	Higgins' Moon (orbits Harvest)	Red Sun	Border
Ariel City	Ariel	White Sun	Core
Desert	Ezra	Georgia	Border
Niska's Skyplex	Ezra (in orbit)	Georgia	Border
Black Market	Moon (unknown)	Georgia	Border
Bellerophon Estates	Bellerophon	White Sun	Core
Li Shen's Space Bazaar	The Black (rotates locations)	Red Sun	Border
Smith's Home	St. Albans	Red Sun	Border
Heart of Gold	Deadwood	Blue Sun	Rim
Trading Station	Lilac (Moon of New Canaan)	Blue Sun	Rim
Maidenhead	Beaumonde	Kalidasa	Rim
Companion Training House	Remote Planet (unknown)	Unknown, likely Blue Sun	Likely Rim
Mining Colony	Haven (Moon of Deadwood)	Blue Sun	Rim
Dock	Miranda	Blue Sun	Rim
Reaver Fleet	The Black	Blue Sun	Rim
Mr. Universe's home	Mr. Universe's Moon (now abandoned)	Unknown, likely Georgia	Unknown, likely Border

THE SCIENCE OF *FIREFLY*

BY MICHAEL BROTHERTON, PHD

PLANET
SHADOW

Train robberies, shootouts, barroom brawls…
Firefly often wraps itself more in the tropes of
American Westerns than those of science fiction, even
if spaceships and the occasional laser gun make an
appearance in the story. Some might therefore be
inclined to label *Firefly* as 'space opera', a Western
that takes place in space, but *Firefly* is fundamentally
science fiction. Science underlies the unique setting
of the 'verse, the spaceships like *Serenity*, and much
of the technology on display.

BELIEVABLE 'VERSE

The creators of *Firefly* did something mighty clever. They wanted to
make a science-fiction show with spaceships voyaging among many
worlds with travel times measured in hours to weeks. They could
have done what so many filmmakers before them had: put the
planets in different star systems and design their spaceships to have
faster-than-light (FTL) capabilities to travel quickly between them.
Such science-fiction shows often skip over the complications of
relativity, including causality, time dilation, and other effects, which
can be troubling to some of the more science-minded fans.

Perhaps most importantly, ships that can move faster-than-light
between alien worlds has been done to death. Such an approach
also requires ongoing world-building—or system-building, as
it were—as each location needs to have little in common with
other planets in the series. That type of world-building can be a
strength, but it also strains creativity and special effects budgets.
The clever idea behind *Firefly*, original and budget-friendly, was to
eschew such derivative universes by creating a contained area of
space for ships to fly in: the 'verse.

ATMOSPHERE-ALTERING TERRAFORMERS

Terraforming is a field of science believed to provide a planet or
moon with an Earth-like atmosphere, gravity, and temperature
range conducive to sustain human, plant, and animal life. Such
an advanced capability might demand remarkable scientific
achievements, but terraforming technology could conceivably be
within humanity's grasp centuries from now.

First, consider the atmosphere (or 'atmo' as they say in the

'verse). Earth has a mixture of nitrogen (78%), oxygen (21%),
and other trace gases, primarily water vapor, carbon dioxide and
methane (1%), that together provide a pressure of 101,000 Pascals.
To be breathable, there needs to be a partial pressure of molecular
O^2 within a certain allowable range, and with no problematic
gasses being too strong.

Terraforming machines, like the processors shown in *Serenity*,
can release oxygen from rocks and minerals in a planet's crust,
or perhaps manufacture oxygen and other molecular gas via
sophisticated nuclear reactors. For life to flourish, the planetary
bodies must also contain water in large enough quantities. Gasses
and liquids like water are called volatiles, and they can also be
brought to a world via cometary impact.

There is another issue involving atmosphere to consider. The
worlds in the 'verse are at different distances from the stars they
orbit. The average surface temperature of a world depends on the
heating-cooling balance. That is, some incidental stellar radiation
is reflected off into space (e.g. from ice, water, highly reflective
clouds, etc.), some is absorbed, which results in heat, and some
thermal radiation is emitted from the world itself.

Additionally, greenhouse gasses, the trace gasses like water,
methane, carbon dioxide, and carbon monoxide, can have a
significant warming effect on a planet's temperature. They act
as blankets, absorbing some of the radiated thermal radiation
and limiting the cooling. Finally, aerosols (e.g. reflective sulfates
and nitrates in the upper atmosphere) can have a cooling effect,
and this component can be engineered to adjust temperatures
downward for worlds otherwise too close to their central star.

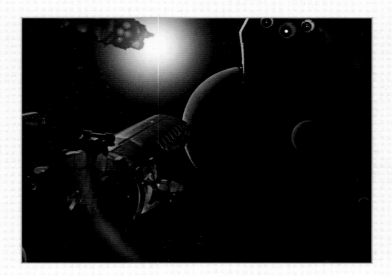

MASTERING THE FORCES OF GRAVITY

In addition to surface temperature and atmosphere, there's also a planet's gravity to consider. Turning a moon less massive than Earth into a world with one Earth gee of surface gravity, some 9.8 meters per second squared, is not a trivial feat. Surface gravity depends on mass and radius. The surface gravitational acceleration g is equal to GM/r^2, where G is Newton's gravitational constant, M is the total mass, and r is the radius. For gravity, not only does it matter how much mass is there, but also how close to it you are.

The terraformers of the 'verse could, theoretically, either crush a moon to high density to give it Earth-like gravity, or have some way of manipulating gravity itself. It may also be that gravity control would permit the compression of a moon to increase its surface gravity, which would result in long-term Earth gravity. For instance, reducing the diameter of Earth's own moon by a factor of about two and a half times would increase its surface gravity from about 1/6 gee to one full gee.

Assuming terraforming technology is plausible, the hundreds of planets and moons of the 'verse are ready to be settled and inhabited. A terraformed planet or moon can hold an atmo, and the details of that atmo can let people breathe and provide adequate temperatures over a wide range in radii from the central star if properly engineered. There's a lot of evidence in *Firefly* that humanity can control gravity, like the floating islands on Bellerophon and the artificial gravity generated on spaceships.

RECREATING EARTH-THAT-WAS GRAVITY

MAGNETIC FIELD

MAGNETIC NORTH POLE

GEOGRAPHIC NORTH POLE

GEOGRAPHIC SOUTH POLE

MAGNETIC SOUTH POLE

MAGNETIC FIELD

MOON

$$F = Gm_1m_2 \char`\^ r^2$$

ARTIFICIAL GRAVITY ONBOARD *SERENITY*

The spaceships in *Firefly* generate artificial gravity, which is a science-fiction trope that is often used because of the expenses involved when creating a zero gee effect for film, be it via physics (*Apollo 13*) or through CGI (*Gravity*). In fact, the gravity onboard *Serenity* appears to remain generally constant despite Wash's fancy flying. The only times there is a shake-up on board, is when there's an unexpected collision. This happens on other shows like *Star Trek*, too, which includes lots of shake-ups for dramatic effect despite the vessels having 'inertial dampeners'.

Currently, there is one way in physics where artificial gravity can be generated in space: through rotation. Forcing an object to rotate requires a force pushing it toward the center of rotation, akin to gravity. If humans want gravity in spaceships in the 21st century, this is the way to do it. There are space stations shown in *Firefly* that rotate, like Niska's Skyplex, and it's likely that they use this rotation to create gravity, perhaps for economy.

However, it's clear that on *Serenity* there is no rotation to provide gravity, so advanced science beyond what is currently understood would be required. Probably the real driving force behind the gravity technology is economic expediency! As in shows like *Star Trek* and *Battlestar Galactica*, it is budget-friendly to 'create' gravity via a technological kludge. Because artificial gravity is so common in science fiction, modern audiences accept it exists and maintain a healthy suspension of disbelief to enjoy their stories.

In the case of *Firefly*, however, artificial gravity for spaceships fits right into the broader world-building where such technology is an essential ingredient to flying through the 'verse. By 2517 C.E., humans have mastered gravity, and most people don't have to worry about leaving kitchen utensils or surgical instruments lying around thanks to the ship's artificial gravity holding them in place.

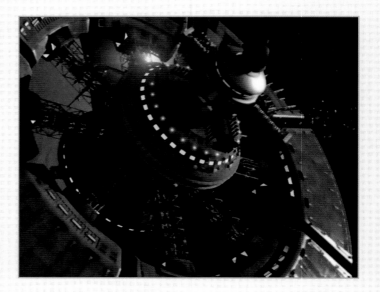

CRYONICS AND FUTURISTIC MEDICINE

While medicine of the 26th century might seem more advanced than that of the 21st century, on the surface there's a lot of commonalities. For example, drugs are still being administered and surgery is still performed by human doctors. Often, the presence of medical technology is tied to the Alliance; the closer you get to the Core or one of its wealthy loyalists, like the Councilor's dermal mender on loan to Inara in 'War Stories', the more commonly found the futuristic equipment will be.

This ties back to the 'how' of how humans safely traveled from Earth-That-Was to the 'verse. Though it's not explicitly stated, we can assume that the White Sun is a significant distance away. To survive the rigors of long-term spaceflight, humans possessed the technology to build massive generational starships to fly to their destination. It's also implied that they may have facilitated their trip using advances in cryonics, with the intent of cryopreserving human and animal tissue to be

revived at a future date. This is the same technology that was probably used to engineer River's containment unit seen in the pilot episode, 'Serenity'.

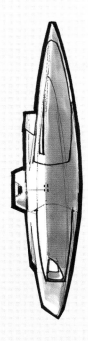
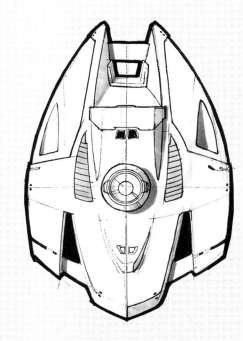

TO THE STARS AND BACK AGAIN

Spaceships in *Firefly* are distinctive from other science-fiction settings because they can move from space to a planet's atmosphere, land on the ground, and then reverse the procedure. Ships possess jet technology to operate in atmo, demonstrated by some thrilling heroics in 'The Train Job', as well as rockets when leaving a world, and a more efficient propulsion system dependent on nuclear fusion to superheat propellant for deep space travel.

These technologies are not too different from what we have currently, but as they exist now they're generally insufficient to conduct interplanetary travel as portrayed on *Firefly* unless they differ in fundamental ways. However, if they are taken in conjunction with gravity control, the entire 'verse opens up. Rockets and fusion engines (which are just another form of rocket, but more efficient) need large fuel-to-ship mass ratios to work effectively. But to be able to adjust gravity? Well, that makes things much, much easier. Just as a ship's gravity is an assumed technology on *Serenity*, perhaps each world's technologically

adjusted surface gravity is something that can be shielded. Being able to ignore a planet's gravity makes it easy to get to space—escape velocity is basically anything you want it to be and only depends on how fast you can clear atmo.

Serenity and other ships in the 'verse do require fuel to fly, however. Although reactors are mentioned, there is no mention of that fuel being radioactive. This means that the power source is a fusion reactor. This device converts hydrogen to helium with the release of energy, as well as the release of neutrons and neutrinos. Hydrogen is available via the electrolysis of water into hydrogen and oxygen. For human health, such systems do require shielding—unless you're a Reaver. (And if you are a Reaver, well, who cares?) This situation means fuel is important, but not rare, expensive, or a deal breaker in normal circumstances. Ships like *Serenity* would be able to move around the 'verse much like gasoline-powered cars move around a country, with fuel being crucial but not overly limiting to spaceflight.

HIGH-TECH LASER WEAPONS AND SUCH

Though the Alliance gunships have munitions, *Serenity* does not. Like medicine, weapons in *Firefly* are both high-tech and low-tech. Most of the time we see familiar weapons: pistols and rifles firing bullets. These long-lasting weapon designs were largely perfected in the 19th century and have not required significant modification. Bullets, for example, carry a lot of chemical energy in the form of gunpowder, and any additional bells and whistles just help deliver the projectile more accurately. Trying to make a quantum leap over the gun is like trying to make a quantum leap over the wheel, or sliced bread. It's conceivably possible, but not easy.

Firefly does showcase a couple of other types of weapons that do have some advantages—as well as some drawbacks—compared to guns: lasers and sonics.

Lasers are common in the 21st century, available in many colors and cheap enough to put on a keychain. In general, the reason lasers don't make good weapons is power. Lasers are focused monochromatic light, and to make them damaging requires them to carry a lot of energy in a short time period. Electricity usually powers lasers, so a compact source of electrical energy like a battery is required. The batteries of the 26th century are good enough to power a laser that can burn through materials at a distance and set things on fire, although they are not so powerful that they can last too long (e.g. Rance Burgess's pistol in 'Heart of Gold').

JAYNE'S GUN
VERA

STOCK

HANDLE

EARLY'S PISTOL

There is a similar issue with sonic rifles. Sound is an auditory experience associated with longitudinal, or compression, waves traveling through atmosphere. There is energy transmitted through sound waves, and some frequencies couple to people better than others. A low-frequency pulse of sound carrying sufficient energy could indeed knock people down and act as a non-lethal alternative to guns. The sonic weapons employed by the Alliance soldiers in Ariel, for instance, are plausible.

SONIC RIFLE

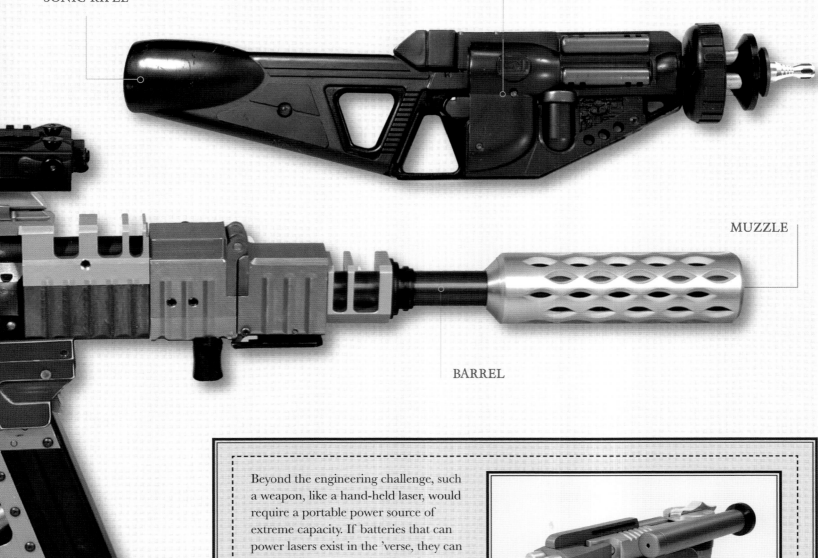

MUZZLE

BARREL

Beyond the engineering challenge, such a weapon, like a hand-held laser, would require a portable power source of extreme capacity. If batteries that can power lasers exist in the 'verse, they can more easily power sonic rifles. Other evidence of advanced sonic technology is the lethal high-frequency device used by the Hands of Blue, which causes hemorrhaging in a human body—a hint that the Hands of Blue are not entirely human.

RIGHT: Burgess' laser pistol which ran out of power in 'Heart of Gold'.

BEYOND THE FICTION OF *FIREFLY*

One of the nice scientifically-informed aspects of *Firefly*—which is not done in most television science fiction—is to go with silence in space. There might be music, but there are no *whooshing* or other sound effects on the exterior shots. Interplanetary space is a near-vacuum, and as we learned from *Alien*, 'In space, no one can hear you scream'. Similarly, no one can hear you whoosh. In *Firefly*, space is referred to as the Black. It could also be called, the Quiet Black.

The world of *Firefly* is a star system dense with hundreds of terraformed planets and moons, worlds and ships perhaps exploiting gravity manipulation, and relatively easy movement with minimal fuel costs among the Earth-like worlds. Travel between moons of a single planet might take mere hours, while moving between planets or the stars of the 'verse could take weeks. This is a mighty clever way of implementing stories on human timescales in a space environment and, when combined with the silence in space, creates a plausible, futuristic setting for humanity to thrive.

In the stories we've read and seen thus far, only a tiny bit of the 'verse has been revealed. The Central Planets, where the most advanced science and technology is found, were only briefly shown. Many details of terraforming, spaceship

technology, medicine and weapons remain unexplored, and provide a rich tapestry for the audience to imagine themselves in a good damn story.

Please see page 256 for Michael Brotherton's biography.

STRAIGHT TO THE 'VERSE'S HEART

The earliest pioneers formed the seat of **human civilization around the White Sun, or Bai Hu (White Tiger). The White Sun System is referred to by many names. It is the Core, the Central Planets, and to most Alliance citizens, home. The region is bordered by an asteroid belt filled with C-, M-, and S-class asteroids called the Halo, and several interlinking satellites that provide access to the 26th-century version of the internet, the Cortex.**

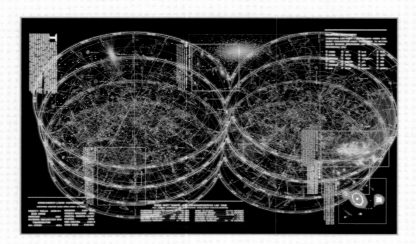

The Central Planets are comprised of three suns, fourteen planets, and the Halo. They are also home to the Anglo-Sino Alliance, the seat of interplanetary government that creates and enforces the law throughout the known 'verse. To accommodate the needs of billions, the Alliance formed two capitol planets: Sihnon and Londinium.

Parliament, the main governing body, is found on Londinium, which is also one of the most populated and oldest planets in the 'verse. Sihnon boasts sprawling cities, cutting-edge Academies, and Companion Houses such as House Madrassa where young men and women are trained in the arts of calligraphy, music, acting, fencing, sex, and massage. All day-to-day government activities, which include the manufacture of currency, are approved and conducted by Parliament on these two planets.

The *Serenity* crew has visited Ariel, Bellerophon, and Persephone. Each is an example of the populous worlds found in the White Sun System.

ARIEL

Ariel is the eleventh planet of the White Sun System. It possesses a strong Alliance presence, common to other Core worlds, such as Osiris.

Of all its cities, Ariel City is a stunning example of what the Central Planets have to offer when compared to a Border Planet. Ariel City is a cultural mecca that boasts museums, fine dining, medical facilities, and towering metallic skyscrapers that glimmer in the sunlight. Despite this, Ariel City is not without its problems: the criminal underground smuggles lab-grown organs in willing hosts in 'The Message', and dissenters supply the *Serenity* crew with hospital uniforms and fake medical IDs in 'Ariel'.

In many ways, Ariel City is a sterile metropolis that, at first glance, reflects what the Alliance wants its citizens to believe. But, while the city streets are immaculately maintained, it is also rife with bureaucracy and government oversight. The Ariel City Junkyard, for example, is a municipal dumping ground for discarded parts, and it is not typically patrolled because the Alliance doesn't expect its citizens to re-use or re-cycle. It is dirty and unkempt, suggesting the Alliance's interference in daily life is so pervasive, anything they don't touch is junk.

St. Lucy's Medical Center stands in sharp contrast to the junkyard. The impeccably clean hospital not only has the latest advances in medical technology, it also features a built-in monitoring station accessible to the Alliance military. The government-run facility is also well guarded, and most of its rooms, such as the medvault, are only accessible with the proper clearance.

BELLEROPHON

The planet Bellerophon is the tenth planet in the White Sun System and the wealthiest planet in the entire 'verse. Located in the Core, its citizens are elite Alliance loyalists whose power and influence are unmatched. Home to Alliance war heroes like Durran Haymer, Bellerophon has a unique landscape. While its socialites live in Bellerophon Estates, which are self-maintained islands floating above a vast ocean, they are bordered by a dry, uninhabited desert with only a few landmarks, such as Isis Canyon.

Security on Bellerophon is high, and each estate owner may signal private security via a silent alarm. The estates themselves are a sprawling blend of high-tech equipment and lush, fragrant gardens. The Bellerophon Estates have a similar design, with the interior of each mansion reflecting its owner's tastes. Haymer's estate, for example, boasts a collection of Earth-That-Was artifacts that included the Lassiter, the first laser pistol ever made.

The Bellerophon Estates are maintained by servants who live on the property, contractors and service professionals, and automated mechanisms and drones.

PERSEPHONE

Many people think of Persephone as a Border Planet. As the second-to-last planet of the White Sun System, the world acts as a gateway between the Core and the Border. In many ways, it is the bridge between the established and the frontier, the wealthy and the poor, the lawful and the criminal.

The Eavesdown Docks are a popular destination for tourists and spacefarers who want to explore the other four systems. The town benefits from its proximity to the resource-rich Central Planets, and its location invites travelers to book passage with docked ships. Its streets boast supply stores that stock everything from fancy dresses to fuel cells; its docks are flush with buskers performing kabuki and street vendors offering fresh meals to passersby. Thieves and dignitaries alike can take advantage of the fact that it is a smuggler's haven, due to a lack of Alliance inspectors. Badger, for example, hires the *Serenity* crew to transport Lord Harrow's cows in exchange for credits in 'Shindig'.

Socialites, farmers, and dandies like Atherton Wing also call Persephone home and frequent many places, such as formal dances under the shimmering light of a holographic chandelier. A nearby hotel, the Plum Orchid, is traditionally decorated and is the perfect place to host guests. Cadrie Pond is another well-known destination, where duelists fight at dawn's first light.

Persephone is a near-perfect match to Earth-That-Was. Despite this, income inequality is more apparent here than elsewhere in the Core. Badger, for example, is a human trafficker who sells slaves, and many workers on the Eavesdown Docks are barely scraping by. This, however, is sharply contrasted by the presence of a ruling class. Sir Warwick Harrow wears a sash to denote his status as a lord; companions, a staple in the Core, are common, and its socialites, such as Banning Miller, have time to spare. What's more, social mores on Persephone are often dictated by the wealthy, which is why Mal unwittingly picked a fight he wasn't sure he could win in 'Shindig'.

RING AROUND THE WHITE SUN

The Border Planets are the worlds that surround the Core, and are found in the Georgia and Red Sun systems. They were also the battlegrounds of the Unification War. Though some skirmishes took place outside the Border, most were fought in these two systems. The Battle of Serenity was fought on Hera, for example, and the planet Shadow was bombed until it was no longer habitable.

Following the end of the Unification War, the Alliance patrols its newly won territories by dividing regions of space into sectors. Each sector is monitored by the captain of an Alliance cruiser. On the ground, areas are divided into territories, with the local law enforcement reporting directly to an Alliance representative or member of the military.

Though the area is patrolled, the Border Planets are numerous and far enough from each other that each one tends to possess its own set of cultures and micro-cultures. Many people have yet to recover from the horrors of war, like the poor townsfolk on Jiangyin, while others have sidled up to the Alliance to ensure their survival.

RED SUN

KALIDASA

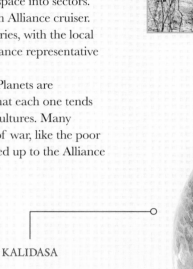

WHITE SUN

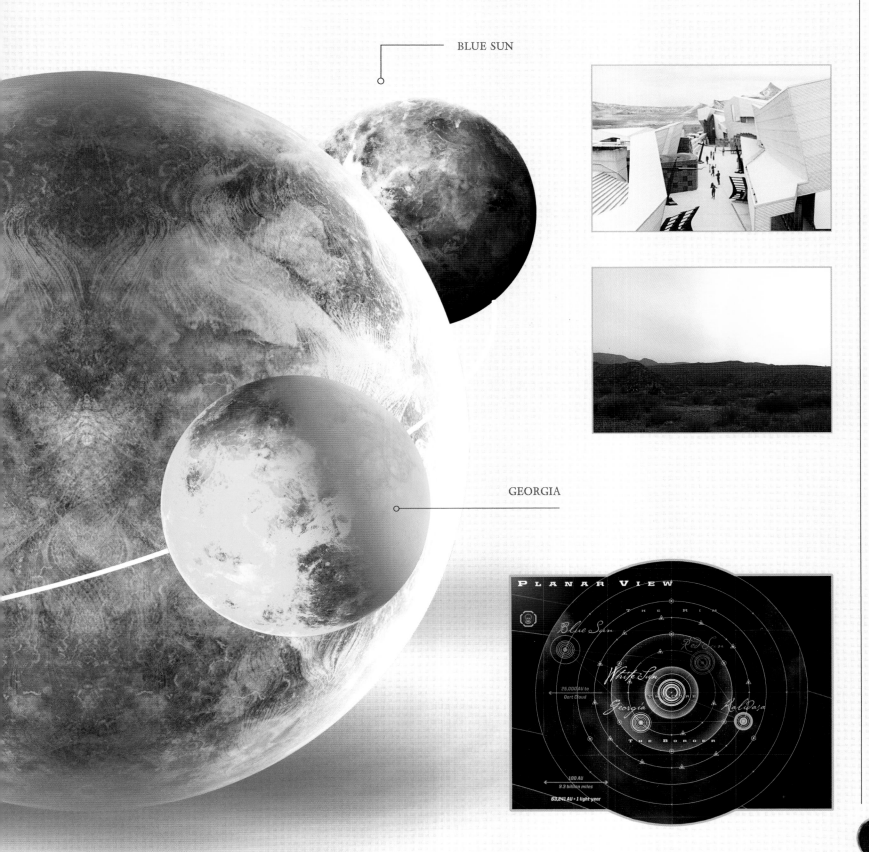

Li Shen's Space Bazaar: Li Shen's Space Bazaar is a space station the size of a small town. Though it has several floors, the bazaar's primary level is a draw for anyone hoping to resupply and do a little business before takin' off elsewhere. The main floor offers several forms of entertainment, including carnival-like attractions, buskers, and food carts. Many Guild traders ply their wares in the bazaar, and the Alliance postal service—one of many satellite offices—is part of a Federal program and run by Postmaster Ammon Duul. Thanks to Li Shen and the folks he deals with, the space bazaar has a reputation for being a safe haven out in the Black. Li Shen's Space Bazaar slowly travels from the Red Sun System to Georgia and back again, supplying the needs of spacefarers and settlers alike.

BLUE SUN

GEORGIA

PLANAR VIEW

THE RIM

Blue Sun

Red Sun

White Sun

25,000 AU to
Oort Cloud

Georgia

Kalidasa

THE BORDER

100 AU
9.3 billion miles

63,241 AU = 1 light year

RED SUN SYSTEM

The Red Sun System is named after its colorful sun, Zhu Que (Red Phoenix), and has two suns, fifteen planets, and one asteroid belt called the Motherlode. Most of the worlds here are overlooked by the Alliance; the lush planet Greenleaf and one of its moons, Dyton, is an exception rather than the rule. This system is also home to the Silverhold Colonies, which are located on the planet Silverhold. Silverhold is the last planet in the system and falls under Lieutenant Womack's jurisdiction. Other planets and moons include Higgins' Moon, Jiangyin, and St. Albans.

HIGGINS' MOON

Higgins' Moon orbits the planet Harvest, the fourth planet in the Red Sun System. It is small and unwelcoming, in part because it is ruled by a shrewd Alliance loyalist named Magistrate Higgins. The moon is home to Canton Mudworks, a facility that produces high-grade mud used in industrial manufacturing. Canton mud is of such high quality it can produce porcelain ship parts or fine china.

Other notable locations include Magistrate Higgins' sprawling hacienda and the town of Canton. Unlike other Border Planets, the Alliance has a special relationship with Higgins to ensure that the mud continues to be excavated from the planet's bogs.

JIANGYIN

Jiangyin is a sparsely populated planet in closest orbit around Zhu Que. It is an example of a Border Planet that has been cut off from the Alliance, in part due to its remote location. Unlike other worlds closer to the Core, Jiangyin is not situated near a shipping lane, so resources are often scarce and hard to find. Though colonists and settlers have made a home for themselves on Jiangyin, skilled laborers and professionals are in such short supply some communities, like the town the Patron runs, have stooped to kidnapping to raise money to survive.

Like other remote settlements, high-tech equipment is in short supply and citizens tend to make do with that they have. The forests provide some wood for shelter, and farmers have found the means to trade with manufacturers, exchanging food for souvenirs.

ST. ALBANS

St. Albans is the sixth planet in orbit around the Red Sun. It's unique because it is covered in ice, and snow falls all year round. The snow attracts wealthier tourists, but it also keeps its original settlers on the surface. Life on St. Albans requires strong survival instincts, because nothing can grow while the snow falls.

On St. Albans, living in isolation is dangerous. The planet's frigid temperatures require its settlers to trade or buy what goods they need. Sometimes settlers book passage on a shuttle to visit Li Shen's Space Bazaar for a supply run. Other times, workers at the local inns will rely on what the owners share with them. For this reason, settlements tend to be small and clustered.

Above: Settler's life on Jiangyin and the harsh cold temperatures of St. Alban's.

GEORGIA SYSTEM

The heart of the Georgia System is a bright yellow sun called Huang Long (Yellow Dragon). The Georgia System has two suns, sixteen planets, and a lot of history. The deciding battle of the Unification War, the Battle of Serenity, was fought on Hera, the fourteenth orbiting planet. As such, the Alliance's interest in this region tends to wax and wane, as many Browncoats in the area still remember what happened when the Independent soldiers attempted to lay down arms.

The Alliance still maintains some military bases in this system, but it primarily does so for its own interests. For example, the *Serenity* crew was initially bound for Boros—which has a strong military presence—but was forced to land on Whitefall instead. Ground units share reports with captains monitoring the skies above, who may intervene in local affairs when necessary.

WHITEFALL

Whitefall is the fourth moon of Athens, formerly run by local criminal Patience who named herself mayor. Unlike Higgins' Moon, Whitefall is ignored by the Alliance, which has allowed crime to flourish. Horses are commonly used for transportation on this moon, and its rugged terrain offers several places for smugglers and thieves to meet—and for hermits to thrive. Disgraced Agent Dobson holed up on Whitefall after he was thrown out of *Serenity*'s cargo hold. He plotted his revenge for months, before being reinstated by the Hands of Blue.

EZRA

Ezra is the first planet in orbit around Huang Long. It is covered with vast deserts and, like St. Albans, resources are often in short supply. Sparsely populated settlements with bars and general stores can be found on the planet's surface. Middlemen like Bolles, or criminals who act as the go-between for smugglers and buyers, often conduct deals to get necessary goods. Usually these supplies are staples that include protein bars or medicines.

Of all the planets in the Red Sun System, Ezra is unique because it is also home to two powerful forces: Adelai Niska, a terrifying crime boss, and the World Council, Ezra's governing body. Niska lives in a space station that slowly orbits Ezra. For many years he was free to operate out of his Skyplex because he successfully infiltrated the World Council—until he met Malcolm Reynolds.

REGINA

The planet Regina is second in orbit around Huang Long. It is a world whose long-term residents suffer from a disease called Bowden's Malady. Something went wrong when the Alliance terraformed it. The first settlers to mine the planet's minerals, in a town called Paradiso, contracted the disease and then passed it on to their children. Now, anyone who remains on Regina is all-but-guaranteed to be diagnosed with the illness. Bowden's Malady is incurable, but a drug called Pescaline-D has been engineered to all-but-erase its effects. The Alliance supplies this drug by transporting shipments from Hancock to Paradiso on a fast-moving train.

Above: Life for settlers can be harsh and unrelenting, with hostile environments, weather and landscapes to contend with.

New settlers on Regina are often drawn to the mining colony because they can't find other work, or their credits have run dry. Life on this planet is harder than most, because on top of limited supplies the people here know they might never leave.

EDGING OUT TO NOWHERE

The Kalidasa and Blue Sun systems are on the furthest edges of the 'verse. Planets and moons in the rim are younger than the Border and Core, and some have yet to be terraformed.

If the Border is the new frontier, then the rim represents the wild and unruly. Most folk have heard stories of brutal murderers who've attacked ships and settlements out this way, never realizing that there's a kernel of truth to them. Reavers, who occupy a territory in the Blue Sun System, occasionally break free from their fleet to target ships.

The Alliance's influence in the rim grew after the end of the Unification War, but has since weakened after it was revealed that they created the Reavers. While they have attempted to govern cities and settlements out on the rim, people are beginning to resist.

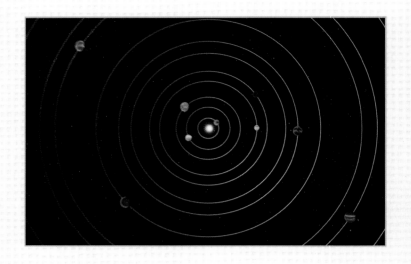

KALIDASA SYSTEM

The Kalidasa System is the biggest of the five. It has two suns, including Xuan Wu (Black Tortoise), and twenty planets.

Kalidasa is populated but has fewer Alliance settlements and colonies than the Border. The government has attempted to incentivize colonization by supplying colonists with supplies and a deed to a homestead, but their efforts have been sabotaged by Reaver attacks. One ship, carrying four families, was bound for Newhall when it was struck by Reavers. The Reavers left one survivor alive, a man so damaged he was destined to become like them, and set a trap for anyone who dared to investigate.

The Kalidasa System is also home to several industrial planets, including Beaumonde, that manufacture everything from toothpaste to socks. By contracting goods and services from other planets, the Alliance hopes to spare the Core from the fate that Earth-That-Was suffered. Once a planet like Beaumonde becomes so polluted life is no longer sustainable, the government will use suppliers, such as the Blue Sun Corporation, to shift manufacturing to a different location.

BEAUMONDE

Beaumonde is a mecca of industrial activity, in part because the Blue Sun Corporation owns and operates several sprawling factories and warehouses on the planet. Its capital city, New Dunsmuir, is said to rival all aspects of the Eavesdown Docks on Persephone—with one exception. Where the Eavesdown Docks tends to attract tourists, New Dunsmuir is not a destination city. It's primarily visited by traders, smugglers, and business-minded folk who need credits. It's so well thought of that Mal urged Saffron to find a job on Beaumonde to be freed from her obligation to Elder Gommen—and their sham marriage.

Though New Dunsmuir does have some attractions, like the Maidenhead, it is a dingy city with a large space dock. Most of its citizens are factory workers, hard luck cases, and middlemen like Fantastic 'Fanty' and Mingojerry 'Mingo' Rample. Many of the resources used, traded, and sold in the city originate from the noisy factories that operate day and night.

Above: **The busy atmosphere that can be found on Beaumonde.**

BLUE SUN SYSTEM

The Blue Sun System is the youngest and smallest of the five. It is named after its Blue Sun (Qing Long), and has two suns, eight planets—including Miranda—and an asteroid field called Uroborus.

The Blue Sun System is home to settlers searching for something the Alliance cannot provide: liberty. Their freedom, however, is marred by the threat of attack. A fleet of Reavers descends on towns and settlements, like the trading post located on Lilac, devastating the local population with its sharp harpoons and fast ships. Stories of Reaver attacks are rampant throughout this area of the 'verse, and settlers aren't sure what's true and what's not. What they do know, however, is that Reavers is just another word for terror. Wherever they roam, death is sure to follow.

Planets include New Canaan, the source of fine brandy, and its moon, Lilac. A bottle of New Canaan brandy is a rare treat, which is why folks like Gabriel Tam savor it. Deadwood and Miranda, however, are perhaps the most noteworthy planets in this sector.

DEADWOOD

Deadwood is the seventh planet in the Blue Sun System. Its name is an accurate description for the sandy soil that covers the landscape; so few hardy shrubs grow on the planet's surface, the planet's de facto official, a rancher by the name of Rance Burgess, sidled up to the Alliance to facilitate trade with the Guild.

A barren, desolate place, most of the folk who live on Deadwood are either godly—or not. When Rance Burgess was around, people flocked to his display of wealth and his fire-and-brimstone speeches. When he wasn't around, his monopoly on trade and technology began to crumble. Since the planet's settlements rely on trade, opportunists vie for power to guarantee their survival.

MIRANDA

Miranda is the eighth planet in the Blue Sun System and, until recently, it'd been wiped from the Cortex. No record of Miranda existed, and it wasn't found on any interplanetary maps.

Miranda is significant because it is proof that the Alliance's intentions to pacify and govern its people aren't as pure as they claim. Following the terraforming process, the Alliance built sprawling metropolises as far as the eye could see. Unlike other Border or rim worlds, Miranda was a beacon of hope for the future, because the planet represented what the Alliance could do outside the Central Planets.

Unfortunately, the Alliance wasn't satisfied with the civilization it had built, so it tasked its researchers with formulating a new way to nullify citizens' aggression. Millions died when their experiment backfired, and the Reavers were born.

Miranda is uninhabitable. Its cities, that once teemed with life, are now necropolises. Most people wouldn't dare visit Miranda to verify the truth, for doing so requires an encounter with pirates, smugglers, or worse—Reavers.

ABOVE: **The sandy soils of Deadwood and the aftermath of the Alliance's experiments on Miranda.**

A CONVERSATION WITH ARTIST BEN MUND

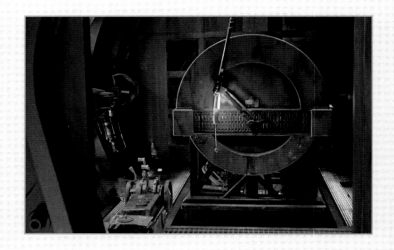

Ben Mund is an artist who has lent his considerable talent to breathing visual life into the ships, planets, and essentials of the 'verse; he has contributed several pieces to the *Firefly Encyclopedia,* including a detailed schematic of *Serenity*'s engine. Ben has also designed many official props over the years, including *Serenity*'s ship papers, blueprints, and wallet, as well as Mal's dogtag set and cigarillo display box. He is also the author of the *Serenity: Atlas of the 'Verse: Volume 1* and has designed money for *Firefly: The Game* from Gale Force Nine, in addition to his work on the *Firefly Role Playing Game*. In this interview, Ben shares his inspiration and why he keeps returning to *Firefly*.

Q: TELL US ABOUT YOUR JOURNEY AS AN ARTIST. WHAT ARE SOME OF YOUR PERSONAL FANDOMS? HOW HAS THAT CHANGED?

A: I started working with paint and canvasboard (and walls) when I was five or six. I liked it from the start. When I was eight, something happened that triggered a new excitement for creating things that don't exist. That was the year I was almost simultaneously introduced to *Star Wars*, *Star Trek*, *Doctor Who*, Tolkien, and Lovecraft. A pretty potent cocktail that's had a long-lasting effect on what excites me in genre art. The Rankin-Bass stills in the illustrated *Hobbit* I got for my birthday. Ralph McQuarrie's paintings in *The Art of Star Wars*. The clean detail in the U.S.S. *Enterprise Officer's Manual* under the Christmas tree.

I loved all of it, and that passion has grown over the years. But it was an element of my design that I didn't get to express commercially until *Firefly*. Quantum Mechanix (QMx) secured the license for prop reproduction and some in-universe expansion, and I picked up some freelance work with them on large-format print books. Since then I've been lucky enough to keep my toe in the genre water I love so much with work on the *Battlestar Galactica* and *Stargate* licenses, as well as other genre work for companies like Steve Jackson Games, Gale Force Nine, and the now-defunct Margaret Weis Productions.

These days I work mostly digitally, though I love adding handwork where the property or project benefits from a blend of both—the world of *Firefly* being a great example. And as clichéd as it sounds, the best part of the work is the people I meet. That *Enterprise Officer's Manual* I got for Christmas as a kid? Twenty-five years later I met the artist who wrote and illustrated it, Geoffrey Mandel. Turns out he was a graphic artist on the *Serenity* movie, and I had the privilege of working with him on *Firefly* projects for QMx. What more could a geeky kid ask for?

Q: DOES YOUR ARTISTIC PROCESS CHANGE FROM PROJECT TO PROJECT?

A: Absolutely. It's one of the exciting and challenging parts of any creative work—you end up needing to learn new things and new techniques to fit a project. You add new tools to your toolbox as you go. You always have those favorites and standbys that give you a foundation, but the new creative tools you add can make specific work better, easier, or both.

Q: WHAT WAS YOUR FAVORITE PIECE TO ILLUSTRATE?

A: I did a set of in-universe *Firefly* playing cards for QMx. That was probably my favorite *Firefly* project because it hit a bunch of check marks for me. I love the property, I have an obsessive fascination with playing cards, and I love to add layers to a project that can be picked up over time. That project fired on all cylinders. I had a blast adding a lot of little details to each card, and since the cards were weathered I even added an Easter-egg silhouette of *Serenity* made out of the weathering patterns that became visible only when you arranged eight of the cards in the right order. That was fun.

Q: AS AN ARTIST, WHAT IS IT ABOUT *FIREFLY* THAT DRAWS YOU TO THIS SETTING?

A: It's what I imagine draws a lot of people to the aesthetic—the great combination of the immediately familiar and the brand new. There's an earthiness to the sci-fi design that makes it easy to connect with.

Q: YOUR STYLE IS INCREDIBLY DETAILED. WHERE DO YOU DRAW INSPIRATION FOR YOUR PIECES?

A: I work professionally in an engineering-heavy industry, so that plays into it in many ways. That kind of attention to detail can lead down an admittedly fun rabbit hole as you try to decide where to draw the line between plausibility and design. But the payoff in genre work is that a lot of fans of the properties also love to dig into details with you, and, I hope, appreciate the level of believability it can bring. A good *Firefly* example is the illustration of Mal's gun in *The Atlas of the 'Verse*. I tried to balance what we saw in the show (it shoots but doesn't eject anything), what we heard in the show (electronic whines), and how the prop was built (magazine-loaded and various other bits and bobs). I designed an entire interior structure to support those items, talking to designers, fans, and gun experts. The result was something that followed its own internal logic to function in that universe the way we see it, and was a helluva lot of fun in the process.

Please see page 256 for Ben Mund's biography.

RIGHT: Ben Mund's amazing exploded view of *Serenity*'s engine—exclusive to this book.

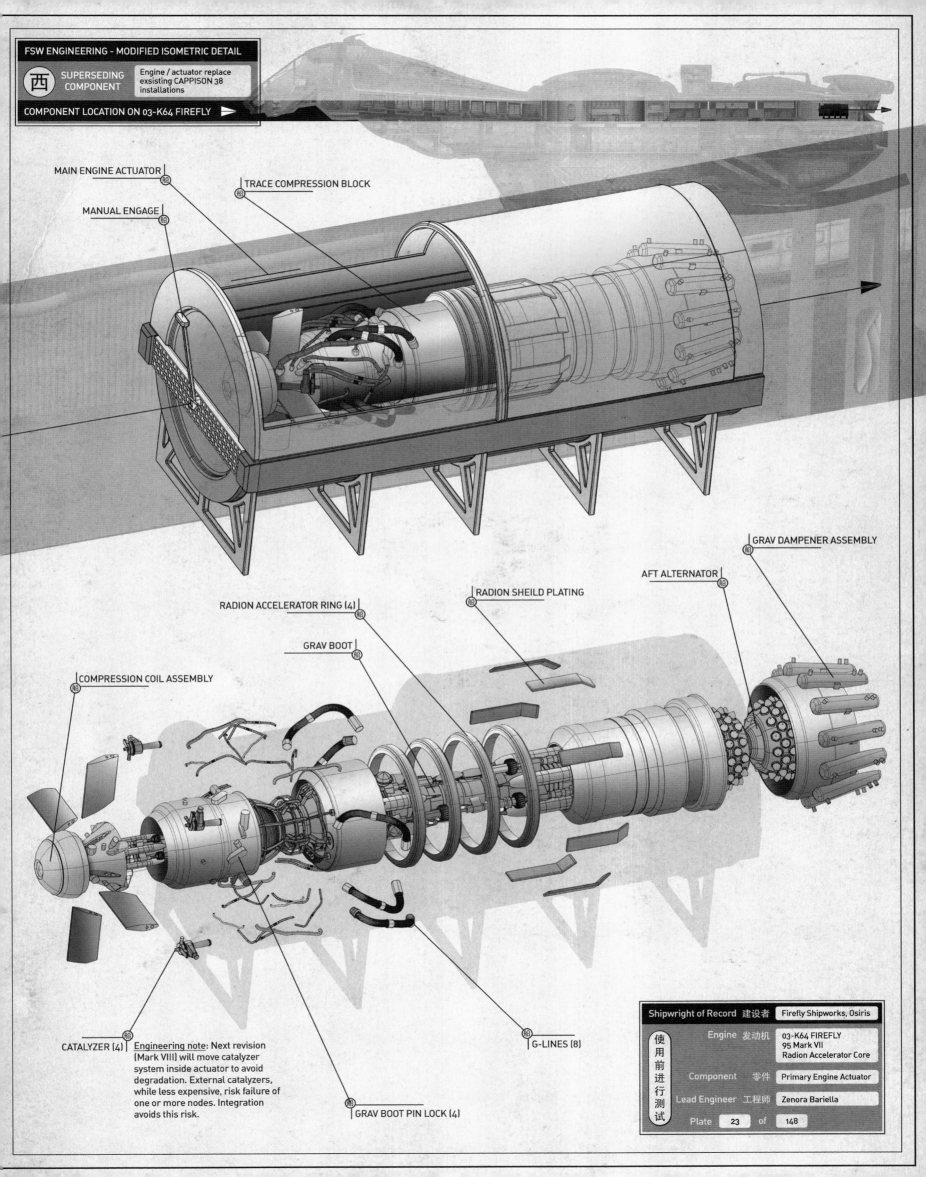

MAIN ENGINE ACTUATOR

TRACE COMPRESSION BLOCK

MANUAL ENGAGE

GRAV DAMPENER ASSEMBLY

AFT ALTERNATOR

RADION SHEILD PLATING

RADION ACCELERATOR RING (4)

GRAV BOOT

COMPRESSION COIL ASSEMBLY

CATALYZER (4)

Engineering note: Next revision (Mark VIII) will move catalyzer system inside actuator to avoid degradation. External catalyzers, while less expensive, risk failure of one or more nodes. Integration avoids this risk.

G-LINES (8)

GRAV BOOT PIN LOCK (4)

Shipwright of Record	建设者	Firefly Shipworks, Osiris
Engine	发动机	03-K64 FIREFLY 95 Mark VII Radion Accelerator Core
Component	零件	Primary Engine Actuator
Lead Engineer	工程师	Zenora Bariella
Plate	23	of 148

使用前进行测试

SHUTTLES, SHIPS & SPACE STATIONS

SERENITY

> *If Whedon was the master of the*
mythology and stories behind *Firefly*, then it was
production designer Carey Meyer and visual effects
supervisor/co-creator of Zoic Studios Loni Peristere
who were the visual magicians, overseeing the design
of all of the brilliant ships, vehicles, and space
stations that are now synonymous with the series.
The two sat down together to reminisce about how
they came to create the myriad of vehicles that were
such an integral part of the show.

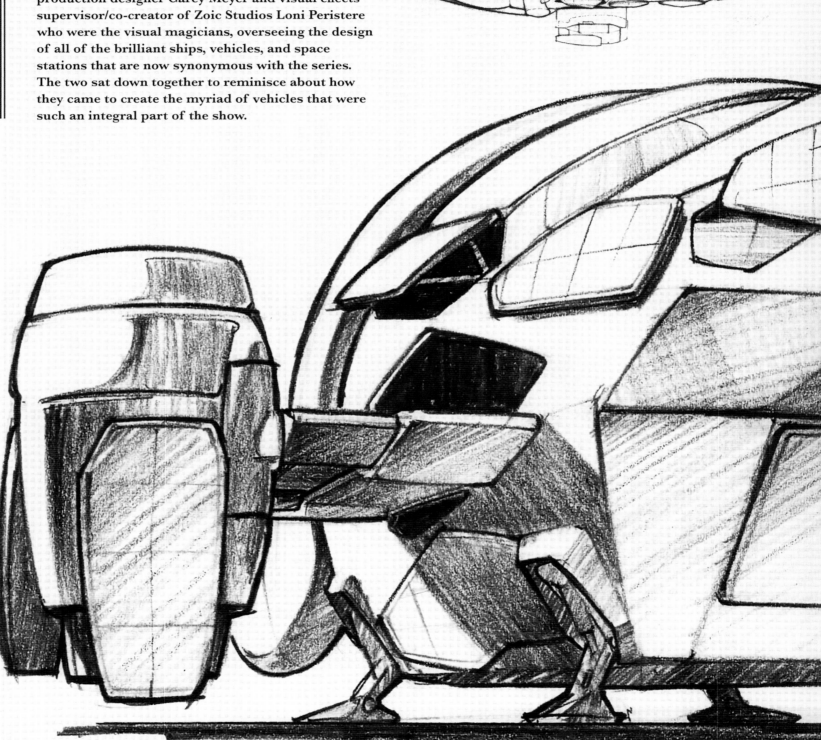

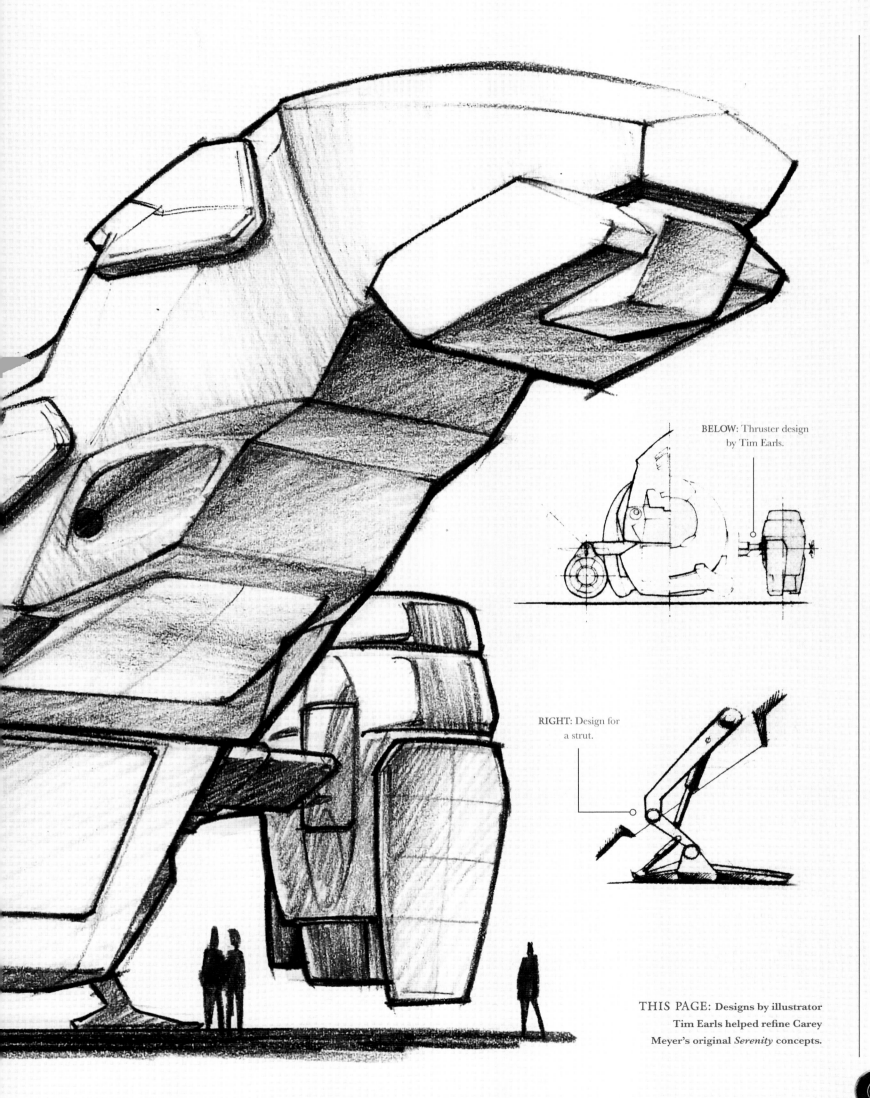

BELOW: Thruster design by Tim Earls.

RIGHT: Design for a strut.

THIS PAGE: Designs by illustrator Tim Earls helped refine Carey Meyer's original *Serenity* concepts.

First and foremost let's make it clear—there really is no *Firefly* series without the Firefly-class transport *Serenity*. In fact the ship was so important to Whedon, he told Meyer and Peristere that it was to be considered a character equal in standing to the cast. That mandate set the tone for how they approached its creation.

Meyer remembers, "When we were first starting the project, Joss was just getting the green light from Fox and we were all working on *Buffy* at the time. After a couple of weeks Joss came up to me and said he really wanted me to work on it and to pitch some ideas for what the ship would look like, because that was the starting point for him. Once he got an idea of what the world was like inside the ship, he could start formulating the stories. Joss said his one key was for it to have an ironic flair to it. It had to be cool, but there had to be some reality to it. So I started playing around with paper airplanes. There was this cool design I had always played around with as a child, and always loved. It's this conical-shaped airplane all made out of paper, and I shoved a balloon into it.

RIGHT: A model of *Serenity* made using a computer-guided laser on layers of laminated paper. It has the apparent density of wood and is finished in grey primer spray paint.

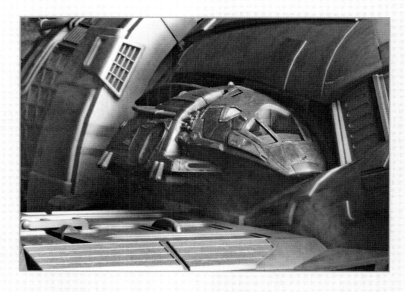

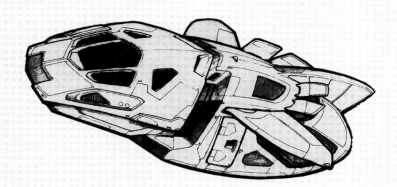

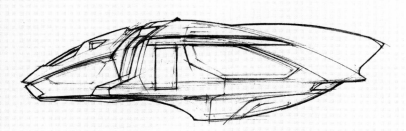

"I still have the original model that I built," he chuckles. "I was up for twenty-four hours building this thing. We came in the next morning at nine o'clock, and I think I nailed it. I brought the plane with the balloon shoved into it and a little sketch of what I was thinking. We all sit down and Joss says, 'Well, it's cool, but I think it's too far. We need to bring it back a little bit.' The shape was very asymmetrical, and he wanted a sleeker line to it. I took that original model and spread clay all over it, smoothing out the original into something resembling what we have today. Then he really fell in love with what we now know as the ring that wraps around the rear."

Meyer continues, "From that point it was a series of sketches for how the rest of it all would look. He wanted a lot of it to look like an insect—a firefly obviously. One of the main designers I was looking at was Lebbeus Woods, who is a futurist architect. Joss liked that look as well, so we started sketching in that style, which got us an overall shape that we were able to cross-section and start developing the interior. From that, Joss was able to ask for a bridge and a hallway that leads to the corridors, a galley, a corridor to the engine room, and the main cargo bay. Once he nailed down the different spaces that were inside, we were able to lay it all out as set designs and work it back into the exterior shape."

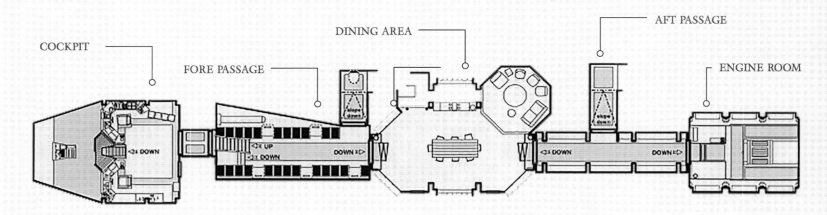

COCKPIT

FORE PASSAGE

DINING AREA

AFT PASSAGE

ENGINE ROOM

Meanwhile Peristere says he was working in concert with Meyer in the digital realm. "I was keying off of what Carey was doing," he explains. "I began to build a temporary version of that ship in 3-D, so once we had a physical model we could immediately bring it into 3-D space. A lot of what we were doing was coming up with how the rooms fit, and fitting that into the 3-D model, adjusting so all the rooms would fit in a logical manner. And Carey had this cool idea that the ship was put together and then reconstructed a little bit, because it had been in a junkyard for a long time. So the idea was that the external panels weren't all original. We spent some time going in the direction of having a lot of variety of textures, with a lot of colors and patinas from other ships. We went too far at first because it was like a quilt of a spaceship, but we pulled back and streamlined it. We also took a look at the logistics of the neck of the ship, and played with how steep it was, and how close to the ground based on how you would drive stuff into the cargo bay when the landing gear was down. Then we had to come up with the right kind of landing gear, and the door/ramp into the cargo bay."

He continues, "In addition, we came up with where the gravity on the ship came from—we used the ring that Carey created.

We called it the 'gravity ring' and put a widget in there that spun around. We built lighting effects for it with our DP on set, so they were built into the set lighting so you could see the changing flicker. We also had to come up with the trans-warp drive, the 'firefly engine'. Carey built these honeycomb shapes on the inside set, so we mirrored that on the outside. We came up with the logic of a cooling process, so we created these panels on the butt of the ship that opened up to reveal the same honeycomb pattern you saw on the inside, on the outside. There were insect-like panels that would show this glowing butt on *Serenity*, which was kinda cool."

Peristere laughs as he reveals an insiders' joke: "I always wanted *Serenity*'s cargo bay to be detachable. Carey thought it was cool, but Joss was worried it was too similar to something that happened in *Star Trek*. I always thought a cargo ship's hold should be like a shipping container, where you can drop one off and pick one up. Believe it or not, I actually built it into the design of the CG model so that it does do that, because I figured at some time I would win that argument. I never won that fight, but it's still there."

Of their final product, Meyer muses, "Joss didn't just want a ship, he wanted a tenth character. I think we pulled it off and to this day he's very emotionally tied to that vehicle."

CARGO BAY

INFIRMARY

PASSENGER QUARTERS

COMMON AREA

THIS PAGE: Top-down plans for the ship layouts, and shots of the detailed sets built from the designs.

ALLIANCE CRUISERS

These massive ships serve as functional cities that house military, police, and civilians, patrolling the space between Alliance planets. After designing *Serenity*, Meyer says these were the next ships they tackled.

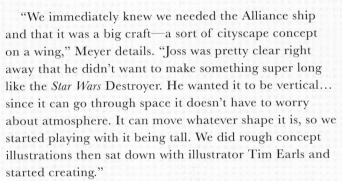

"We immediately knew we needed the Alliance ship and that it was a big craft—a sort of cityscape concept on a wing," Meyer details. "Joss was pretty clear right away that he didn't want to make something super long like the *Star Wars* Destroyer. He wanted it to be vertical… since it can go through space it doesn't have to worry about atmosphere. It can move whatever shape it is, so we started playing with it being tall. We did rough concept illustrations then sat down with illustrator Tim Earls and started creating."

Peristere continues, "The whole concept of a city in space was interesting to me. I love the notion of revealing a ship in an entirely new way, and one which embraced the fact that in space there is no up, down, right, or left. There are no hard and fast rules of what you are looking at. I love how we introduce I.A.V. *Dortmunder* seeing two towers, thinking they are just great shapes, but then we reveal they are essentially Empire State buildings—these massive things! I love the idea that the tiny fighter craft show just how big this thing is. There's no need for scale in space—you can build ships as big as you like—so the idea of having this giant thing moving through the Black was really cool. I was actually disappointed we didn't use the ship more, because we spent a lot of time working out the design of all of it, like the interesting bays on the underside where the fighter craft were stationed."

Carey adds, "The other concept we were playing with was that the textures and colors were completely divergent. The Alliance ship was stark grey with blacks and whites, while *Serenity* was very warm and had texture and felt real."

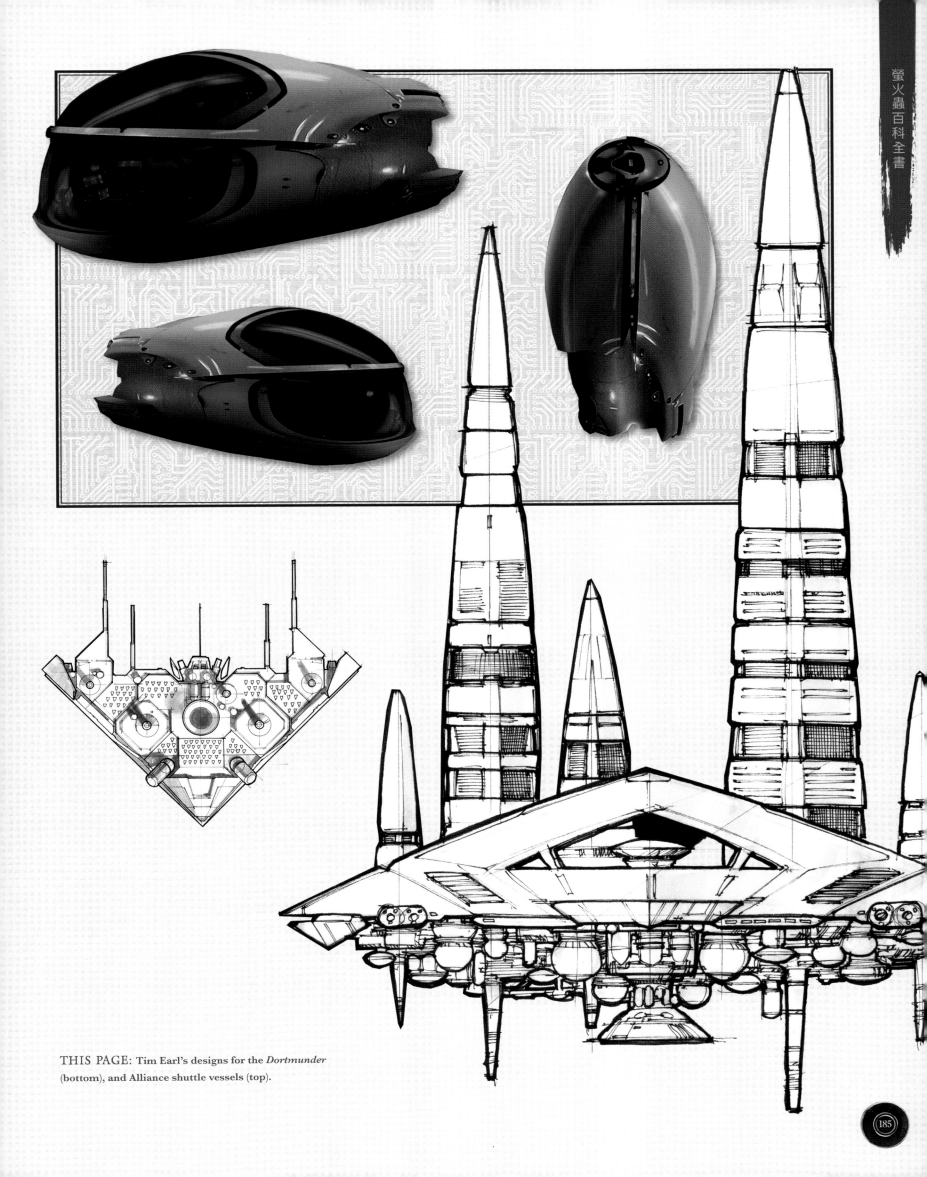

THIS PAGE: Tim Earl's designs for the *Dortmunder* (bottom), and Alliance shuttle vessels (top).

REAVER SHIPS

To represent the nightmarish savages that **terrorize the outer planets, it was essential for Meyer and Zoic to come up with a visual concept for the Reavers' ships that was just as terrifying as the monsters that lurk within.**

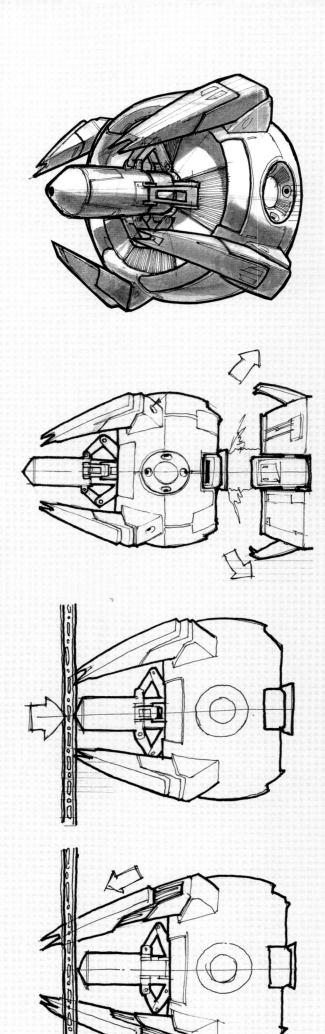

"We said that *Serenity* is this rough-and-tumble ship patched together with pieces of another ship; but it was all from another Firefly-class ship," Meyer says about their design rationale. "With the Reaver ship, we decided they would make a ship out of ten ships. The original idea was that the main body was made from a really old super liner cruise ship. They took it and ripped it apart and put engines at the front, so it was a complete fabrication of ripped-up other ships."

He continues, "Around that time in-house we were building the *Serenity* interiors on stage, and I worked out a short-hand with illustrator Tim Earls, who had finalized some designs for *Serenity* and the Alliance Cruisers. He had a good feel for the world we were creating, so when Joss started talking about the Reaver ship, it was literally as quick as saying to Tim, 'Let's go even further than what *Serenity* was.' We talked about a wide-body 747 and started deconstructing that, along with the idea of a wild boar."

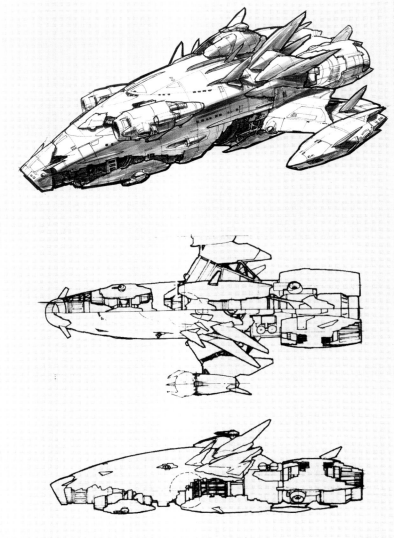

"Then we added the idea they wanted to paint their ships with war paint," Peristere details. "And that they would purposefully rip open their containment engine so it would leak. They didn't care that they would get radiation poisoning, so the idea was to be as menacing as possible by design. They haphazardly construct the meanest-looking things they can. They create a mask of intimidation so you get scared."

Carey smiles as he remembers, "When I saw the first pre-viz of the Reaver ship chasing *Serenity* I just about fell out of my chair. It was the coolest thing I had seen in sci-fi."

LEFT: Tim Earls' design concepts for the Reavers' grapple claw.

THIS PAGE: The initial designs of the Raver ship, and how it appears on-screen.

SPACE BAZAAR

In 'The Message', the *Serenity* crew visits a space station, described in the script as a Space Bazaar. Inside, it's a colorful, bustling marketplace full of people, shops, and stalls. The exterior design is similarly striking, and had a very definite inspiration, as Meyer reveals: "It was a whole other idea of how a city in space would work, with bits added on and added on, like the modern-day International Space Station works today, as opposed to a thought-out Alliance ship. It wasn't like a Reaver ship, meant to look mean," he clarifies, "but a conglomeration of thousands of people's ideas. We referenced the book *City of Darkness—Life In Kowloon Walled City* [by Ian Lambot and Greg Girard], which is based on a housing development in Hong Kong that had its own police force and its own laws. It was literally this block of humanity that sat in the middle of a city, with its own boundaries. We really went at the bazaar with that book in mind."

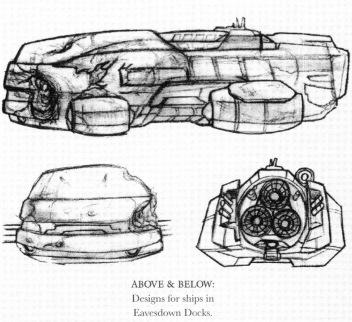

ABOVE & BELOW:
Designs for ships in
Eavesdown Docks.

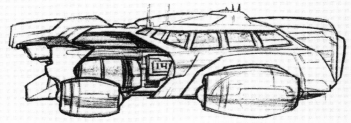

PERSEPHONE'S EAVESDOWN DOCKS

In the episode 'Serenity', Mal's crew lands at a quasi-Skid Row-type docking station filled with a motley assortment of ships. Peristere says all of those vehicles were designed and created for the scene. "Between our department and Carey's department we threw around different sketches for that particular place. We asked what other kinds of ships would you find there? We came up with transportation vessels for people and other kinds of cargo ships. We pulled a bunch of real-world reference and then started deconstructing that material. It became a first set of library rules [vehicles] that inform the series."

ALLIANCE SHORT RANGE ENFORCEMENT VESSEL (A.S.R.E.V.)

These small gun ships were housed within larger Alliance vessels, and were originally glimpsed in 'Trash' before one had a starring role in the memorable chase sequence in 'The Message'. Meyer explains that these ships represented the point where he handed off the intricate design work to the Zoic team.

"We were so deep into production of the show that Loni completely took over in terms of getting the design process finished on these kinds of vehicles," Meyer explains.

"So we brought in some superstar freelance designers [like Ron Cobb] to help us out," Peristere continues. "With this ship, the idea was to take the technology of today and advance it several hundred years and imagine what would be functional both in space and in atmosphere. I wanted to think about what would work in both spaces. Again we employed a joint strike fighter VTOL system where a panel opened up in the wing so it could lift off vertically instead of needing a runway. At the same time we wanted a sleek, bad-ass look that was intimidating and looked like a creature. We wanted it to be familiar, yet fresh and functional."

NISKA'S SKYPLEX

For the episodes 'The Train Job' and 'War Stories', the design team needed to create a space station that was a contrast to the Alliance ships, but with a menace all its own. Meyer explains, "It was another design that was both an exterior CG model and interior sets—especially for 'War Stories'. But Loni just took it to the nth degree on the outside."

Peristere continues, "For this space station we imagined that an independent contractor had taken it over, and it had been retrofitted many times. It's almost like a house you rebuild five or six times, and then *Serenity* has to squeeze and slide in. We created these tubes that were like a claw that would grab *Serenity* and take it into its folds; inside a deep, dark place."

Meyer says his favorite design aspect was featured inside the station. "The whole station had a central core of a long, long tube that everything glommed onto. Loni knocked it out of the park in Niska's office when they throw the guy over the balcony and you look down and it's basically that core. Amazing."

LEARNING TO TECHNOBABBLE

Spaceships have a lot of moving parts, and sometimes it's not always clear what names and terms mean. To speak like Kaylee, an eager mechanic will need to know what a compression coil is—or at least have a good idea.

TERM	DEFINITION
CONDUCTOR CAP	Thick casing designed to stop an electric or electro-magnetic output resulting from an accidental or intentional discharge. When applied to a port, outlet, or live cable, the conductor cap prevents a current from being emitted through that conductor.
CONSOLE ACCESS, OR CONTROL PANEL	Flat, programmable surface granting a user the ability to program, maintain, monitor, or control a system, object, or vehicle.
COOLING DRIVE	Ship's system that lowers the temperature of the engines to prevent them from overheating.
COMPRESSION COIL	Complex ship part attached to the engine. The compression coil is a piece of the system designed to turn an engine to generate power. In a Firefly-class ship, the engine has two compression coils on either side of it that are part of the steamer. Each coil contains a crucial part called a catalyzer. The poor condition of the compression coil is initially a bone of contention between Captain Reynolds and Kaylee, which eventually results in tragedy during 'Out of Gas'.
CORE CONTAINMENT	Primary ship's system engineered to prevent the effects of radiation from harming the crew. Reavers fly ships without a core containment system. Knowledge of this trait gives targeted victims the opportunity to detect nearby Reaver ships to plan an escape.
DRIVE FEED	Wires on a ship that transmit power to the cockpit. Part of the navigational system.
EXTENDERS	Mechanical parts that stabilize an engine to prevent the ship from shaking and rattling.
FULL BURN	Act of maximizing the power of a ship's engines.
GOING DARK	Act of turning off most of the ship's power to avoid detection by another ship.
GRAV-DAMPENER	Ship system responsible for creating and maintaining artificial gravity while flying through space.
GRAVITY DRIVE	Ship system responsible for creating and maintaining artificial gravity while flying through space.
HYDRAULICS	Ship system designed to feed liquids like oil or fuel around the different parts of the ship. 'Cutting the hydraulics' refers to cutting wires that are part of this system, which effectively shuts down another system or part.
NAVCOM	Short for navigational computer. An important ship part responsible for plotting flight paths, maintaining a ship's trajectory, identifying celestial bodies, spotting oncoming vessels, etc.
PRESSURE CATCH	Type of switch—attached to doors, for example—that acts as a locking mechanism.
SYNCHRONIZERS	Mechanical parts used to help decrease irregularities in two ship systems or to help parts work in tandem. Kaylee finds synchronizers in 'Ariel' in the junkyard.
WETWIRE	Opposite of hardwire. Instead of permanently attaching wires to an interface, console, or part, wires are temporarily connected to repair a ship's system or temporarily create a desired effect.

WALKING IN SPACE

Chris Gilman's company, Global Effects, has produced high-end spacesuits and armor for countless movies and TV shows, from *Bram Stoker's Dracula* to *Armageddon*. Chris recalls the origins of the suits used in *Firefly*. "They were originally created for Kurt Russell's movie *Soldier*. The movie's costume designer asked us to come up with some sort of 'soldier spacesuits'. I thought it was a perfect job for us as it combined two areas I'm really interested in: armor and spacesuits. The suits are a variant of the S10 high-altitude flight suit."

Originally the *Firefly* production team rented the *Soldier* suits unmodified, but Shawna Trpcic asked Chris if they could create a new look for our crew when outside the ship in space. "We came up with a custom designed helmet for use on the *Soldier* suits. We wanted to give the impression that the helmet could retract back over your head, so we incorporated pleats of the suit material up on the back of the helmet so it would look collapsible. The helmet is basically in two parts, there's the front shell and faceplate, and the pleated back section, which is on a plastic cap.

The texture of the shell surface is in the molding and the finish is a drab olive, golden green color to match the suits. There's a drybrush effect over the top to make the helmets look used and armored. A fan system in the backpack forces air up the helmet hose and over the inside of the faceplate. All of our helmets have fans as they would fog up without this and create a big problem. They saw some pieces we did for *Armageddon* and liked the vents on them, so we sculpted some smaller ones for the helmets. The light tubes on the side were rigged by our guy on set, at the request of the production. They're a couple of flashlights and some tubing we usually use for air hose."

Jayne's yellow spacesuit is somewhat different. There were only two of the *Soldier* suits available for rent, so Jayne's suit is an exact replica of an SR-71/10-30 suit, originally made for Dolph Lundgren, who's a similar size to Adam Baldwin. The helmet is the same launch/entry model as those worn by current shuttle crews and is a basic grey color with a black stipple effect. The neck seal ring is a replica of that on an Apollo suit. "Replica spacesuits are surprisingly complicated to make. The *Firefly* suit has about 300 to 400 components. Our replica Shuttle EMU suits have over 1,200, but the real EMU has over 19,000."

Costume designer Shawna Trpcic: "We couldn't afford to make our own spacesuits. Joss said, 'Well, they're scavengers anyway, so just scavenge them from a couple of different shows.' I designed my own helmets to go with the suits, so that at least they would look a little different from the original. We tried to make them look like they'd been through a lot."

HEALTH SERVICES AND MEDICINE

In the 26th century, accessibility to **medical services is thematically tied to the three primary regions of the 'verse: Core, Border, and rim.**

The Core (or Central Planets) is flush with medicines, prestigious institutions such as AMI on Osiris, and high-tech machines, like the 3-D neural imager Simon used to scan River's brain in 'Ariel'. Much of the techniques and practices doctors employ in the White Sun System are rooted in 21st century practices, with a futuristic touch.

The experimental procedures performed on River were conducted by the government to create sleeper agents. Though the blastomeres Tracey Smith smuggled in his chest were tied to a criminal organization on Ariel, the technology to grow organs for transplant is accessible to everyday Alliance citizens. When combined with the access to prestigious medical schools, called Medacads, and hospitals where a Medical Elect not only acts as administrator but also as an Alliance informant, the White Sun System is a mecca for health care.

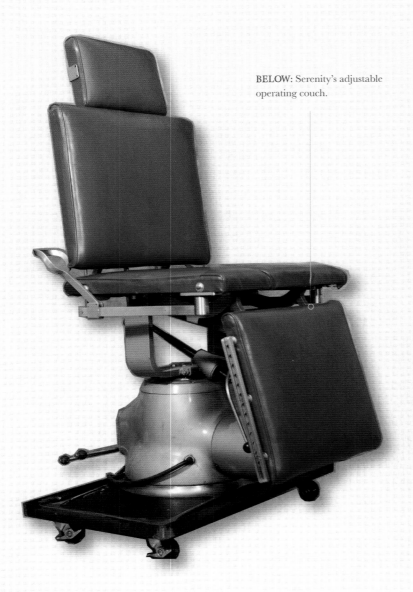

BELOW: Serenity's adjustable operating couch.

THE UNIVERSAL ENCYCLOPEDIA

Chris Colquhoun of Applied Effects explains why this prop seems strangely familiar. "It's a Franklin personal organizer. Randy [Erikson] asked me to modify it. I laid it out in Illustrator and had a design for the left side. My chemical etcher etched the brass plate away from the lettering. It was sprayed semi-flat black, as production wanted a slightly matt finish, and then I cleaned the paint off the tops of the letters, leaving the brass showing. I sealed it all with Crystal-Clear."

The organizer shell was completely gutted and the new brass face-plate installed in the left side. On the right side, a piece of Plastruct with a grid pattern was fitted. The piece of translucent material was intended as a futuristic Etcha-Sketch, a page which could be written on and erased. For shots where a data screen or animated graphic was required, it was created in post-production.

"The data sticks were made to fit into the pen-recess on the top. I made them from some rod, some PDA styluses and some heat shrink and I also turned some of the pieces on the lathe. They had to read on camera so we made them all different colors."

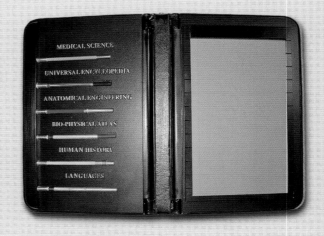

Cities, settlements, and colonies on the Border Planets are not as well-stocked as they are in the Core, and the lack of basic resources affects everything from medicine to the availability of doctors and hospitals. Simon, for example, is well-trained but still refers to his medical reference library stored in his Universal Encyclopedia. If he was working in a hospital, he would have access to his peers' knowledge and might consult with them instead.

The absence of skilled doctors outside of the Core is common and can be deadly. On Jianying, townsfolk snatch unsuspecting, skilled citizens and force them to perform their trade. On Higgins' Moon, the wealthy Magistrate possesses everything he needs, but the indentured servants forced to work at Canton Mudworks do not. If a Mudder got sick, that person would be discarded and replaced. If a Core citizen fell ill, the Alliance would take care of them in exchange for their loyalty.

Income inequality in the Border Planets not only impacts accessibility of medicine, it can also mean the difference between living and surviving. On Regina, for example, the terraforming process was flawed and miners contracted a debilitating disease called Bowden's Malady. The government agreed to provide shipments of Pescaline-D—the medicine that'd help offset the uncurable disease's effects. This agreement, however, creates a system of dependency. Settlers stuck on Regina can't leave unless they're wealthy enough to move to the Core. Thus, miners who need the medicine to work must keep working to find relief. This stands in sharp contrast to what the Alliance military has access to on their cruisers. While the towns and settlements may be suffering, their medical facilities are top notch and not accessible to everyone.

Access to medical services and equipment is even more sporadic in the rim. Due to Deadwood's proximity to the White Sun System, Rance Burgess sidled up to the Alliance to gain access to technology, like the DNA tester he forcibly used on Petaline. Miranda, on the other hand, was a high-tech city that failed due to the Alliance's hubris. They sought to pacify the population and end all forms of aggression but, by administering the PAX to the general population, they unwittingly murdered millions and created the Reavers.

In a post-Unification War environment, the Alliance's motivation shifts from battling Independents to retaining control of the known 'verse. Controlling access to vital resources, like medicine, doctors, and hospitals, is one way of keeping its citizens in line. The government also expands its reach by constructing bigger cities outside of the Core, to not only show its power but to also help distribute resources in short supply.

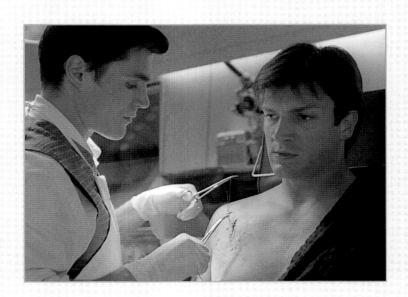

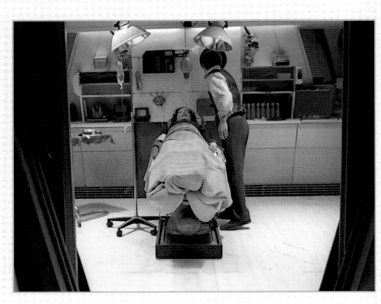

Despite medical advances, colonists and citizens alike still contract diseases and suffer from ailments, including heart disease or psychological disorders like post-traumatic stress or a psychotic break. These are treated in a variety of ways, depending upon what medical facilities and skilled personnel the patient has access to.

TERM	DEFINITION
APHASIA	Condition that affects the language center of the brain and removes the ability to speak, write, and understand written and verbal forms of language. Caused by stroke, head injury, and other forms of brain damage. May be temporary or permanent. An aphasic patient is someone who is suffering from this condition.
BOWDEN'S MALADY	Degenerative disease that afflicts bone and muscle. On Regina, it's a localized illness contracted by settlers who live in Paradiso. The town's original miners contracted the disease and passed it on to their children. New miners are all but guaranteed to suffer from the illness.
CRYO SLEEP	Induced state of rest caused by lowering the body temperature of a living patient down to extreme levels. The patient remains in stasis until revived. Cryo sleep is induced to transport people over long distances, but may also be used to postpone the effects of an illness until a cure can be found or administered.
CYANOSIS	Skin with a bluish or purple tint caused by low oxygen levels in the blood. Someone who suffers from cyanosis may be described as cyanotic.
DAMP LUNG, OR DAMPLUNG	Slang for a respiratory illness that causes fluid to accumulate in the lungs. Similar to pneumonia. Jayne Cobb's brother, Mattie, suffered from the Damp Lung.
DILATE	Become wider, more open, e.g. this medicine will dilate your pupils.
TACHY	Short for tachycardia. State where the heart is beating irregularly. To 'go tachy' is for the heart to beat out of sync.

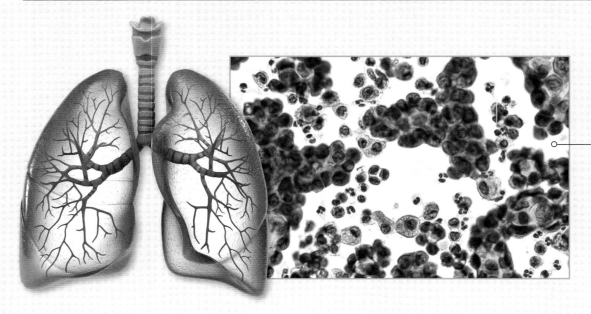

DAMP LUNG: Respiratory illness that affects the lungs.

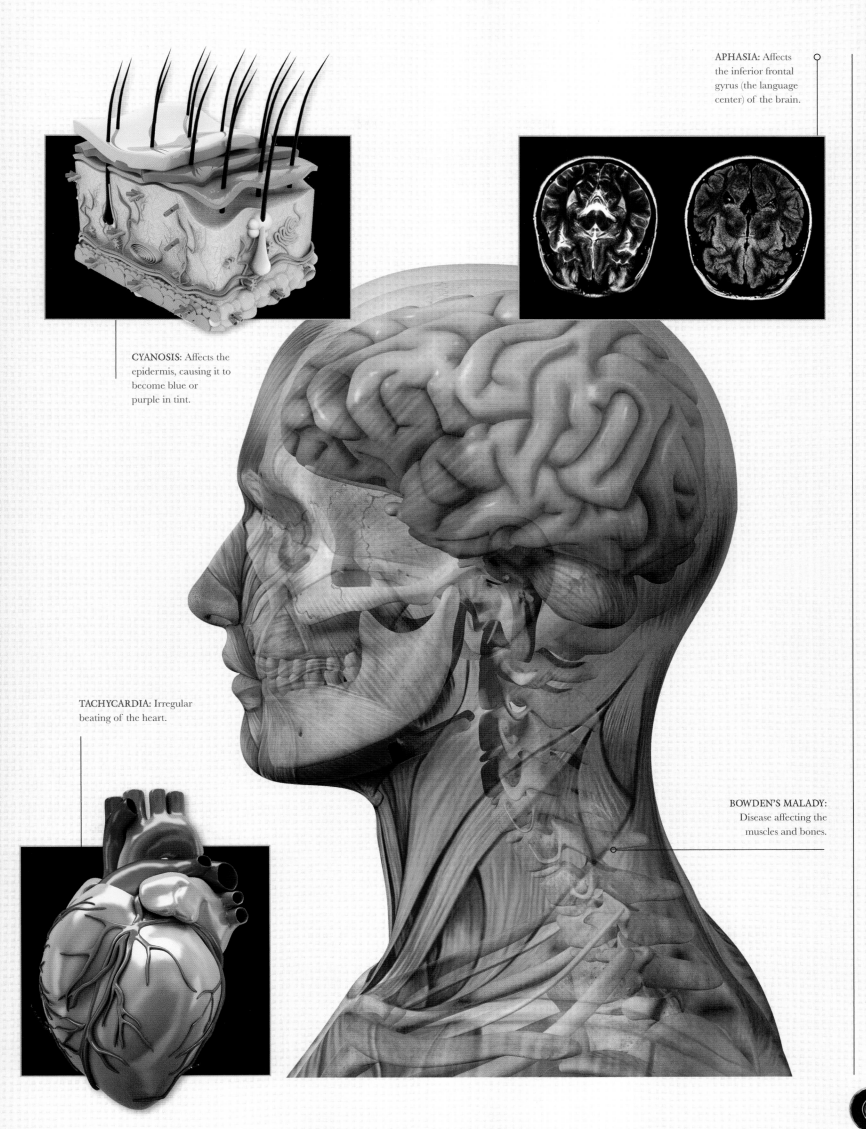

APHASIA: Affects the inferior frontal gyrus (the language center) of the brain.

CYANOSIS: Affects the epidermis, causing it to become blue or purple in tint.

TACHYCARDIA: Irregular beating of the heart.

BOWDEN'S MALADY: Disease affecting the muscles and bones.

CRYO BOX

Cryonics or Cryogenics?

Cryo is a catch-all term that could mean cryonic or cryogenic. Cryogenics is a field of physics concerned with studying the effects of low to extremely low temperatures. Cryonics, on the other hand, is a field of biology that deals with lowering the temperature of human tissue to preserve it for future use. Most often, when cryo is referred to its an abbreviation of cryonics. For example, St. Lucy's Medical Center on Ariel has a Cryo Lab dedicated to cryonics, and Simon had placed River in a cryo-cube that employed this technology.

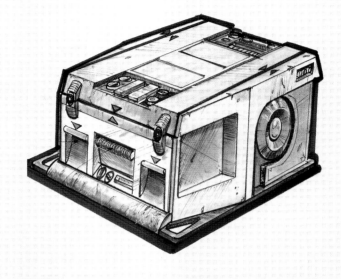

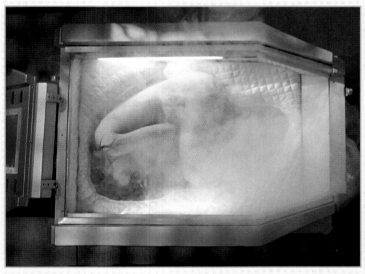

RIGHT: Design for the cryo box locks.

RIGHT: The final and finished item.

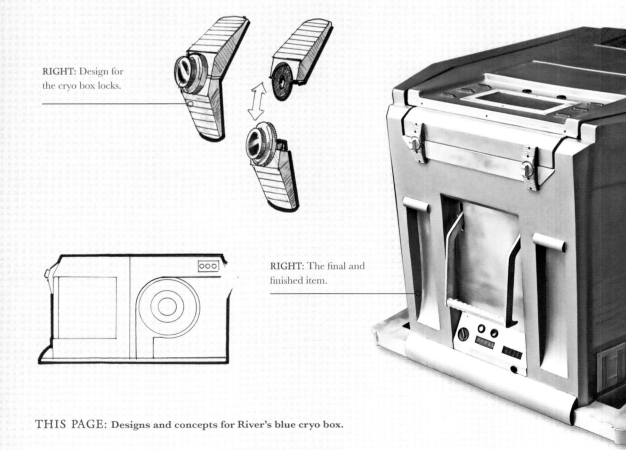

THIS PAGE: Designs and concepts for River's blue cryo box.

MEDICAL SUPPLIES AND DRUGS

Prop master Randy Eriksen tasked
Applied Effects with the job of making Simon's surgical instruments for the pilot show. Applied's Chris Calquhoun explains: "We were just told: 'medical tools', a scalpel and a bullet-grabber. A year after the first *Star Wars* movie came out I customized an X-Acto hobby knife handle, and I used to make all kinds of cool little tools and stuff that were based on the look I came up with like a zillion and a half years ago. I've incorporated the look into a couple of props since then, but never so prominently as in Simon's medical instruments. This is me 'going off' on the lathe. As well as the lathe work, there are some little milled parts too. The scalpel was originally designed with a laser cutter, but was later changed to a more traditional blade." The colored bands are sections of silicone sleeving stretched over the handles. It is a more durable surface than paint and stands up to on-set rigors far better.

The scalpel and bullet-grabber were first, then the laser probe device was ordered: "I picked a style and made it fit in with the other instruments. I turned some aluminum tube and made an end-cap and fitted an LED, some batteries, and a little switch on top. The graphic on the display is a 'geekness' flow chart—so you can tell how geeky you are in comparison to other sci-fi fans! It's too small to read on TV and I put it in just for fun."

Randy Eriksen on Simon's surgical tools: "Applied Effects made Simon's surgical tools, which were totally awesome. They were inspired by desperation. I was standing in Applied's shop talking to Chris and I noticed his X-Acto knife. I said that it was cool and we should just do them like that. We had a scalpel, a scope and a grabber. They are so good and you didn't really see them on the show much. They look much better in real life than they do on the screen. Then again, they would focus on something that we didn't pay any attention to and was awful and kind of embarrassing. Oh, you'd see that!" The medical equipment used in the 'verse ranges from lab-grown organs to 3-D neural imagers. This list is a small sample of what you can expect to find in a hospital.

TERM	DEFINITION
BLASTOMERES	Illegal wetware. Blastomeres are experimental, lab-grown organs that mature in a living human host. Tracey Smith had his organs removed to accommodate the blastomeres. Once they reached maturity, the wetware would be surgically removed and Tracey's original organs would be reattached—provided he reached the rendezvous point on Ariel in a timely fashion.
CRYO-BOX	Walled, insulated structure designed to preserve the body of a single human in a cryonic state with the intention of reviving the patient. The equipment is high-tech and requires the help of a trained specialist and medical doctor.
CARDIAC INFUSERS	Type of medical equipment used to direct fluids into the heart. Used in emergency situations.
CORTICAL ELECTRODES	Medical device attached to the temples. Designed to stimulate brain activity in the cerebral cortex. Used in life-or-death situations.
DERMAL MENDER	High-tech medical equipment designed to refasten pieces of flesh together. At the conclusion of 'War Stories', Simon uses a dermal mender on loan from the Councilor to reattach Mal's ear.
DNA TEST DEVICE	Portable, self-contained device designed to extract DNA from an expecting mother to determine the identity of the father. Rance Burgess used this device on Petaline to confirm his suspicions.
E.C.G. OR E.K.G.	Short for electrocardiogram. Common test that scans the electrical activity in the heart to identify and diagnose health problems.
EXTRACTOR	Surgical instrument designed to remove a bullet.
FINAL SCALPEL	Surgical instrument used in operations. Simon Tam has a final scalpel in his medical kit.
HYPO	Short for hypodermic.

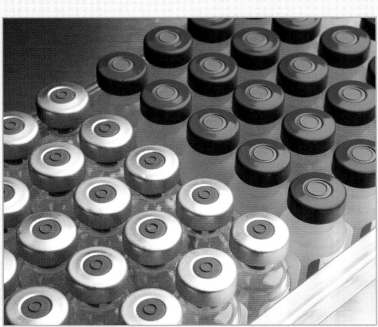

TERM	DEFINITION
HYPO GUN	Plunger designed to pierce the skin with a needle. Typically used to inject medicine or drugs into the body.
HYPO KIT	Medical equipment that includes a hypo gun, needles, and sterilization equipment.
LASER PROBE	Exploratory medical instrument used in surgery.
LASER SAW	Surgical instrument involving the use of lasers to cut bone and tissue.
NEURAL IMAGER	High-tech diagnostic equipment that allows a medical technician or doctor to create a holographic image of a patient's brain.
PULMONARY STIMULATORS	Medical equipment designed to send an electrical charge to the heart to reset it or bring the heart rate up.
RETINAL SCAN	Method to verify identification using biometrics on a subject's eye. The results are more authoritative and foolproof than any data or reports gleaned from scanning an ident card.
WEAVE	A material used to bandage and cover wounds in place of gauze.

Pharmaceutical drugs are commonly found in the Core. Due to their scarcity in the Border and rim, they are worth more on the black market. Several drugs are named throughout the *Firefly* story, but few are clearly defined.

ADENOSINE
Type of medicine administered to patients to increase blood flow to tissues or organs, to speed up the healing process. Adenosine is a type of vasodilator.

ADRENALINE
Synthetic or naturally-produced hormone administered to patients in emergency situations. The patient feels a burst of energy as their heart starts beating faster.

ALPRAZALINE PUSH
Given to patients to help regulate blood pressure. Often administered to relieve suffering from acute blood loss either from a wound or during surgery. Alprazaline push is a type of vasoconstrictor.

BYPHODINE
Causes a patient to appear medically dead to the untrained eye.

DILAVTIN
Administered to patients to prep them for surgery.

G-23 PAXILON HYDROCHLORATE OR PAX
Experimental chemical compound designed to pacify a population and weed out aggression. When added to the air processors on Miranda, 99.9% of the population lost the will to live and died. The other 0.1% became overly aggressive and began mutilating themselves and murdering researchers. They then escaped into the Black. The Pax created the Reavers.

IMMUNOBOOSTER
Drug engineered to improve performance of the immune system.

PESCALINE-D
Medicine administered to offset the effects of Bowden's Malady. While there is no cure for the degenerative disease, Pecaline D allows a patient to function normally without suffering from its effects.

ADDITIONALLY, THE FOLLOWING DRUGS HAVE EITHER BEEN MENTIONED, STOLEN, OR USED THROUGHOUT THE SERIES:
Amirymadel, Atropine, Bipamomarinol, Cepleyan, Cimitriptilayn, Fillioxalyn, Hydrozapam, Isoprovalyn, Propoxin, and Romadyl.

BEYOND STANDARDIZED MEDICINE

On the other side of cryonics and blastomeres, pushing the boundaries between science and science fiction, are the secret Alliance Academies. Most Acads aren't suspicious to the average citizen, because they're billed as places of learning. Ironically, that is true to some extent because the Alliance is using those facilities to learn—just not in the way people think. The Acads are facilities designed to experiment on human beings. Thus far, the government has successfully manufactured psychic abilities in their subjects and has devised a way to engineer sleeper agents by manipulating a subject's mind.

River Tam is an example of their efforts. After stripping her amygdala—the almond-shaped area of the brain responsible for regulating fear and aggression—the surgeons cut into her brain to artificially induce telepathic abilities. Though successful, they also stole her mental faculties and experimented on her without her consent. River, and other patients like her, are pawns being used to further the government's agenda.

In addition to psychic assassins, the Alliance has also pushed the boundaries of cybernetic technology. Lawrence Dobson's lost eye was replaced with a mechanized one. Henry Evans, who became Derrial Book, had a camera implanted in his eye that recorded data and transmitted it back to the Independent Faction's High Command during the Unification War.

The Alliance took cybernetics one step further by creating (what they believed to be) the perfect blend of man and machine: the cyborg. Known only as the Hands of Blue, these two 'men' are programmed to do the Alliance's bidding without the burden of human emotion. When they are tasked with the retrieval of River Tam, they are free to kill when needed to protect the Alliance's secrets.

The High-Frequency Neuralizer used by the Hands of Blue is a one-of-a-kind weapon built by the weapons manufacturing arm of the Blue Sun Corporation. It projects a high-pitched frequency that causes a target's blood vessels to rupture in a localized area. The Hands of Blue are immune to the effects of most sonic-based weapons, and this may be due to their engineering.

In many ways, the Hands of Blue are the exact opposite of the Operative, whose faith in the Alliance was absolute—up until he met Malcolm Reynolds. Faith, however, can be shaken. Broken. Shattered. The Hands of Blue possess no emotion and do not flinch when their victims scream. They, perhaps, are not only a warning of what's to come, but a sign of the Alliance's willingness to manipulate the healing art of medical science to further their own agenda. For all the benefits medicine in the 'verse has to offer, the cutting edge is a little too sharp.

THIS PAGE: The terrifying blankness of the Hands of Blue on their quest to locate River and Simon.

BRIMMING WITH CULTURE

FROM EARTH-THAT-WAS TO NEW EARTHS

Culture in the 'verse is complicated, and its variability shifts depending upon its location. Though the 'verse is well-populated, most people live in the White Sun System. Micro-or-fringe cultures, like the Triumph Settlement, are formed either out of a need for survival or to practice a religious belief free from the Alliance's influence—provided they had the money to travel. The economics of life in the 'verse is as variable as its peoples. Some cities prefer the digital transfer of credits; towns tend to accept cash or coin; poorer folk trade services and goods when they can.

The formation of these cultures has occurred over two-to-three centuries following humanity's exodus from Earth-That-Was to the Core. As time passed, people spread out and moved to habitable, earth-like planets and moons in the Border and rim. Some colonists were encouraged to leave the Central Planets, to ensure that the Alliance had a presence outside of the Core. Others sought freedom, adventure, or a simpler way of life. Then, when the Unification War broke out, social mores shifted as a response to the conflict that spanned dozens of worlds.

If you lived in the Core, you supported Unification. If you lived in the Border or rim, you didn't. Unfortunately, war is never that cut-and-dry, and the 'verse's many citizens have yet to grapple with the horrific losses suffered on both sides. This, in particular, has spurred a subculture of Independent veterans of the Unification War: Browncoats, who refuse to accept the Alliance won.

Cultural nuances are widespread and apparent from the clothes people wear, like the telltale brown coats, to the food they eat. Even something as simple as the myth of Earth-That-Was might seem universal at first glance, but the story of what spurred the creation of the 'verse varies from culture to culture.

Some myths are religious or philosophical. Others are embedded with a moral lesson or teaching. Though the details, formats, and performances of these stories may change, Earth-That-Was myths form the one thread that ties humanity together.

The story of Earth-That-Was was performed in a Balinese puppet show during 'Heart of Gold'. In a darkened theater, performers attach two-and-three dimensional figures to sticks. Then they guide the puppets' movements behind a lit screen to act out scenes. The show, performers, and puppets have since adapted other cultural influences into the *Firefly* performance, and the show was performed in Mandarin Chinese.

EP: HEART OF GOLD

Little by little, the tribes used the Earth up. Barren, she had little left to offer them.

Swollen of her, they left. And for the first time since the Great Burn that birthed her, she was alone.

The Earth cried, and terrible were her tears. Acid and caustic, the spawn of the tribes' rape. They flowed a century.

The fire that finally came did so as a blessing.

American English translation of the shadow puppet play

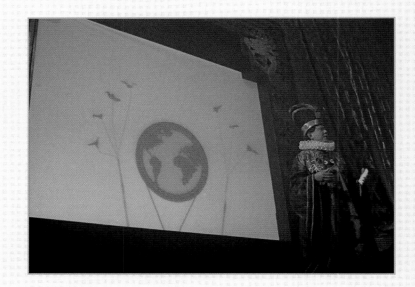

Saffron leverages the awe and wonder of looking at the stars in her hyper-sexualized version of the tale, told to seduce Wash in 'Our Mrs. Reynolds'.

One aspect that makes Firefly so believable is the presence of faith. Inara practices Buddhism, a religion that's commonly observed in the well-populated Core, and Shepherd Book is a Christian preacher. Additionally, Christian sects were hinted at in 'Safe', 'Our Mrs. Reynolds', and during funeral proceedings in 'The Message' and 'Heart of Gold'. In the Core, though it's not explicitly stated, it's likely that other religions exist due to the large number of people and cultures who live there.

EPISODE: OUR MRS. REYNOLDS

SAFFRON: Do you know the myth of Earth-That-Was?
WASH: Not so much.
SAFFRON: That when she was born, she had no sky, and she was
              open, inviting, and the stars would rush into her,
              through the skin of her, making the oceans boil with
              sensation, and when she could endure no more
              ecstasy, she puffed up her cheeks and blew out the
              sky, to womb her and keep them at bay, 'til she had
              rest some, and that we had to leave 'cause she was
              strong enough to suck them in once more.

Though the details of the story may change, a kernel of truth can be found in each version of the tale. Earth-That-Was wasn't habitable any longer, and humanity was forced to find a new home among the stars. This mass exodus was governed by an amalgamation of Chinese and American governments that formed the Anglo-Sino Alliance.

POLITICS AND GOVERNMENT

The Anglo-Sino Alliance is the governing **body that oversees the Union of Allied Planets. Their reach encompasses all celestial bodies in the 'verse, spanning the White Sun, Georgia, Red Sun, Kalidasa, and Blue Sun systems.**

Though the Alliance began with the intent to unify billions of people, it is a neo-fascist government run by Parliament, blending 20th-century American and Chinese political systems from Earth-That-Was. Its leaders are primarily located in the Central Planets on Sihnon and Londinium, the 'verse's capital planets. While the top-positioned rulers tend to remain within the Core, major and minor dignitaries can be found in the Border Planets and rim, like Magistrate Higgins who runs Higgins' Moon and the Councilor who coordinates with the planet Ezra's World Councilors.

The Alliance military works in conjunction with the rulers by policing shipping lanes and maintaining a close watch on the Border and rim. Alliance cruisers, such as the I.A.V. *Dortmunder*, possess superior firepower, dozens of ships, and a well-equipped crew and captain fully capable of maintaining the peace should a skirmish break out.

RIGHT: **The very embodiment of Alliance officialdom.**

People have strong feelings about the Alliance due to their role in the Unification War that ended a short while ago. The Unification War, which was instigated by the Alliance, was fought over the philosophy that the planetary systems would be better off under a single governing body than a series of separate political systems. People within the Core often believed that the wealth, resources, and opportunity they enjoyed would be brought to the Border Planets and rim if Unification came to pass. However, in a post-War environment income inequality is greater than ever, since the worlds outside of the Core suffered the greatest losses during the conflict and work is scarce.

Because the Alliance has a strong foothold in the Core, their interest in the Border and rim waxes and wanes according to its interests. They have made many attempts to encourage Alliance loyalists to colonize the Border and rim by gifting settlers with expensive supplies and genetically-engineered seed (Gen-Seed), but have had mixed results establishing a stronger foothold outside the Central Planets. Dignitaries, like a prefect or a Magistrate, are given more power in the Border than they would in the Core because the government is anxious to settle and expand their reach.

The Alliance's power is hindered by the fact that terraforming isn't always successful. It is also weakened by the scarcity of resources, population, and the vastness of space. These factors combined lead to a ruling body that is viewed very differently by folk outside of the Core. The Anglo-Sino Alliance does have a strong military and many different types of law enforcement, like Federal agents and lieutenants, to punish transgressors.

To prevent rebellion and stamp out dissent, the Alliance employs a variety of propaganda techniques. It errs on the side of caution and paranoia to protect its interests, using technology and biological warfare to experiment on its citizens before putting them to good use, as was the case with River Tam, Kalista, Jubal Early, and the Hands of Blue.

Though the government may seem impenetrable, the Alliance is plagued with corrupt officials and law enforcers who accept bribes and twist the rules to their own advantage. The Unification War has left many scars, and groups of underground resistance fighters are not fooled by government propaganda. Working to the Alliance's advantage, however, is its size, vast resources, and intimidating presence, which combined keeps the majority of citizens in check.

Most people do not resist the Alliance, because they have been lulled into apathy in a post-War environment. Citizens from the Central Planets view the Border as a backwater dump, and the rim as a criminal's haven. Though they never stepped foot outside of the Core, their opinions have been formulated by years of justifying Unification which, in turn, has strengthened the Alliance's grip. Those who do travel widely wonder why they leave because, despite the government's aggressive and unethical tactics, the White Sun System is brimming with possibilities for a better, Alliance-monitored, way of life.

MUSIC, FOOD AND ENTERTAINMENT

MUSIC

In the 26th century, what people eat, listen to, and play is impacted by their cultural practices. Songs from Earth-That-Was, now ancient by most people's standards, are played to honor the past and mark an important moment. 'Amazing Grace', for example, is a beautiful Christian hymn that was written by John Newton in 1779. The song is often performed at church services and funerals and sung by Lucy at Nandi's funeral in 'Heart of Gold'. A traditional Irish jig, such as 'The Sailor's Wife', might be played at an outdoor dance, like River did in 'Safe'.

For fancier occasions, Classical Chinese music, including 'High Mountains and Flowing Water', may be performed on a dulcimer, lyre, or flute, while classical European music composed by Beethoven or Haydn may be played by an orchestra.

Sometimes, however, folk songs are composed spontaneously to encourage soldiers to fight in battle or, in Jayne Cobb's case, to give people hope. The 'Hero of Canton' is a tune that tells the story of how Jayne robbed Magistrate Higgins and gave the money back to the Mudders. Though that wasn't what really happened, the downtrodden people of Canton needed something to hang onto to save them from falling into despair. Higgins, a cruel man who punishes transgressors by confining them to a small, dark prison called a 'hot box', does not want for anything, and treats the factory workers as his slaves by supplying Mudder's Milk. Simon Tam described it as: "Liquid bread. Kept them from starving, and knocked them out at night, so they wouldn't be inclined to insurrection."

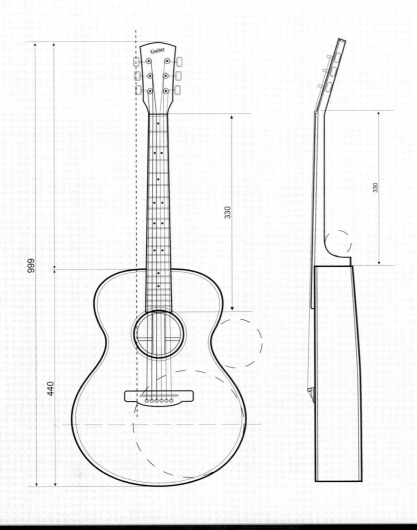

Composer Greg Edmonson: "We used classical music for the ballroom stuff Beethoven, Haydn. For filming they bought a performance, probably by a European orchestra, and then used the playback on set. Otherwise, they would have had nothing to dance to. Right about the time I got hired, they were already substantially into filming. They said, 'Here's the playback that we used. If you want to write something and replace this, feel free.' The problem was, number one, there was no time, and number two, I didn't have a symphony orchestra to do it with. So I said, 'I will find the scores to this music and go in and add instrumentation, so that it doesn't just sound like something you could just go into a Tower Classical store and pick up today.' I overlaid ethnic instruments, I would double a flute line with a shakuhachi or something, so that it sounded like classical music, except with a little bit of an ethnic twist. A shakuhachi is like a Japanese flute, but it's not polished like an orchestral flute, it's more of an organic, rough-sounding instrument."

SHAN YU

According to Shepherd Book, Shan Yu was a psychotic dictator and warrior poet from Earth-That-Was who wrote many books about war and torture. Adelai Niska also referred to his work and justified the use of torture by drawing inspiration from his poetry. Some historians speculate that Shan Yu is known by another name—Attila the Hun—a brutal warlord whose 5th-century conquests and failures were well documented by many cultures back on Earth-That-Was.

BELOW: Portrait of Attila the Hun, speculated to be Shan Yu.

ABOVE: Music is an integral part of the many cultures of the 'verse.

The Hero of Canton:

The Mudders are one of many examples of the wealth inequality rampant throughout the 'verse. Their town is sparsely decorated and their buildings are crude, while Higgins lives in a lush, well-maintained hacienda. Though they pass the time by drinking and listening to music, the Mudders are worked to the bone day and night. It's no wonder they believed Jayne was trying to save them. That glimmer of hope has kept them going ever since.

FOOD AND DRINK

Alcoholic beverages, like the Chinese spirit Ng-Ka-Pei, are common throughout the 'verse, and people drink it to relax, celebrate, and have fun. Shimmerwine was served at a dance during 'Shindig'; a bartender broke out a bottle of Canton whiskey for Jayne Cobb in 'Jaynestown'—very different from the mudder's milk he usually served; and Gabriel Tam purchased an expensive bottle of New Canaan brandy for Simon in an unaired segment for 'Safe'.

In general, however, the availability of food and alcohol tends to be better in the Core than anywhere else. The Blue Sun Corporation is an interplanetary company that manufactures, distributes, and sells everything from T-shirts to Fruity Oaty Bars. While the Blue Sun Corporation doesn't specialize in fresh fruits and vegetables—those are grown in abbeys, estates, farms or ranches—their power and influence is unmistakable. Although the Blue Sun Corporation tends to operate in secret, it works in tandem with the Alliance, and has even gone so far as to embed subliminal messages in its advertising.

Food scarcity is one of the biggest sources of discord in the Border and rim. Many farmers and ranchers had thrown their lot in with the Independent Faction during the War, and either never returned home or found out they had no home to go to.

Now, many Border folk grow what they can and hunt the rest. The Alliance does distribute protein bars from time to time, but each one is stamped with a government seal. If it showed up on the black market, a seller without the proper paperwork could be arrested for distributing goods. Same thing is true of ranchers who sell cattle. If a cow isn't registered properly, local law enforcement has a right to arrest the auctioneer and track down the owner.

The economics of eating fresh food, such as strawberries, or visiting a bioluminescent lake, often deter poorer folk from relocating to wealthier regions of the 'verse. Not only would they have to pay for passage, they'd also have to find affordable room and board while securing a job. Since many people from the Border and rim aren't as well-educated as those who grew up in the White Sun System, their chances of finding work are slim.

Flying millions of miles through space has also affected what people eat. Protein powders, which come in several flavors and can be reshaped or mixed into a drink, are commonly found because they're cheap. Soup and canned goods, such as beans, also travel well and don't spoil. If a crew sees better days and has more credits than they know what to do with, they might spend their money on apples or the ingredients to make bao.

RIGHT: A pot of
re-usable chopsticks.

GALLEY WARE

The galley is the heart of the ship. Bad things as well as good can
happen to a heart, and *Serenity*'s galley has seen the best of times and
the worst of times for our intrepid crew. Birthdays, arguments, conflict,
love, and war.

The set was designed to be a little part of home in space. It's a
warm, inviting space and the huge table brings Thanksgiving and
Christmas family gatherings to mind. You can almost see Kaylee
stenciling the flowers on the bulkheads.

Essential dressing for any galley set are the tools of the trade: pots,
pans, knives, and spoons.

ABOVE & FAR RIGHT: The cosy dining area provides a place for
the crew to gather after a hard day's work to eat, drink, and talk.

The set was dressed by the *Firefly* Art Department, using items from prop rental houses in the Los Angeles area. Many of these rental houses have 'themed' sections, such as medical or police equipment. These props would be from the restaurant section.

The chopsticks used in the mess are typical *Firefly*: a motley crew of mix-and-match items from many different cultures. Some are expensive Core Planet lacquer-ware, others the basic wooden sticks of a farmer out on the Rim.

The orange/brown, oriental serving containers appear in virtually every episode, as do the big pans and spoons hanging on the rack.

The two aluminum dredgers are standard kitchen equipment, used in *Firefly* as salt shakers. One has a bent handle, damaged when Zoe was blown up in 'Out of Gas'.

In many ways the galley is the most important set in the show. For many of the cast and crew, the happiest times on *Firefly* were in the mess hall, gathered around the table laughing.

LEFT: **A metallic cooking pot found in *Serenity*'s kitchen.**

ENTERTAINMENT

Space also has an impact on what people do for fun, because flying through the Black can be hard on the body and the mind. Some travelers read the Bible, practice their Chinese calligraphy, or work out, while others pamper themselves when they can. Most, however, play games to pass the time. These include basketball, horseshoes, and Chore Poker (a.k.a. Tall Card).

When they do land on a planet or moon, they might stroll past a kabuki performance or a street-side merchant, then head straight for the bar to drink beer, play a game of Chinese Checkers, and watch a belly dancer. Some might even request a Companion's services to help them forget who and where they are, at least for a little while.

THIS PAGE:
The crew entertain themselves in many ways, including playing cards and basketball in the cargo hold.

COMPANIONS AND THEIR HOUSES

> *"A Companion chooses her own clients;*
> **that's Guild law. But physical appearance doesn't matter so terribly. You look for compatibility of spirit... There's an energy about a person that's difficult to hide, you try to feel that..."**
> *Inara Serra*

A Companion is the 26th-century equivalent of a French courtesan or a Japanese geisha. They are government-sanctioned entertainers and, as such, enjoy a high-ranking social status. Unlike other sex workers, Companions are generally accepted and command respect.

When the Companion Houses were first formed, the Companions possessed more freedoms than they do now. Companions may choose their own clients; they can also attach a black mark to a client's name in the Companion Registry to indicate that client has been banned from procuring services. Their activities, health, and whereabouts are monitored to varying degrees, depending upon their connection to the Alliance.

During their youth, Companions in the Core are selected to live in a House—such as House Madrassa on Sihnon—to study at an Academy before achieving their credentials. Companions who hail from the Border or rim tend to be older and are often brought to a House located in the Central Planets for indoctrination. Though sex is a component of their services and considered a sacred union between two souls, all Companions are required to learn several different customs and earn high marks in academic fields that include: psychology, linguistics, music, art, theater, fencing, world cultures, biology and human anatomy.

Because a Companion is trained to exude an aura of mystery, rumors often swirl in their wake. For example, it is widely believed that a Companion cannot abandon her profession and remain in the Central Planets. This is not true, because a Companion might remain Registered yet be asked to leave her House. And, while most Companions are women,

some men also serve in that role. Registered Companions are rarely seen outside of the Core, and are treated as government representatives. Though most people aren't aware that some Companions are secret agents acting on the Alliance's behalf, they do know that where a Companion travels, secrets are sure to follow.

All Companions are required to document their status. They do this by compiling their Guild credentials, which grants them certain legal rights wherever they might travel. These include a Companion License, which is renewed on an annual basis following a mandatory physical examination at a hospital in the Core. Other paperwork includes a Companion's medical history and academic record, which can be presented upon request. A Companion's health is crucial to their ability to entertain clients and, as such, they are given an immunization package that includes a standardized selection of drugs and medicine.

Though the details and specifics of their job vary from Companion to Companion, their appointments are often highly ritualized. The Companion Greeting Ceremony, which involves the ritual pouring and preparation of tea, is performed to welcome a new client during their first meeting. Most Companions are also practicing Buddhists, but do not require their clients to share their faith.

Companions who've trained at a House, but perform services with an expired license, are treated as prostitutes, and may be bound by law. Sex workers who've never trained or obtained a license are considered whores and are treated similarly, if not worse, to an unregistered Companion.

CLOTHING AND FASHION

Clothing speaks volumes about a person's identity: Mudders wear mud-soaked coveralls; Sir Warwick Harrow wears a sash denoting his status as a lord; the Alliance wear utilitarian uniforms. Culturally speaking, the most profound statement a 26th-century citizen can make is by paying attention to the clothes they wear. At first glance, most people will assess where someone is from, just by the condition and style of their outfits. For this reason, many members of the Independent Faction continue to wear their long, brown coats—even after the War ended.

LEFT & RIGHT:
Shawna Trpcic's costume designs for the Councilor.

RIGHT:
Costume design concept for Inara.

MAL'S COSTUME

Costume designer Shawna Trpcic: "The direction from Joss was American, go back to the frontier and pioneer of the land. We researched World War One and Two pilots and Civil War and frontier characters and, out of all those different images, we came up with five or six different types of sketches and Joss picked them out. It was pretty much Civil War pants and a Civil War jacket, but made out of leather like a frontiersman. It was a mishmash of a bunch of different things and a little Han Solo thrown in—because we like him [laughs]! The Han Solo influence is in the holster and the gun belt, which isn't a copy at all, that's where the design came from—slung over the side like a cowboy."

ZOË'S COSTUME

Costume designer Shawna Trpcic: "Zoë wore the same straight pants as Mal toward the beginning of the series, and then we tightened them up and made them a little bit sexier as we got a little more freedom. But same idea—she's a warrior. She's not Xena, but we wanted to highlight her figure and her strength and her poise with really clean lines. So the leather vest fit tight and could resemble a bulletproof vest and actually acted as one in the pilot, 'Serenity'. So she was from the same background as Mal, but obviously different."

KAYLEE'S COSTUME

Costume designer Shawna Trpcic: "At first, I thought that she was going to be Asian, so I got a bunch of books on Chinese and Japanese youths and girls—one book in particular was called

Fruit. I was also inspired by the World War Two figure Rosie the Riveter and Chinese Communist posters, with Chairman Mao and everybody smiling. We blended all these ideas together.

"I loved it when Kaylee wore her little flirty dress [in 'The Message']—I loved it when I got to break out of the army green or metric yellow jumpsuit. I also found some fabric downtown in a remnant store, and we just made a bunch of T-shirts from it, because that was kind of her uniform. The frilly little dress I made out of actual antique Japanese kimono fabric, from the pattern of a 1970s flower girl dress."

JAYNE'S COSTUME

Costume designer Shawna Trpcic: "Your bounty hunter, your warrior, your guy just making it on the cusp. Anything from Robert De Niro's character in *Midnight Run* to every hardcore guy doing a thing—with the coats, again, we went to the past to define the future. It was a World War Two jacket, a World War One flight cap, modern-day army boots—pieces from a lot of different eras. I had a lot of fun with the graphics for Jayne's T-shirts.

"The costume production assistant was really good on the computer, and he and I were on the same page with our take on art. I would come to him with five or six different images and he would blend them all together on the computer and come up with a couple of different choices, then we'd show them to Joss and let him make the final decision. That was our way of making our tough guy a little more lyrical and a lot less of an echo of every other bad guy—with the goofy T-shirts. One of them did say 'soldier', but a lot of them said, 'fighting elves', all in Chinese. We had someone downstairs in the Fox library who could translate for us."

JAYNE'S HAT

Costume designer Shawna Trpcic explains the genesis of Jayne's hat: "He had a World War Two pilot's hat in 'The Train Job'—it's a green canvas cap with flaps. I went to the production coordinator in the office—I saw her knitting something for her mom for Christmas—and I said, 'Look, I need a hat for Jayne.' My thing is the ombre—ombre is a way of dyeing something where you start dark and it gets lighter and lighter. That's the idea that I wanted. Elyse, the girl who sewed it for me, brought me different yarn samples, and we put it together from there, and she knitted it from the pattern using that World War Two fighter pilot's hat. And of course, it had to have a pompom on top. Joss said it shouldn't look really stupid, like we're trying too hard, but it should look like a labor of love. So I went to my grandmother's slippers that she used to make me every Christmas—they are goofy because they're these knit slippers with this giant pompom on them, but I love them, because they're from her. That was how we were supposed to see Jayne's hat. You can tell that he loves it because it's from his mom, and he doesn't even think about the fact that here he is, this hired killer, wearing a pompom on his head."

WASH'S COSTUME

Costume designer Shawna Trpcic: "Wash's look was taken from Harry Dean Stanton's character in *Alien*. That was one thing that Joss threw out there. We created our own variation with the flight clothes, but the Hawaiian shirts, that's very Harry Dean Stanton. Wash's character is more lyrical and he's a lighthearted guy, and so we tried to use colors, oranges and greens, that weren't as intense or earthy as Zoë and Mal."

INARA'S COSTUME

Costume designer Shawna Trpcic: "Inara was taken from a lot of different cultures. I went to the past once again to find pictures of a lot of women in lingerie; I took from a lot of different periods, all the way back to Grecian times and all the way up to modern-day geishas. So we combined a bunch of them, and then I just took Morena Baccarin's body and designed on it. She was my Barbie doll, she has this incredible body. I had this little figure, and I would draw on it and just use my imagination, and then we'd collect amazing fabrics from all different sources and blend them to try to come up with her look."

BOOK'S COSTUME

Costume designer Shawna Trpcic: "We went through a few different designs trying to come up with our nondenominational and yet recognizable preacher. He was more like a pastor than, say, a Catholic priest, but we wanted people to recognize him because at one point Book says, 'I thought the outfit gave it away,' about what he does. So we ended up with a blend of a lot of different religious leaders. The grey was to echo the Alliance colors. And when I could, I showed off his body, I threw a T-shirt on him, because the guy is in incredible shape."

SIMON'S COSTUME

Costume designer Shawna Trpcic: "Simon was the dandy, if you will. His was a classic look. Certain things in men's fashion throughout thousands of years haven't changed, so his classic lines were just to show his schooling, that he wasn't sloppy, that he was neat, and that even if he became more casual, his sweaters fit well and his pants fit well and it just happens to be a very Banana Republic look," she laughs. "We toughened him up as he became more and more part of the group with the big nubby sweaters. We really wanted to separate him from the others, who are very earth-toned and very down to earth. They had cotton and he was always very put-together with wools and the stiffer fabrics and the more expensive satins and silks. At first, Joss wanted him to have a vest on, so we used Asian fabrics and Asian buttons to reflect the Asian influence, but his character went through a transformation as the show went on, especially as he started the relationship with Kaylee. We got him to be more romantic and softer, but still staying in those color tones."

RIVER'S COSTUME

Costume designer Shawna Trpcic: "The first thought was, when she came on to the ship, that [once dressed] she would be wearing Kaylee's clothes. We got hippie-looking clothes, but in jewel-colored tones and in grays and blues, to make them kind of colder, to show that she was from a different world than the *Serenity* crew, and then we started to find her own look. In 'Safe', I lightened her up with pinks, but still staying with the garnet sweater, still staying with the jewel-like tones. We made the majority of the stuff, except for the classic hippie dress, and used boots to differentiate River from the softness of a normal girl in those kinds of soft fabrics. I like to contrast the really soft and flowing fabrics with the hardcore boots, because that's who she is—she's this soft, beautiful, sensitive girl, but with this hardcore inner character."

BADGER'S COSTUME

Costume designer Shawna Trpcic notes, "Originally, Badger was supposed to be played by Joss. So we designed it for Joss." However, Mark A. Sheppard wound up playing the role. "Mark was incredibly perfect for the role and fit Joss's clothes like they were made for him, so we just altered a little bit here and there. I love pink, and when I bought my house, somebody put two sculpted pink flamingos out front as a welcome, and I adopted them as my mascots. I put my little pink flamingos touch on Badger for his second visit in 'Shindig', but the bowler hat, all that was from Joss. How he tied his cravat and those special touches—that was Mark. We had the cravat, we had the scarf, we had everything, but he added his own little style to it."

For sharp-eyed viewers, do Trpcic's flamingos turn up elsewhere in *Firefly*? "No. I was going to do a Jayne T-shirt with a pink flamingo on it as a print, but we got shut down."

RIGHT: Costume design for Mal as an Independent soldier.

THE BROWNCOATS

Costume designer Shawna Trpcic: "We actually designed the Serenity battle before we designed Mal's individual look. That was a lot of [original *Firefly* designer] Jill Ohanesson's input. We went everywhere from chain mail to these red vests with the Asian closures and Civil War pants and torn-up rags for keeping warm. We had images from around the world, from wars in Genghis Khan's time to Civil War time, and captured a little bit of everybody's armor and everybody's layers to try to convey the homespun look of the Serenity battle."

THE MUDDERS

Costume designer Shawna Trpcic says that the biggest costume challenge in all of *Firefly* were the 'Jaynestown' Mudders. "We had to cover about 350 extras in mud each day and then collect those clothes at the end. We couldn't really wash them; we were able to anti-bacterialize the inside, so they could at least put clean clothes against the body. But it was pretty gross and muddy and really dirty. The mud is what we call 'clean mud'—it's a mixture that we made ourselves from a lot of different materials—and we splattered the clothes before the people came in. I had an ager, Julia Gombert, and she aged all the clothes and came out with us to the set and finished the job while people were wearing them so it looked more natural. We tried to use as much cotton as possible, mainly because a lot of it was rented, so we wanted to use something we could shake off and throw into the washing machine to save on the dry cleaning costs; also, to make sure we didn't destroy any fabrics, because we really had to respect our renters. So the costumes were cotton and wools—wools are pretty easy to clean, although they're not as easy to throw in a washing machine—and rubber, of course. Some of the stuff was from the movie *Waterworld*, which was supposed to be wet and gooey, so that was perfect, because it was already aged and it was rubber or plastic or something that could handle it."

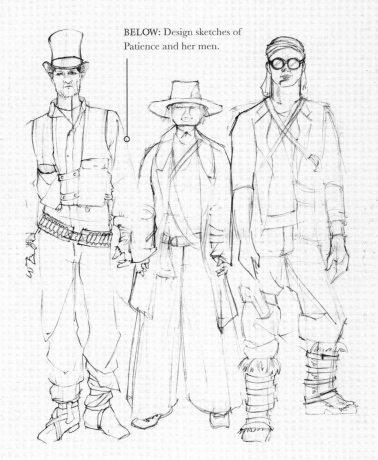

BELOW: Design sketches of Patience and her men.

BELOW: The design takes motifs from Nazi uniforms.

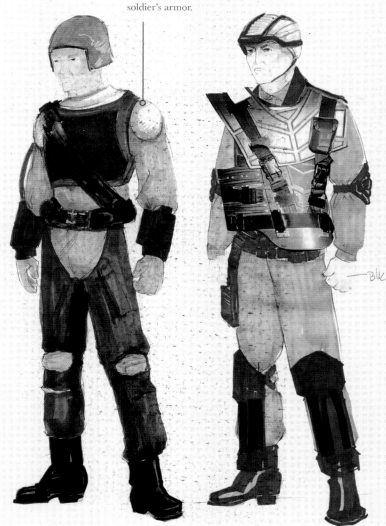

BELOW: Design for Alliance soldier's armor.

THE ALLIANCE

Costume designer Shawna Trpcic: "The classic image was Nazi Germany, and to try to avoid it just being totally German, we again went to different wars. The first sketches that we did were way too Nazi," she laughs. "You don't need to be so obvious when you're conveying a bad guy, and Joss was like, 'Okay, pull it up a little…' but we took the hat shapes and things from that World War Two time period."

INTERVIEW WITH KEITH R.A. DECANDIDO

In this interview with Monica Valentinelli, **Keith R.A. DeCandido talks about his life as a writer, his work on the *Serenity* novelization and the *Firefly* RPG, and how he connects with Whedon's creation.**

Q: TELL US HOW YOU BECAME A WRITER. CAN YOU SHARE SOME OF YOUR EARLIEST INFLUENCES?

A: It's mostly my parents' fault. They're librarians, and they fed me wonderful things to read as soon as I could read on my own: Le Guin's *Earthsea* trilogy, Heinlein's YA fiction, Tolkien's *The Hobbit*, and Wodehouse's Jeeves stories. I was doomed.

I first started writing when I was six years old. It was a book I put together on construction paper called *Reflections in My Mirror*. It was terrible (I was six!), but I still have it to keep me humble. I continued to write, and eventually it was good enough that someone paid me for it.

Over the twenty-four years that I've been writing fiction, I've written a great deal of tie-in fiction in more than thirty different licensed universes (*Firefly* obviously being among them), and I've also got several fictional milieus of my own creation that I write in. Among the latter: the 'Precinct' series of high fantasy police procedurals, including four novels (with three more planned) and a mess of short stories; the 'Super City Police Department' series about cops in a city filled with superheroes and super-villains, including one novel, three novellas, and two short stories; a cycle of urban fantasy short stories featuring Cassie Zukav, a weirdness magnet in Key West; a cycle of Sherlock Holmes pastiches set in modern New York City featuring Shirley Holmes and Jack Watson; and a new urban fantasy series debuting this year starring Bram Gold, a nice Jewish boy from the Bronx who hunts monsters.

Q: HOW DID YOU FIND YOUR WAY TO *FIREFLY*?

A: I was interested from the jump for two reasons: Joss Whedon (of whom I was a big fan via *Buffy the Vampire Slayer* and *Angel*) and Ron Glass (of whom I was a big fan going back to his days on *Barney Miller*).

Q: YOU WROTE THE FIRST NOVEL SET IN THE *FIREFLY* UNIVERSE. CAN YOU DESCRIBE YOUR PROCESS?

A: Well, it was the same process as every movie novelization I've done (*Serenity* is one of eight I've written). First, I read over the script. Then I figure out where and how I can expand it.

See, a movie only has about a novelette's amount of story. In order to novelize a film, you *have* to add to it. In the case of *Serenity*, it was pretty easy because I had more than a dozen hours of *Firefly* to work with as backstory. In particular, the script had several references to the Battle of Serenity Valley—all but one of which wound up being cut from the final film, but I didn't know that at the time—so I started the novel by dramatizing that battle via a novelization

of the opening scene of the pilot episode 'Serenity' (as well as the original opening scene that was later deleted and altered). In addition, I detailed River and Simon's backstory, combining the information we got verbally in 'Serenity' and also in flashback form in 'Safe' with the early scene of Simon rescuing her in the movie.

One other thing I try to do in movie novelizations is immersive third-person POV. The one thing prose can do that dramatic presentations can't is internal point of view. So I made sure to get deep inside the characters' heads, going so far as to alter the narrative style to suit the character's POV. So when I was in Mal, Zoë, Wash, Kaylee, or Jayne's head, it was the laconic, slang-laden style of those characters. When I was in Inara, Simon, or the Operative's head, the narration became more formal. And when I was in River's head, the narration was batshit crazy.

Q: TO FLESH OUT THE SETTING AND CHARACTERS, YOU HAD ADDED SOME DETAILS TO THE NOVEL. WERE THESE APPROVED AHEAD OF TIME? OR WERE THEY YOUR CONTRIBUTIONS TO THE 'VERSE. CAN YOU DESCRIBE THEM?

A: I sent a memo to Whedon when I started the process asking if it was okay to do certain things. Once I got a reply to that, I tailored the novel accordingly. (As an example, I was told in no uncertain terms that I could not tell Book's backstory in any way, so I didn't even have a scene from Book's perspective.)

Two things I was given free rein on were the backstories for Mr. Universe and for Fanty and Mingo. That was fun. I also dramatized some off-camera things, like the Operative's interrogation of Fanty and Mingo, Simon's meetings with the people who helped him rescue River (mentioned in 'Serenity'), and the Operative's massacre of Haven.

Q: WHAT WAS YOUR BIGGEST CHALLENGE WRITING THE *SERENITY* NOVELIZATION?

A: Getting it done in two-and-a-half weeks. I didn't get much sleep...

The hilarious part is that that wound up being unnecessary. In order to make the April 2005 release date, I had to turn the book in on the Monday before Thanksgiving 2004, which was only three weeks after I got the gig. I busted my butt—and several other body parts—getting the thing in, and e-mailed it to my editor on the due date. She sent it off to Universal for approval and into the production queue to get that started. Then the very next day, Joss Whedon shows up on the Internet to announce that the movie was pushed back to September 2005, and I screamed. (The worst part was that we couldn't verify this until the following Monday because everyone had gone home for Thanksgiving...) Still, I was able to fix some things and make some adjustments that I probably wouldn't have gotten to make if the movie had stayed an April release.

Q: WAS THERE A SCENE YOU'D WRITTEN THAT STOOD OUT TO YOU? WHAT WAS IT AND WHY?

A: I think the scene on Lilac when our heroes are robbing the place, and we get River's POV. I love writing telepaths, and writing River's impressions of the crew, not just from their actions and words but also from the thoughts of theirs she could sense, was tremendous fun to do. I'm particularly proud of these two paragraphs:

'As for Captain Reynolds, he had a lot more to him; he was the only person River knew who lived with pain as much as River herself did. Where Jayne lived in the present, Mal lived in the past. More precisely, he lived in one particular time and place: Serenity Valley on Hera, where the last battle of the War was fought.

'Mal had never left that valley. He named his ship after it so he wouldn't ever have to leave it. And woe be to anyone who tried to take him away from it.'

Q: *FIREFLY*'S LITERARY VOICE IS DISTINCTIVE. WHAT TECHNIQUES DID YOU USE TO ENSURE YOUR PROSE SOUNDED LIKE THE SHOW?

A: Making sure that the word choices matched that of the show. I binged the entire series after I read the script to get the characters' voices in my head. Every line of dialogue that wasn't from the script, every bit of narration that was in a particular character's perspective, I wanted to make sure that those words matched what we'd seen from them on screen. If I couldn't hear Adam Baldwin saying it, it didn't go in Jayne's mouth or head.

Q: IN ADDITION TO THE NOVEL, YOU ALSO WROTE AN ADVENTURE FOR THE *FIREFLY* RPG. WHAT WAS IT ABOUT?

A: Basically, it's a heist story. A rich couple, Quon and Zan, who were Browncoat sympathizers during the War, had a falling out, with Quon switching sides to the Alliance. Quon is a collector of ephmera from Earth-That-Was, with a museum of his items on Ariel. Zan hires our heroes to steal back the one possession from their marriage that she actually wants—the last Ming vase—with the crew welcome to steal and keep whatever else they can get their grubby little hands on.

The trick is that the museum's security includes answering trivia questions about Earth-That-Was—some of which may be 'wrong' due to the passage of time. (As an example, one of the exhibits in the museum is an iPod, which is labelled as a record player.)

Q: WAS IT CHALLENGING OR EASY TO VISUALIZE THE CHARACTERS YOU'D WRITTEN ABOUT INTO AN ADVENTURE?

A: Actually, it was remarkably easy both times to slide into the characters' voices. One of the hallmarks of Whedon's work is that his characters have very distinct voices and speaking patterns, and that makes a tie-in writer's work much easier. And for the RPG, I deliberately picked an adventure that would have resonance as a heist story, as a link to the War, and as something that would give a GM the chance to be silly and have fun (coming up with the trivia questions).

Q: IF YOU COULD WRITE ONE NEW STORY SET IN THE *FIREFLY* 'VERSE, WHAT WOULD THE PLOT BE?

A: A sequel to 'Jaynestown' in which Magistrate Higgins enacts a plan to get revenge on the *Serenity* crew for screwing him over in that episode.

Keith R.A. DeCandido has written in more than thirty different licensed universes, from *Aliens* to *Zorro*, as well as his own original worlds. His contributions to the 'verse include the novelization of *Serenity* in 2005, an essay for the Smart Pop collection *Finding Serenity*, and an adventure for the *Firefly* RPG game supplement *Things Don't Go Smooth*.

Find out more at DeCandido.net.

CHINESE IN *FIREFLY*

Most people of the 'verse are bilingual.

Though other languages exist—such as Cantonese and Czech—the two most prominent spoken languages are American English and Mandarin Chinese. Below are the words and phrases used in *Firefly* and *Serenity*, with English translations and a pronunciation guide.

KEYS TO UNDERSTANDING PINYIN

TONAL MARKS		
1st tone	mā (mother)	High flat tone or even inflection
2nd tone	má (sesame)	Up tone, or rising inflection from low to high
3rd tone	mǎ (horse)	Down and up tone, or descending then rising inflection
4th tone	mà (scold)	Down tone or descending inflection from high to low
5th tone	ma (final particle used in yes-no questions)	Shortened neutral tone

UNUSUAL PINYIN DECIPHERED	
q	'chee' as in 'cheap'
x	'shee' as in 'sheep'
zi	'tze' as in 'ritzy'
ci	'tse' as in 'cats'
zhi	'jr' as in 'jury'
chi	'chr' as in 'church'
shi	'shr' as in 'shred'
ri	'zhr' as in 'azure'
yu	'ü' as if saying 'ee', 'oo', and 'er' simultaneously
iu	'yo' as in 'Leo'
o	'uo' as in 'woman'

COMBOS	
LETTER	PRONUNCIATION
chi	'chr' as in 'church'
ci	'tse' as in 'cats'
iu	'yo' as in 'Leo'
ri	'zhr' as in 'azure'
shi	'shr' as in 'shred'
yu	'u' as if saying 'ee', 'oo', and 'er' simultaneously
zhi	'jr' as in 'jury'
zi	'tze' as in 'ritzy'

CONSONANTS	
LETTER	PRONUNCIATION
b	'baw'
c	'ts as in 'hats'
ch	'chir' as in 'churn'
d	unaspirated 't' as in 'stop'
f	'faw'
g	'guh' as in 'gull'
h	as in 'hay' and also acceptable as in 'hero'
j	'gee' as in 'gee whiz'
k	'kuh'
l	'luh'
m	'maw'
n	'nuh'
p	'paw'
q	'ch' as in 'cheat'
r	'ir' as 'er' in 'bigger'
s	'suh'
t	'tuh'
w	'wuh'
x	'shee' as in 'sheep'
y	as in 'yes' but pronounced with rounded lips as if before a 'u'
z	'ds' as in 'fads'
zh	'j' as in 'Joe'

VOWELS	
LETTER	PRONUNCIATION
a	'ah' as in 'father'
ai	long 'i' as in 'eye'
an	'ahn' as in 'sonogram'
ang	'ahng' as in 'angst'
ao	'ow' as in 'chow'
e	'uh' as in 'bush'
ei	'ay' as in 'way'
en	'un' as in 'ton'
eng	'ung' as in 'tongue'
er	'ar' as in 'are'
i	'ee' as in 'tea'
ia	'ya' as in 'gotcha'
ian	'yan' as in 'Cheyenne'
iang	'yahng' as in 'y' followed by 'angst'
ie	'yeh' as in 'yet'
iong	'young' as in 'you' followed by 'ng'
iu	'yo' as in 'Leo'
i after h or r	'r' as in 'grr'
i after s, c, or z	'z' in 'buzz'
i elsewhere	'ee' as in 'beet'
o	'uo' as in 'woman'
ong	'oong' as in 'too' followed by 'ng'
ou long	'o' as in 'so'
u	'oo' as in 'too'
uai	'why'
uan	'wan' as in 'want'
ueng	'wung' as in 'one' followed by 'ng'
ui	'way'
un	'one'
u after q, j, x, or y	'oo' as in 'goo' quickly followed by 'ee' as in 'see'
u elsewhere	'oo' as in 'pooh'

螢火蟲

CHINESE–ENGLISH TRANSLATIONS

PROVIDED BY JENNY LYNN
PRONUNCIATIONS AND *SERENITY* TRANSLATION PROVIDED BY TONY LEE

EPISODE 01: SERENITY

MANDARIN CHINESE	ENGLISH (PRONUNCIATION)	SPEAKER
Āi ya! huài le	Oh no! Something's wrong (eye yah hu-eye luh)	Zoë
Bì zuǐ	Shut up (bee zwei)	Mal
Duì bù qǐ	Sorry; excuse me? (dwei bu chee)	Simon
Hún dàn	Asswipe (hoo-wen dahn)	Jayne
Kuáng zhě de	Totally insane; acting like crazy people; nuts (kwong zuh duh)	Wash
Nǐ men dōu bì zuǐ	All of you shut the hell up (nee muhng doh bee zwei)	Mal
Nǐ tā mā de. Tiān xià suǒ yǒu de rén dōu gāi sǐ	Dammit, everyone under the sun ought to die (nee tah mah duh tee-an shee-ah sh-woh yoh duh rhn doh g-eye sz)	Mal
Qǐng jìn	Come in (ching jeen)	Inara
Shì	Yes [affirmative] (sz)	Kaylee, Wash
Tā mā de	Damn it (tah mah duh)	Mal
Wǒ men wán le	We're in big trouble; it's all over for us (woh muhng woo-on luh)	Zoë
Xiǎo mèi mèi	Dear little sister (shee-ow may may)	Mal, Inara
Zhù yì	Watch out; be careful (jhwu yee)	Zoë

EPISODE 02: THE TRAIN JOB

MANDARIN CHINESE	ENGLISH (PRONUNCIATION)	SPEAKER
Dǒng ma?	Understand? (dohng mah)	Jayne
Gǒu cào de	Dog-humping (goh chow duh)	Jayne
Kě wù de lǎo bào jūn	Detestable old tyrant (kuh woo duh la-ow bow juh-un)	Kaylee
Qǐng zài lái yī bēi wǔ-jiā-pí?	Can I have one more glass of Ng-Ka-Pei, please? (ching j-eye l-eye yee beh woo jiah pee)	Mal
Zhè zhēn shì gè kuài lè de jìn zhǎn	This is a happy development (jhuh j-ng sz guh ku-eye luh duh jeen juhn)	Mal
Zhēn de shì tiān cái	An absolute genius (jhuhng duh sz tee-an ch-eye)	Kaylee

EPISODE 03: BUSHWHACKED

MANDARIN CHINESE	ENGLISH (PRONUNCIATION)	SPEAKER
Fēng le	Crazy; loopy in the head (fohng luh)	Jayne
Hún dàn	Asswipe (hu-wen dahn)	Jayne
Tiān cái	Genius (tee-an ch-eye)	Kaylee
Tiān xiǎo de	In the name of all that's scared; heaven knows (tee-an shee-ow duh)	Wash
Wǒ de mā	Mother of God; my God (woh duh mah)	Jayne
Wǒ de tiān a	Dear God in heaven; oh my God (woh duh tee-an ah)	Mal
Zāo gāo	Crap; what a mess (juh-ow gow)	Wash
Zhēn dǎo méi	Just our luck; what rotten luck (jhuhng dow may)	Mal

EPISODE 04: SHINDIG

MANDARIN CHINESE	ENGLISH (PRONUNCIATION)	SPEAKER
Bǎo bèi	Darling; sweetheart (bow bay)	Atherton Wing
Cái bù shì	No way (ch-eye boo sz)	Kaylee
Gǒu shǐ	Crap; dog shit (goh sz)	Atherton Wing, Inara
Lǎo péng yǒu, nǐ kān qǐ lái hěn yǒu jīng shén	Old friend, you're looking wonderful (luh-ow puhn yoh nee kun chee luh-eye huhn yoh jing shuhn)	Inara
Pì gǔ	Butt (pee goo)	Badger
Shén me?	What? (shuhn muh)	Kaylee
Tī wǒ de pì gǔ	Kick me in the ass; kick my ass (tee woh duh pee goo)	Mal
Wā	Wow (wah)	Mal
Wěi	Hello; hey (way)	Wright
Wén guò pì	Smelled a fart (Woo-uhn goo-oh pee)	Badger
Xiè xiè	Thank you (shee-eh shee-eh)	Kaylee
Yú bèn de	Stupid (yew-ee buhn dahn)	Mal

EPISODE 05: SAFE

MANDARIN CHINESE	ENGLISH (PRONUNCIATION)	SPEAKER
Bù tài zhèng cháng de	Not very normal; not entirely sane (boo tuh-eye juh-ng chong duh)	Simon
Chú fēi wǒ sǐ le	Over my dead body (Chuh-woo fay woh sz luh)	Gabriel Tam
Chuī niú	Bullshit (Chuh-way nee-oh)	Gabriel Tam
Dà biàn huà	World-changing (dah bee-an hoo-wah)	Simon
Fèi huà	Nonsense (fay hoo-wah)	Mal
Gǒu shǐ	Crap; dog shit (goh sz)	Simon
Jiàn tā de guǐ	Like hell; nonsense; preposterous (jee-en tah duh goo-way)	Simon
Jīng cháng méi yòng de	Consistently useless (jing chong may yohng duh)	Mal
Lǎo tiān, bù	Oh God, no (luh-ow tee-an boo)	Wash
Lè sè	Garbage (luh suh)	Simon, Kaylee
Liú kǒu shuǐ de biǎo zi hé hóu zi de bèn ér zi	Drooling idiot son of a whore and a monkey (luh-yoh koh sh-way duh bee-yow tz h-uh hoh tz duh buhn ur tz)	River
Mǎ shàng	Now; right away (mah shuhng)	Mal
Mèi mèi	Little sister (may may)	Simon
Nà méi guān xī	It's all right (nah may guh-wahn sh-yee)	Gabriel Tam
Nián qīng de	Young one (nee-an ching duh)	Patron
Niú fèn	Cow dung (nee-oh fuhng)	Simon
Piān zhí de jiū chá yuán	Stubborn disciplinarian (pee-an tz duh joh chee-ah yew-an)	Simon
Shuài	Handsome (sh-why)	Kaylee
Tiān xiǎo de	God knows what (tee-an shee-ow duh)	Gabriel Tam

MANDARIN CHINESE	ENGLISH (PRONUNCIATION)	SPEAKER
Āiya	Damn; oh no (eye yah)	Wash
Bāo	Steamed, stuffed bun (bow)	Wash
Dà xiàng bào zhà shì de lā dù zi	To have the explosive diarrhea of an elephant (dah shee-ung bow zah sz duh lah doo tz)	Mal
Dāng rán	Of course (dahng ruhng)	Simon
Děng yī huí er	Hold on a second; wait a little while (duhn yee hoo-way er)	Wash
Guǎn nǐ zì jǐ de shì	Mind your own business (guh-won nee tz jee duh sz)	Mal
Hún dàn	Bastard (huh-wen dahn)	Mal
Jiàn huò	Cheap floozy; hussy (jee-an hoo-wo)	Zoë
Jīng cǎi	Brilliant; splendid (jing ch-eye)	Wash
Nǐ bù gòu gé, nǐ hùn qiú	You don't deserve her (or you're not good enough), you fink (nee boo goh guh nee hoo-wen choh)	Kaylee
Rén cí de fó zǔ	Merciful Buddha (rhn tsz duh fu-oh z-woo)	Inara
Wǒ de mā hé tā de fēng kuáng de wài shēng	Holy mother of God and all Her wacky nephews (woh duh mah huh tah duh fohng kwong duh why shuh-ng)	Wash
Zěn me le	What's going on; what's wrong? (zuhn moh luh)	Simon
Zhēng qì de gǒu shǐ duī	Steaming crap pile (jhuhng duh goh sz duh-way)	Bandit

MANDARIN CHINESE	ENGLISH (PRONUNCIATION)	SPEAKER
Gū yáng zhōng de gū yáng	Motherless goats of all motherless goats (goo yahng joh-ng duh goo yahng)	Wash
Gè zhēn de hún dàn	A real bastard (guh jhuhn duh hoo-wen dahn)	Jayne
Hú chě	Shut up [as in "get out"] (hoo ts-uh)	Zoë
Yē sū, tā mā de …	Jesus-mother-of-a-jumped-up … (yeh soo tah mah duh)	Jayne
Xióng māo niào	Panda piss (sheong mah-ow nee-ow)	Bartender
Zhè shì shén me làn dōng xī	What is this trash? (jhuh sz shuh moh lahn dohng shee)	Wash

MANDARIN CHINESE	ENGLISH (PRONUNCIATION)	SPEAKER
Dǒng ma?	Understand? (dohng mah)	Mal
Fèi wù	Junk; trash (fay woo)	Zoë, Mal
Gǒu shǐ	Crap; dog shit (goh sz)	Rival Captain
Guǐ	Ghost; hell (goo-way)	Jayne
Jiù shēng xì tǒng gù zhàng. Jiǎn chá yǎng qì gōng yìng	Life support failure. Check oxygen levels immediately (jee-oh shee-an shee tohng goo juhng jee-an tzah yahng chee gohng yeen)	*Serenity* (ship's emergency beacon)
Qù nǐ de	Go to hell; screw you (ch-yew nee duh)	Wash
Suǒ yǒu de dōu shì dāng	All that's proper (swoh yoh duh doh sz dung)	Mal

MANDARIN CHINESE	ENGLISH (PRONUNCIATION)	SPEAKER
Lǎo tiān yé	Jesus (luh-ow tee-an yeh)	Simon
Mèi mèi	Little sister (may may)	Simon
Nǐ hǎo	Hello; how are you? (nee how)	Agent McGinnis
Qīng wā cāo de liú máng	Frog-humping son of a bitch (ching wah tz-ow duh lee-oh muhng)	Mal
Tiān shā de è mó	Goddamn monsters (tee-an sah duh uh moh)	Simon
Xī niú	Cow-sucking (shee nee-oh)	Jayne
Yān guò de hún dàn	Castrated bastards (yee-an goo-oh duh hoo-wen dahn)	Simon
BONUS TRANSLATION		
Yòu tián, yòu shuǎngkuài. Hē Lán Rì Kělè!	Sweet and refreshing. Drink Blue Sun Cola! (yo tee-an yo swuhng kwhy. Huhr lun rzz kuh luh)	Blue Sun Corporation's jingle in ad

EPISODE 10: WAR STORIES

MANDARIN CHINESE	ENGLISH (PRONUNCIATION)	SPEAKER
Fàng zòng fēng kuáng de jié	Knot of self-indulgent lunacy (fahng joh-ng fohng kuh-wong duh jeh)	Mal
Hé chù shēng zá jiāo de zāng huò!	Filthy fornicators of livestock! (huh ch-woo shuhng jee-ow duh zung hoo-wo)	Book
Mèi mèi	Little sister (may may)	Simon
Niú shi	Cow dung (nee-oh sz)	Mal
Tā mā de hún dàn	Mother-humping son of a bitch (tah mah duh hoo-wen dahn)	Mal
Tài kōng suǒ yǒu de xíng qiú dōu sāi jìn wǒ de pì gǔ	All the planets in space flushed into my butt (tuh-eye kohn sh-woh yoh duh shing cho doh suh-eye jeen woh duh pee goo)	Wash
Zāo gāo!	Damn it! (juh-ow guh-ow)	Mal

EPISODE 11: TRASH

MANDARIN CHINESE	ENGLISH (PRONUNCIATION)	SPEAKER
Bèn tiān shēng de yī duī ròu	Stupid inbred stack of meat (bahn tee-an shuhng duh yee duh-way luh-oh)	Saffron
Bù huǐ hèn de pō fù	Remorseless harridan (boo hoo-way huhng duh puh-oh foo)	Simon
Fàng xīn	Don't worry (fahng shing)	Zoë
Hóu zi de pì gǔ	Monkey's ass (hoh tz duh pee gu)	Saffron
Kuài qù hěn yuǎn de dì fāng	Go far away very fast (kuh-why ch-yew huhn yew-an duh dee fahng)	Simon
Nǐ men dōu shì shǎ guā	You're all idiots (nee muhn doh sz sah goo-ah)	Inara
Qiáng bào hóu zi de	Monkey-raping (chung bow hoh tz duh)	Mal
Shén shèng de gāo wán	Holy testicles (suhn shee-an duh guh-ow wahn)	Mal
Suǒ xì	Petty; trivial (swoh shee)	Inara
Tā shì suǒ yǒu dì yù de biǎo zi de mā	She's the mother of all the whores in hell (tah sz sh-woh yew-ee duh bee-ow tz duh mah)	Kaylee
Wáng bā dàn de biǎo zi	Son of a mother's whore (wong bah dahn bee-ow tz)	Saffron
Yī qǐ shēn hū xī	Let's all take a deep breath (yee chee suhn hoo shee)	Mal
Zhàn dǒu de yī kuài ròu	Dangly piece of flesh (zuhuhn doh duh yee kuh-why luh-oh)	Zoë

MANDARIN CHINESE	ENGLISH (PRONUNCIATION)	SPEAKER
Dǒng ma?	Understand? (dohn mah)	Lieutenant Womack
Gǒu shǐ	Crap (goh sz)	Lieutenant Womack
Nǐ gào sù nà niú tā yǒu shuāng měi mù?	Why don't you tell the cow about its beautiful eyes? (nee guh-ow soo nah nee-oh tah yoh sh-wahng may moo)	Kaylee
Tiān xiǎo de	Heaven knows; in the name of all that's sacred (tee-an shia duh)	Mal
Xiōng cán shā shǒu	Ruthless killer (sheong ts-un sah soh)	Kaylee
Wǒ de mā	Mother of Jesus (woh duh mah)	Wash
BONUS TRANSLATION		
Jǐng tì xiǎo tōu. Zhùyì nǐ de cái wù. Zhè ge hángzhàn dào qiè héng xīn	Pickpockets alert. Mind your valuables. Pickpockets are at work in this station (jing ti sheow toh. Jwu yi ni duh tsai woo. Zh-uh guh huh-ung zhun dow chiyeh h-uhn shee-in)	Public announcement in Li Shen's Space Bazaar
Simmering Sam's jīn tiān tè jià wǔ cān, hóng shāo yútóu tang. Sì lóu, xī biān, shí jiǔ hào tān wèi	Simmering Sam's lunch special today, fried fish head soup. Level 4 West, Stall 19 (Simmering Sam's jin tee-an tuh jee-ah woo tz-ung, hohn suh-ow yew-ee-toh tuhng. Sz low, shee bee-an, sz joh how tahn weh)	Public announcement in Li Shen's Space Bazaar
Liù lóu chóng hài. Zàn shí guān bì. Suǒ yǒu shāng diàn gǎi zài shí èr lóu yíng yè. Hěn bào qiàn zào chéng gè wèi de bù biàn	Level 6 closed for vermin explosion. All businesses temporarily relocated to Level 12. We apologize for any inconvenience this may cause (luh-yoh low chohng huh-eye. Jhun sz gwahn bee. Swoh yoh shung dee-an g-eye z-eye sz er low ying yeh. Huhn bow chee-an jhow ch-uhn guh weh duh boo bee-an)	Public announcement in Li Shen's Space Bazaar
Dào Devendra yuè qiú qù de dì yī jiǔ qī liù hào bān jī, zuì hòu guǎng bō. Qǐng suǒ yǒu de lǚ kè lì kè dào dì èr shí liù hào xīngjì jiāotōng zhàn dēng jī	Final boarding call for shuttle flight 1976 en route to Devendra Moon. All passengers report immediately to interstellar transport station 26 (dow Devendra yu-eh choh duh dee yee joh chi luh-yoh how bun jee, jhway hoh gwong boh. Ching swoh yoh duh luh-yee kuh lee kuh dow dee er sz luh-yoh how shing jee jeeow tohng jhun duhn jee)	Public announcement in Li Shen's Space Bazaar
Pái zhào: líng bā èr yī hào, zōng sè huò chuán de zhǔrén, qǐng zhùyì. Nín de zhuó lù dēng hái liàng ze. Qǐng shù guān diào	Attention, the owner of a brown transport barge, register number 0821, please report to your vehicle, your landing lights are on (P-eye jhow: ling ba er yee how, jhohn suh whoh chwon duh jhru-rhn, ching jhoo-yee. Nin duh zwoh loo duh-ng h-eye lee-ong zuh)	Public announcement in Li Shen's Space Bazaar

MANDARIN CHINESE	ENGLISH (PRONUNCIATION)	SPEAKER
Dǒng ma?	Understand? (dohn mah)	Jayne
Gēn hóu zi bǐ diū shǐ	Engage in a feces-hurling contest with a monkey (guh-uhn hoh tz bee dee-oh sz)	Inara
Làn dàn jiàng	Weak-ass sauce (luh-ung duhn jee-ung)	Mal
Màn màn di, rén lèi yòng jìn le dà dì de zī yuán. Huāng wú le, tā wú kě gōng yìng. Lüè duó zhě, mǎn zài ér qù. Chuàng shì jì, chǎn shēng de dà dì, shǒu dù gǎn dào gū lì. Dì qiú wèi rén lèi de róu lìn ér tòng kū liú lèi, suān kǔ de lèi shuǐ, màn liú le yī shì jì. Huī miè zhī huǒ, rú tiān jiàng fú zhōng yú lái dào	Little by little, the tribes used the Earth up. Barren, she had little left to offer them. Swollen of her, they left. And for the first time since the Great Burn birthed her, she was alone. The Earth cried, and terrible were her tears. Acid and caustic, the spawn of the tribes' rape, they flowed a century. The fire that finally came did so as a blessing. (mun mun dee, rhn leh yohn jin luh dah dee duh tze yew-an. Hwahn woo luh, tah woo kuh gohn ying. Luh-woh dwoh zhuh, mun z-eye er ch-yew. Chwong sz jee, chohn shuhn duh dah dee, shoh doo guhn dow ch-yew lee. Dee choh weh rhn leh duh roh lin er tohn koo luh-yoh leh, swahn koo duh leh shwei mun luh-yoh luh yee sz jee. Hoo-wei mee-yeh tz whoh, roo tee-an jee-ang foo jhohn yew luh-eye dow)	Play's Narrator
Mèi mèi	Little sister (may may)	Nandi
Niào shǐ de dǔ guǐ	Piss-soaked pikers (nee-ow sz duh doo goo-way)	Wash
Wáng bā dàn	Dirty bastard sons of bitches (wong bah dahn)	Nandi
Zhēn měi nài xīn de fó zǔ	Extraordinarily impatient Buddha (jhuhn may nuh-eye shing duh foh juh-woo)	Nandi
Zhù fú nǐ, mèi mèi	Blessings on you, dear sister (Jhuh-woo foo nee may may)	Nandi

MANDARIN CHINESE	ENGLISH (PRONUNCIATION)	SPEAKER
Bì zuǐ, ni hěn bù tǐ tiē de nán shēng	Shut up, you inconsiderate schoolboys (bee juh-way nee huhn boo tee tee-eh duh nuh-uhn shuh-uhn)	Inara
Fèi fèi de pì yǎn	A baboon's ass-crack (fay fay duh pee yee-an)	Jayne
Xiōng měng de kuáng rén	Violent lunatic (sheong mohng duh kwong rhn)	Inara

SERENITY MOVIE

MANDARIN CHINESE	PRONUNCIATION	ENGLISH	SPEAKER
Bai tuo, an jing ee dian	bye twoh, uhng jing yee dee-an	We will enjoy your silence now.; please be quiet.	Academy Teacher
She me	shuh muh	What; I'm sorry	Academy Teacher
Dong le ma	dohng luh mah	Are we clear on that?	Mal
Bi zui, rong wo men fa cai	bee zwei, zuh-uhn woh muhn fah ch-eye	Shut up and make us wealthy	Mal
Ai ya, tian a	eye yah, tee-an ah	Merciless hell...	Wash
Ni yao si ma? Ni yao wo kai qiang?	nee yow sz mah? Nee yow woh k-eye chee-ong	You wanna bullet? You wanna bullet right in your throat?	Mal
Bian da ta men de bei jou gou le	bee-an dah tah muhn duh beh joh goh luh	A switch to those girls' backsides is just good enough…	Inara
Gou huang tong	goh hwong tohng	Enough of this nonsense	Jayne
Ren ci de fo zu, qing bao you wo men	Rhn tze duh fwo zoo, ching bow yoh woh muhn	Oh merciful Buddha protect us…	Inara
Zhe ge ji hua zhen ke pa	jhuh guh jee hoo-wa jhuhn kuh pah	There's nothing about this plan that isn't horrific	Wash
Ren ci de shang di, qing dai wo zou	rhn tze duh suhn dee, ching dye woh jhoh	Merciful God, please take me away	River
Wo xiang ming er, ming xin, bi yan shi tou	woh sheong ming er, ming shing, bee yen sz toh	I will close my ears and my heart and I will be a stone	River
Xiao xin tian weng	shee-ow shing tee-an wohng	Little albatross	Mal
Gou le	goh luh	Enough!	Mal

Please see page 256 for Jenny Lynn's and Tony Lee's biographies.

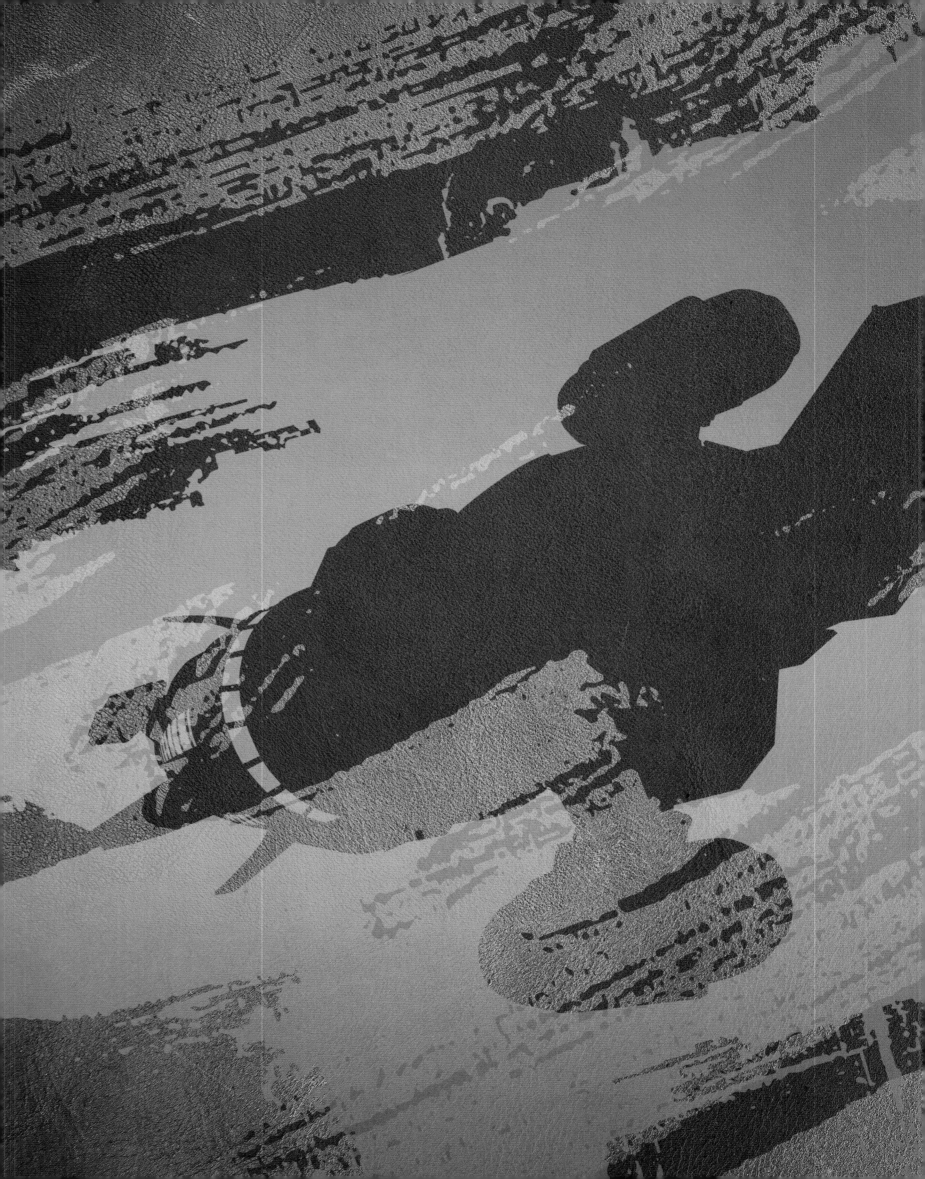

book four

SCRIPT EXCERPTS & ANALYSIS

INTRODUCTION
BY THE AUTHOR

Though Firefly is often thought of as a cult phenomenon, what's remarkable about its continued popularity is that the first run of the show aired weekly for approximately only four months. Fans have fueled a *Firefly* renaissance to keep the show, and its beloved characters, alive by supporting a film, comics, games, and novels. As time passes, however, the love of the show shifts and changes along with the franchise. For some Browncoats, the *Firefly* TV show is a warm-but-distant memory; for others, it's the reason why they wear an orange-striped hat or a pair of overalls to a local convention. Of course, any fan can tell you why they love *Firefly*—it's because of the show's great characters.

Joss Whedon is one of those rare writers who can balance multiple characters and storylines in a single show to great effect. Each character he creates, whether they're part of the main cast or not, is marked by their distinctive dialog and mannerisms. Mention Kaylee to any *Firefly* fan, for example, and they'll respond with "Shiny!"

There's no question about it: Browncoats love the *Serenity* crew, because they feel emotionally connected to the cast. And, as every good storyteller knows, there is nothing better than an audience who will cheer for your characters. When examining the *Firefly* scripts, the characters and plots emerge in a fresh light, ensuring the show is seriously considered as a work of art that inspires new generations of fans and creators alike.

BELOW: Joss Whedon's crew of *Serenity*.

ROOTED IN THE AMERICAN OLD WEST

Firefly is an American Western TV show set **500 years in the future. Though the show is often categorized as a science fiction or space Western, the science-fiction elements are used as world-building tools to highlight class distinctions and locations in the 'verse. Primarily, the show taps into the American Western genre and explores several of its tropes.**

As Whedon asserted in an interview, he was inspired by John Wayne's *Stagecoach* (1939) and, after feedback from the network, added a touch of *The Wild Bunch* (1969) to make *Firefly* more action-centric. The film *Stagecoach*, which has long been considered a landmark Western film, was adapted from a short story written by Ernest Haycox called 'Stage to Lordsburg' first published in 1937. The director, John Ford, also stated that he was thematically inspired by Guy de Maupassant's famous story 'Boule de Suif' (Ball of Fat or Dumpling), which was published in 1880 and inspired by the Franco-Prussian War (1870-1871).

Stagecoach—John Wayne's career-launching film—was so popular it was remade in 1966, featuring such luminaries as Ann-Margret and Bing Crosby, and again in 1986 as a made-for-TV film starring Kris Kristofferson, Willie Nelson, and Johnny Cash.

'STAGE TO LORDSBURG'

'Stage to Lordsburg' is a short story written by Ernest Haycox (1899-1950). Haycox, who hailed from Portland, Oregon, was a military veteran who was stationed along the U.S.–Mexican border in 1916 before joining the front lines in Europe during World War One. He is best known for penning over two dozen novels and 300 short stories about the Old West and American Revolution, which were printed in publications such as *The Saturday Evening Post*. This story is Haycox's best-known work and is considered one of the cornerstones of the Western genre.

Though *Stagecoach* is noted for its historical importance, it's not without its problems due to its racist, savage depictions of Geronimo and the Apache tribes. Instead of re-imagining a futuristic American Western frontier filled with indigenous peoples, in *Firefly* the conceit is that all of humanity has been forced to flee from an Earth that was 'all used up' to the stars. Each world and moon they discovered is bereft of alien life; for them to be habitable, the barren worlds had to be terraformed first.

By removing aliens from the science-fiction setting, Whedon sidesteps the horrors of colonizing a populated frontier. This worldbuilding technique allows Whedon to examine the pseudo-utopian goals of the Anglo-Sino Alliance as an omnipresent-yet-invisible threat to Mal and his crew and depicts the government as the primary villain in the *Firefly* story. Though *Firefly*'s antagonists take many forms that include other bandits like Patience, con artists like Saffron, and crime bosses like Adelai Niska, Whedon shows the biggest threat of all—Reavers—was chemically created by a neo-fascist government intent on removing all forms of aggression. To further underline

how toxic the idea of a technology-based utopia can be, Reavers originate from Miranda, a planet filled with sprawling, high-tech cities-turned-necropoli.

Revisiting the plot of *Stagecoach*, it's easy to spot the elements Whedon drew upon to create *Firefly*. The story is about nine characters riding together on a stagecoach to Lordsburg, New Mexico, through hostile territory. The characters include Lieutenant Blanchard, a member of the U.S. Cavalry; a former Confederate soldier named Hatfield; and Dallas, a prostitute who has been driven out of town. There is no stagecoach in *Firefly*, but the crew does fly around on a spaceship called *Serenity*. There is no American Civil War present either, but there is a Unification War lingering in the background that can be loosely compared to real historical events.

While the Union forces in the American Civil War and *Firefly*'s Alliance were both better manned and possessed superior firepower, for example, the Unification War was fought to unite all the planets and moons under one rule of law, whereas the American Civil War was fought over the right to own slaves. Additionally, the

Anglo-Sino Alliance is an amalgamation of Chinese and American governments from Earth-That-Was, whereas the Union is a coalition of Northern states in America. Though the Chinese influences are subdued and there is a lack of Chinese characters on screen—it's implied that every citizen is bilingual and fluent in Mandarin Chinese.

The Wild Bunch, on the other hand, is a departure from *Stagecoach* in many ways; its pace is quicker and more violent, the outlaws are veterans, and it's set in 1913. The so-called Old West the characters once knew is eroding, and it's being replaced by 20th-century wonders. Despite the feeling of loss and change, the outlaws perform one last job: stealing a cache of silver from a railroad office.

Elements of *The Wild Bunch* are present in both 'Heart of Gold' and 'The Train Job', but also in the world-building of the 'verse. Not only does the Alliance possess more technology—everything they have is futuristic, cutting-edge, and a symbol of the times. Despite these wonders, Whedon defaults to well-worn territory to add an element of fear: science is bad. Throughout *Firefly*, the Alliance government is depicted as neo-fascist and loyalists—Rance Burgess, Durran Haymer, Magistrate Higgins—who've benefited from sidling up to them are awful people in one way or another. While this form of resistance (good) vs. government (evil) storytelling can be reductive, the emphasis on deep characterization gives the audience a broader range of antagonists who are distinct from one another.

Combined, tropes present in both influential films are examined through Whedon's lens. As one example, *Firefly* touches upon the grizzled veteran trope present in both movies in a few ways. Mal and Zoë are Independent veterans of the Unification War; Shepherd Book is an Alliance veteran-turned-preacher; Jayne is an experienced mercenary. *The Wild Bunch*'s secondary theme—betrayal—is a key aspect of Malcolm J. Reynolds' character and is prominent in the first scene of 'Serenity' (Pilot). Betrayal and redemption are two very common themes in Westerns, because they give the audience an imperfect character to identify with, one who they wind up rooting for in the end.

While the plots of most *Firefly* episodes are action-centric, there are homages to the slower-paced *Stagecoach* in episodes like 'Bushwacked', 'Out of Gas', and 'Objects in Space'. In particular, 'Out of Gas' is a deep dive into Mal's character and foreshadows the events of *Serenity* (2005).

STRUCTURE AND TECHNIQUE

While there are many technical aspects to scriptwriting for a television show, the ebb and flow of scenes is affected by the presence (or absence) of commercial breaks. The television show format is important to consider when thinking critically about *Firefly* because, unlike a movie, each episode acts as a short story that, when combined, relays a larger narrative or point. *Firefly* TV episodes employ a five-act structure centered on a task the crew needs to accomplish. True to form, things never go smooth and the crew often finds themselves in a heap of trouble—only to squeak out of their terribly bad luck in the last and final segment by performing some thrillin' heroics.

When a television show's episodes are strung together, they form a season. Knowing how many episodes are to be made ahead of time provides writers with more tools in their storyteller's kit, which includes the ability to slowly tease and build up to a thrilling finale. This was not the case with *Firefly* because the show was cancelled three months after the first episode, 'The Train Job', aired in 2002. Cancellations or technical snafus, which are not an unusual occurrence, force writers to think quickly to bring the season to a satisfying close for their fans. The threat of cancellation, which Whedon has spoken about in an interview, was a driving force for each episode to keep *Serenity* and her crew sailing in the Black.

Fans and critics often point out that the show's strength is its characters. In fact, Whedon excels at balancing multiple characters on screen while ensuring they are each characterized in their own way. Whedon does this in both *Buffy the Vampire Slayer* (1996-2003) and in *Angel* (1999-2004) by centering the story on an individual character or lead. Everyone else in the show typically orbits the main character to help them, stand in their way, force them to grow, or cause them to fall.

On screen, this technique is used to help audience members 'see' the stories through the eyes of the main character. This allows the addition and subtraction of new characters over time, but it also gives the audience an anchor to fixate upon. In *Buffy*, each friend and advisor plays a role in the hunt led by Buffy Summers. Without Buffy, there would be no show. In *Angel*, each character lends their talents to help Angel solve his cases—but without him, Angel Investigations wouldn't exist. Whedon employs this same lead-centric technique in *Firefly*. The reason why he's able to balance screen time for nine memorable characters is because the show is centered upon Malcolm J. Reynolds. All the other characters are seen through his eyes, for better or for ill, and their mission—find a crew, find a job, keep flying—are the Captain's marching orders. He decides who stays and who goes, and acts as the glue keeping everyone together.

Without Mal, there'd be no *Firefly*.

MAL AND THE *SERENITY* COMIC 'NO POWER IN THE 'VERSE'

Chris Roberson is the co-creator of *iZombie* with artist Michael Allred, writer of several *New York Times* best-selling Cinderella miniseries set in the world of Bill Willingham's *Fables*, and the co-writer of *Hellboy and the B.P.R.D, Witchfinder, Rise of the Black Flame*, and other titles set in the world of Mike Mignola's *Hellboy*. He had this to say about how he viewed Mal's role when he wrote 'No Power in the 'Verse', which takes place after the events of the show and movie.

Mal is in a tough spot at the beginning of 'No Power in the 'Verse.' Ever since most of their contacts were killed off by the Operative in the *Serenity* movie, he and the rest of the crew have found it difficult to get jobs, or to fence stolen goods, or generally do the things they need to do in order to keep *Serenity* flying. And Mal has started to get tired of turning and running every time the Alliance comes after them. As we saw in his confrontation with Rodgers in the 'Leaves On The Wind' comic miniseries, he is "developin' a taste" for turning and meeting the Alliance head on.

He's still got his crew to look after, and wants to keep them safe, but the urge to independence that drove him to volunteer in the Unification War in the first place is itching at him. So at the outset of 'No Power in the 'Verse' Mal is beginning to tire of always running away, but by the end of the storyline the continued outrages and abuses on the part of the Alliance have pushed him to the point where he is ready to take a more active role against them.

UNRAVELING MALCOLM REYNOLDS

Similarly shaped to Whedon's other works, Firefly revolves around one complicated character: Malcolm J. Reynolds, and the decisions he makes that affect his crew. The story follows the perspective of a ship's captain and former military sergeant; what the audience sees, hears, and feels about the rest of the crew is guided by how Mal views them. But who is Mal? Is he a hero? A villain? A thief with a heart of gold or, as Inara once called him in 'Trash', a petty thief? These questions are explored in every episode, and the answers often depend on what the Captain decides to do next. To understand who Mal is, however, it's important to revisit his character during the Unification War, long before he found a ship and got a crew.

The opening scene of 'Serenity' presents Mal at a crucial turning point. Though the Battle of Serenity acts as both a flashback and teaser to set the tone for *Firefly*, it is also a defining moment of change. 'Malcolm' became 'Mal' because his faith was shattered when, despite all his best efforts, he lost both the battle and the War.

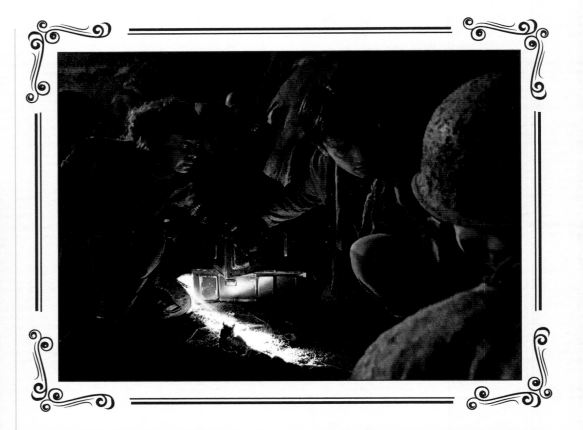

EP. 01 'SERENITY'

EXT. SERENITY VALLEY – NIGHT
Battle rages. Dead bodies, explosions — we see rapidfire images of bloody conflict. The INDEPENDENTS hold a narrow gulch that overlooks a desert valley, which the ALLIANCE troops swarm through, trying to take the position. From above, a small Alliance SKIFF flies by, strafing the ground and several men.

ANGLE: behind an outcropping: are six soldiers, all in conference, sweaty, haggard, shouting over the din. Amongst them are SGT. MALCOLM REYNOLDS, clearly in charge, ZOE, his unflappable corporal, BENDIS, a terrified young soldier, and GRAYDON, an exhausted but tough radio operator. Around them, other soldiers are laid out, firing, keeping back the onslaught of Alliance troops.

GRAYDON
Sergeant! Command says air support is holding til they can assess our status!

MAL
Our status is that we need some gorramn air support! Get back on line and —

ZOE
That skiff is shredding us, sir —

GRAYDON
They won't move without a lieutenant's authorization code, sir —

Mal breaks past them, moves to a corpse of at least two days in officer's gear. He rips a rank symbol off the corpse's arm. Hands it to Graydon, flipping it over so we can see a series of numbers and letters on the other side.

MAL
That's your code. You're lieutenant Baker, congratulations on your promotion, now get me air support!
Turns to the two other soldiers.

MAL (cont'd) (to one)
Pull back just far enough to wedge 'em in here. (to the other) Get your squad to the high ground, you pick 'em off.

ZOE
High ground's death with that skiff in the air.

MAL
That's our problem and thank you for volunteering. (to the scared guy) Bendis, you give us cover, we're going duck hunting.

A soldier falls back between them, dead.

MAL (cont'd) (to all)
Just focus. Alliance said they were gonna waltz through Serenity Valley and we've choked 'em with those words. We've done the impossible and that makes us mighty. Just a little while longer, our angels'll be soaring overhead, raining fire on those arrogant cods, so you hold. You HOLD! Go.

Two of them scamper off, Bendis moving into position, back to the rock, ready to give cover fire but still scared shitless.

Mal and Zoë move over to a small cache of arms and he picks up a rifle.

ZOE
Really think we can bring her down, sir?

MAL
Do you even need to ask?

Unseen by her, he pulls a small cross from a chain on his neck, silently kisses it, puts it back.

MAL (cont'd)
Ready?

ZOE
Always. (shouts) Bendis! BENDIS!

But he is too scared. Can't move.

ZOE (cont'd)
Rut it.

She pops up herself, firing a machine gun, strafing the area. A moment, and Mal goes, also firing, Zoë behind.
As they run to an anti-aircraft gun, three Alliance troops come into view.
They each shoot one but one gets in close to Mal and they tangle, Mal adroitly outfighting him, knocking him on his ass and moving on as Zoë follows, firing a burst into the gut without even stopping.

She reaches a little cover, throws herself down. He goes higher, for a clear view of the sky.

ANGLE: THE SKIFF streaks through the night sky, firing short, deadly bursts. A single-person fighter, it looks like nothing so much as a boomerang.

Mal shoots the soldiers by the anti-aircraft gun, then jumps in and grabs it. There is much with buttons and dials and whirring and clicking. He sights up...

MAL
Give me a lock...

ANGLE: THROUGH THE SCOPE:
More of the skiff, but with calibrations and infravision and whatnot. A moment, and Mal fires.

ANGLE: THE SKIFF is hit direct, explodes, fragments of it coming straight for camera—Mal bolts, slamming into Zoë and diving with her out of the way as a huge flaming chunk of skiff spins over them and into his position, exploding.

They hit the ground and roll, fire raining down around them.

ANGLE: behind the outcrop—
They return, Bendis still unmoving.

ZOE
Nice cover fire.

MAL
What's the status on—

But they see that Graydon is dead.

MAL (cont'd)
Zoë.
She starts pulling the radio off his corpse. Mal moves to Bendis, gets in his face.

MAL (cont'd)
Listen to me. Look at me! Listen. We're holding this valley. No matter what.

BENDIS
We're gonna die...

MAL
We're not gonna die! We can't die, Bendis, and do you know why? Because we are so very pretty. We are just too pretty for God to let us die, look at that chiseled jaw, come on...

BENDIS
I'm sorry...

Mal hears something — a growing roar. He smiles.

MAL
You won't listen to me, listen to that. That's our angels, come to blow the Alliance right to the hot place.

Bendis hears it too. It changes him, hope suffusing his expression.

MAL (cont'd)
Zoë, tell the eighty second to —

ZOE
They're not coming.

Mal stops. Zoë lowers the radio.

ZOE (cont'd)
Command says it's too hot. They're pulling out. We're to lay down arms.

Mal is uncomprehending at first.

MAL
But...what...

The noise grows louder. IN SLO MO, Mal rises, the first light of day hitting his face as he scans the valley.

ANGLE: THE VALLEY
As out of the sunrise come dozens of Alliance ships, filling the sky.

ANGLE: MAL as he sees everything lost—everything he believes, everything he fought for... In the background of the shot, we see Bendis, also looking in horror, be strafed with bullets and fall out of frame.

Mal just stares.

Excerpt by Joss Whedon

Betrayed by the Independent Faction, Mal kept fighting against an enemy he knew he couldn't possibly defeat. This key scene, however, gives us crucial insight into his character; it presents Mal both before *and* after he was irrevocably hurt at the very beginning of his narrative arc. When *Firefly* opens, it is six years after the end of the Unification War, and the former sergeant still hasn't come to terms with his loss.

Mal, like his wartime partner Zoë and his buddy Monty, has chosen to live life on his own terms outside of Alliance control. Though the Browncoats lost, every action Mal takes highlights how he refuses to accept reality despite the years that have passed. He wants nothing more than to live life outside the rule of law, because he will not acknowledge the Anglo-Sino Alliance—the interplanetary body of government who makes and enforces those laws—is now in power.

Though he may regard himself as a futuristic Robin Hood, Malcolm Reynolds is not a heroic icon. Unlike Robin Hood, Mal is not a hopeful resistance leader who performs acts of charity by stealing from the Alliance to give to the poor and downtrodden. When he does, as at the end of 'The Train Job', it's because he's reminded of his connection to humanity. Instead, the jobs Mal takes are often a means to an end, that end being to keep flying on his terms. First, Mal rejects all trappings required to live as an Alliance citizen, and chooses to make *Serenity* his mobile home. In 'Serenity', for example, we learn that the crew is performing illegal salvage.

While Mal *could* obtain legal papers, he chooses not to. He could apply for a permit to salvage ships legally, but from 'Serenity' (Pilot) we know he didn't. In 'Safe', we find out that Mal falsified his ship's papers to avoid the Alliance, and we know from 'Bushwacked' that he does have a record. Not only has he turned his back on the Alliance, Mal refuses to settle down and form emotional or physical attachments. Thus, Mal is a drifter, captaining a ship of people who have chosen to live on the fringes of society for their own differing reasons.

Each character, like Mal, is either running from their past—like Inara, Simon, and River—or they're heading to a new destination because they're motivated by money, faith, curiosity, or love. This storytelling technique forces the crew to be constantly on the move and opens up multiple possibilities for plots and schemes that aren't anchored to a moon or planet.

PERSONIFYING THE LOST CAUSE

Malcolm J. Reynolds thematically symbolizes the Lost Cause of the Confederacy, an ideology generated from the American Civil War (1861-1865) that inspired much of the conflict between the Anglo-Sino Alliance and the Independent Faction. The Lost Cause of the Confederacy is a romantic ideology that depicts Confederates as honorable, virtuous heroes who tragically lost against an unbeatable force.

Historically, the Lost Cause is problematic because the true reason why the Civil War was fought is rendered opaque: the crime of human slavery falls into the background, and the conflict is blamed on the North's oppressive attempt to dictate how Southerners should live.

In *Firefly*, a comparison can be drawn due to the Unification War's roots in real history. The Alliance wages war to unify the known 'verse under their rule and force the Independent Planets to comply. Slavery, however, is present in *Firefly*, but is depicted to the audience after the War.

In the show, chained slaves march together in the background in Badger's office, and Mal—clearly demonstrating his anti-slavery stance—confronts two slavers on Santo in 'Shindig' by stealing from them and starting a fight. In this way, Mal's character subverts the narrative and intimates that the Independent Faction was the true underdog of the Unification War, and the Alliance should never have won.

Serenity is the crew's home, after all, and provided she is space-worthy they can fly wherever they fancy.

Despite Mal's bitterness, he is a character who reluctantly needs other people. For him, home is truly where the heart is; the sense of belonging is a recurring theme in the show. This is often reinforced in punchy moments of dialogue. For example, at the beginning of 'Ariel', Mal doesn't want his crew to leave the ship—until Simon gives him a job. Deep down, Mal understands that the crew is dependent upon his decisions to get the credits they need to keep flying. In this way, the crew aren't just people he's hired or stowed on board—they're his family.

This portrayal of the crew-as-family is omnipresent in every episode when they gather to eat a meal, but more directly when a drugged Mal asks Book to stay at the end of 'Out of Gas', and when he angrily confronts Jayne for betraying Simon and River at the end of 'Ariel'. Note in this scene how Mal elevates the other crewmembers to his status, to remark how important they are. If they get hurt, Mal does, too.

EP. 09 'ARIEL'

EXT. SERENITY — DAWN As she takes off and shoots towards the atmosphere.

INT. SERENITY — CARGO BAY/ AIRLOCK — DAY Jayne comes to in the airlock. Trapped between the closed ramp and the double airlock doors. He stands, sees Mal through one of the windows.

JAYNE
The hell are you doin'?!

MAL
(via intercom) Job's done. Figured it was a good time for a chat.

He works the controls, cracks the ramp open. The airlock area fills with WIND. Jayne reacts to that...

MAL (cont'd)
Seems to me we had a solid plan. Smooth,

you might say. What I can't figure is what you were doing 'round the back exit.

JAYNE
What? I couldn't make it out the front, I had to improvise. Open the damn door!

MAL
You called the Feds.

JAYNE
(indignant) What—I got pinched!

MAL
Kind of thing that happens when you call the Feds.

JAYNE
(selling it well) I would never do that. My hand to God, may He strike me down where I stand.

MAL
You won't be standing there long. Minute we break atmo, you'll be a lot thinner, you get sucked out that hole.

A loud KLAXON BLARES, a RED ALARM LIGHT goes on—Jayne SLAMS his fists against the air-lock doors—

JAYNE
Mal! C'mon! This ain't no way for a man to die. You wanna kill me, shoot me! Just let me in!

MAL
Heard tell they used to keelhaul traitors back in the day. I don't got a keel to haul you on, so...

JAYNE
Okay! I'm sorry, all right?!

MAL
Sorry? What for, Jayne? Thought you'd never do such a thing?

JAYNE
The money was real good—I got stupid. I'm sorry.

Mal says nothing.

JAYNE (cont'd)
Be reasonable. Why you taking this so personal? It's not like I ratted you to the Feds.

MAL
But you did. You turn on any of my crew, you turn on me. And since that's a concept you can't seem to wrap your head around, means you got no place here. (then) You did it to me, Jayne. And that's a fact.

The fight goes out of Jayne. Jayne takes a long moment, looking at the ramp. He really thinks he's going to die here. Mal starts to go, when—

JAYNE
What are you gonna tell the others?

MAL
About what?

JAYNE
'Bout why I'm dead.

MAL
Hadn't thought about it.

JAYNE
Do me a favor... (beat, genuine) Make something up. Don't tell them what I did.

A long beat. Then Mal hits the controls and the ramp starts to close.

MAL
Next time you decide to stab me in the back...have the guts to do it to my face.

With that, Mal goes, leaving Jayne between the ramp and the airlock doors. Jayne doesn't bother calling after Mal; he knows he's lucky to be alive. He simply sits. Someone will come let him out...eventually.

Script Excerpt by Jose Molina

This scene from 'Ariel' is one of many examples showing how Mal is often at home and in charge on *Serenity*. This is one of the reasons why 'Shindig', which primarily takes place on the planet Persephone, is a crucial episode in helping us understand how Mal feels when he's *not* comfortable and in familiar surroundings. Not only does the episode highlight how Mal fares in 'polite' society, 'Shindig' also offers a glimpse into a different class structure formed by Alliance loyalists, like Sir Warwick Harrow, who reap the benefits of their government connections and ability to navigate a complex political landscape.

It also, however, allows us to peek inside Mal's heart by putting the spotlight on Inara.

THE HEART OF *SERENITY*

Inara Serra is often regarded as the heart of the ship but, unlike a damsel-in-distress, she has autonomy: she rents her own shuttle, chooses her clients, and can leave at any time. Often the crew flies to planets and moons at Inara's request as part of her agreement. In 'Shindig' she sets a date with Atherton Wing and ultimately decides not to settle down on Persephone. In 'War Stories' Inara has an appointment with the Councilor on Ezra. In 'Heart of Gold' the crew helps Nandi at Inara's request. Over and over again, Inara forces the crew to stick closer to civilization so they can all find work, and creates yet another source of conflict with Mal, who wants to steer clear of the Alliance ('Trash'). Inara, on the other hand, admits she's puzzled by the Captain, and states to Shepherd Book that he's something of a mystery ('Serenity').

Unlike Malcolm Reynolds, Inara's character arc hinges on her feelings for Mal and the reason why she left House Madrassa. Though the latter wasn't explored until the *Serenity* comics published by Dark Horse Comics, Inara's feelings for Mal are finally revealed when she cries after Mal sleeps with Nandi in 'Heart of Gold'. Following this, she decides to leave *Serenity* and returns to a Companion House, until she's forced to reunite with Mal during his surprise visit to confront the Operative.

Mal, whose peace is typically found on *Serenity*, is very uncomfortable in Inara's world. We see this through the way he argues with her. Unlike Mal, Inara is loyal to what the Alliance has to offer. A registered Companion, Inara supported Unification ('Serenity'), follows Guild Law, and entertains ranking members of the Alliance as her clients. Thus, Inara acts as a mirror that forces Mal to question his life's choices. Is the Alliance *all* bad? Or are just *parts* of the government unacceptable? And, if only parts of them are evil, can he ignore those bits and rejoin society?

To convince Malcolm Reynolds there may be a downside to rejecting the Alliance's manufactured society, his character must finally accept the losses he suffered both on and off the battlefield. Mal, however, never falters as the Alliance turned his home, Shadow, into a black rock. If he wanted to settle down, he'd have to find a new one on an entirely different planet and, in a way,

he already has because that's what *Serenity* means to him. Thus, when he is forced to remain behind in 'Shindig' and off his ship, Mal becomes increasingly nervous when talking to Inara to the point where he acts and speaks erratically.

Deep down, he knows he cannot take care of Inara in the way she has come to provide for herself. By rejecting the Alliance whole cloth Mal had convinced himself he's taken the right, even noble, course of action—at least most of the time. By unwittingly calling for a duel with Atherton Wing, however, Mal knows he screwed up. He doesn't know the rules and has no idea how to break or bend them to his advantage—not like Inara.

During the following exchange in 'Shindig', Mal's insecurity is shown through his confusion and awkwardness.

He's on Inara's home turf and, perhaps more importantly, in a world he has already fully rejected. To follow through on his desire to stand up for the woman he loves, Mal must embrace what he doesn't want to have anything to do with. This ideological gulf is a central point of conflict for his relationship with Inara and is on display in two scenes that take place in Mal's hotel room.

When strung together, the romantic conflict between Mal and Inara emerges more vividly, in part because the pair are rarely alone together and for this lengthy amount of time.

EP. 04 'SHINDIG'

INT. LODGING—HALL AND ROOM—NIGHT Inara slips quietly down a hallway, like a modern hotel hall, only with Chinese numbers on the doors. And, oddly, round SHALLOW HOLES INSTEAD OF DOORKNOBS (the holes don't go all the way through the doors). She stops at a closed door.

Now we get to see how a hotel key works. She is holding a small metal sphere with a small protruding round shaft. The sphere is about two thirds the size of a regular doorknob. She holds it near the hole in the door and magnets pull it in. THE SHAFT FITS INTO THE HOLE ON THE DOOR AND, THUS, THE SPHERE BECOMES A DOORKNOB! The mechanism hums and A SMALL LIGHT COMES ON. She turns it, unlocking and opening the door.

She enters quietly and we see the room, again, not too different from a modern hotel room. A sword lies on the bed.

Mal, suit coat off, shirt sleeves rolled up, stands, back to her, brandishing a second sword with ridiculous flourishes.

Inara makes a noise and Mal JUMPS. He spins to see her. His sword swings, hits the wall and the tip embeds in the plaster. The sword hangs there.

MAL
What are you doing here?

He tugs at the embedded sword, trying not to be obvious.

INARA
Atherton's a heavy sleeper, night before a big day. He's got the killing you in the morning, then a haircut later.

MAL
It's such a comfort having friends visit at a time like this.

Mal tugs the sword free. Inara looks around the room.

INARA
I knew the accommodations would be nice. Atherton doesn't skimp.

MAL
Don't s'pose I like being kept by him s'much as others do. How come you're still attached to him?

INARA
Because it's my decision. Not yours.

MAL
Thought he made it pretty clear he's got no regard for you.

INARA
You did manage to push him into saying something, yes. Made a nice justification for the punch.

MAL
He insulted you. I hit him. Seemed like the thing to do. Why'd this get so complicated?

INARA
Well, it's about to get simpler. There's a back door. I have the desk clerk on alert. He'll let us out.

MAL
I'm not gonna run off.

Inara looks at him, surprised.

MAL (cont'd)
No matter what you've got into your head, I didn't do this to prove some kinda point to you. I actually thought I was defending your honor. And I never back down from a fight.

INARA
Yes you do! You do all the time!

MAL
Yeah, okay. But I'm not backing down from this one.

INARA
He's an expert swordsman, Mal. You had trouble with that wall. How will your death help my 'honor'?

MAL
But see, I'm looking to have it be his death. 'S why I need lessons.

Mal picks the other sword off the bed and throws it to her. She catches it expertly.

MAL (cont'd)
Figure you'd know how. Educated lady like you.

INT. MAL'S LODGING—PRE-DAWN
The furniture has been pushed to the walls. In the center of the cleared room, Inara and Mal face off, holding swords.

INARA
Attack.

He attacks, swinging the sword. She slips out of the way.

INARA (cont'd)
How did I avoid that?

MAL
By being fast like a freak.

INARA
No. Because you always attack the same way, swinging from the shoulder like you're chopping wood. You have to thrust with the point sometimes, or swing from the elbow.

MAL
Swinging from the shoulder feels stronger.

She touches his arm, adjusting his swing, controlling it. It's an intimate touch.

INARA
It's also slower, Mal. You don't need strength as much as speed. We're fragile creatures. It takes less than a pound of pressure to cut skin.

MAL
You know that? They teach you that at the whore academy?

Inara backs away, breaking the contact.

INARA
You have a strange sense of nobility,

Captain. You'll lay a man out for implying I'm a whore, but you keep calling me one to my face.

MAL
I might not show respect to your job, but he didn't respect you. That's the difference. Inara, he doesn't even see you.

INARA
Well, I'm sure death will settle the issue to everyone's satisfaction.

MAL
This <yu bun duh> [stupid] duel is the result of rules of your society, not mine.

She's angry now, waving her sword as she gestures.

INARA
Mal, you always break the rules. It doesn't matter which 'society' you're in! You don't get along with ordinary criminals either! That's why you're constantly in trouble!

Mal backs away from her sword.

MAL
And you think following rules will buy you a nice life, even if the rules make you a slave.

Inara, turns away, frustrated almost to tears.

Then, Mal, avoiding her eye:

MAL (cont'd) Don't take his offer.

Inara turns and stares at him.

INARA
What?

MAL
Don't do it. Because, in the case it comes up, that means he's the fella killed me. And I don't like fellas that killed me. Not in general.

He starts practicing again, unable to look at her.

MAL (cont'd)
I said before I had no call to stop you. And that's true. But, anyways…don't.

INARA
I need to get back. He'll be up early.

And she exits, leaving him alone. He swings the sword.

MAL
Right. He's got that big day.

Script Excerpt by Jane Espenson

Gazing into Inara's character through Mal's eyes, it's challenging to understand why he treats her so badly and calls her 'whore', despite her requests to respect her boundaries and her wishes. 'Shindig' offers one explanation for his treatment of her: Inara is an upstanding member of the Alliance with an impeccable record, who represents the winner of the War the Captain refuses to accept. While it isn't explicit in the show, it's implied later that Mal was a wealthy rancher back on Shadow before he joined the Independents.

Though he had a home, he didn't have the option of returning to his old life. The Alliance had ensured his entire *planet* was no longer habitable, an incalculable loss that Inara never had to deal with. Thus, every time Mal rebukes Inara, he pushes her further away, and this often becomes a source of bickering between the two. If a registered Companion wants to be in a relationship with Mal, then she must give up that Alliance-sanctioned life—which Inara later does in the *Serenity* comics published by Dark Horse Comics.

Inara's character arc is similar to Mal's in that by joining *Serenity* and abandoning House Madrassa on Sihnon she has also willingly left the comforts of high society behind. Her reasoning for leaving her Companion House was one of the show's mysteries, mentioned by Nandi in 'Heart of Gold', and later explored in the comics.

Though Companions have more freedoms and protections than prostitutes, Mal does not hail from the Central Planets where their services are treated as viable and respected. He turns his nose up at her profession, but also admires her. This adds to Mal's internal conflict: Inara is a subtle-yet-constant reminder that perhaps not everything in the Central Planets is automatically bad or to be shunned.

For these reasons, the conflict between Mal and Inara intensifies in 'Shindig' because Inara entertains a request to remain on Persephone from the charming Atherton Wing. Mal is secretly upset because his rival has almost everything that he doesn't: money, security, good looks, superior swordsmanship, fine clothes, manners. Each detail is fuel for Mal's motivation to meet Atherton at Cadrie Pond for their duel.

Outskilled and outmatched, Mal shouldn't win this fight—just like the Independent Faction was destined to lose in the Unification War—but against all odds he does. Winning the duel, followed by Inara's decision to stay on board *Serenity*, reassures Mal he made the right decision to stick to his convictions. Mal often uses small wins to stay the course, and takes whatever he can get to justify his decisions to himself.

BELOW: Inara has many skills—including martial arts.

PRIDE AND STUBBORNESS

Mal's refusal to deal with the Alliance emerges in subtle and significant ways. The potential cost of his stubbornness is on display in 'Safe', when Shepherd Book is shot and requires emergency medical attention. Note two details in this scene. First, Inara is the character who talks sense into Mal. And second, perhaps more importantly, Simon and River are not present on *Serenity*. Visiting an Alliance cruiser doesn't put the crew at risk of being arrested; to thwart the Feds from scrutinizing him further, Mal's already falsified his ship's papers. To ask the Alliance for help, however, means that Mal is so desperate he's willing to forgo his character's greatest commodity: pride.

EP. 05 'SAFE'

EXT. SERENITY— EFFECT The ship moves through space, fast.

INT. SERENITY—INFIRMARY
Book is laid out on the examining table, apparently unconscious. Zoë stands over him, cleaning the wound. He opens his eyes, watches her for a moment before she's aware he's awake. She looks grim.

BOOK
(re: her expression) That bad?

She looks at him, a little caught.

ZOE
Battle wounds are nothing new to me, Preacher. Seen men live with a dozen holes in 'em that size.

BOOK
That right?

ZOE
It surely is. Knew a man with a hole clean through his shoulder once. He used to keep a spare hanky in there.

BOOK
Where's the Doctor? Not back yet?

ZOE
We don't make him hurry for the little stuff. He'll be along.

Book's losing it, starting to drift away again.

BOOK
He could hurry a little...

INT. SERENITY—BRIDGE Wash is piloting. Mal leans over his shoulder. They're looking at a star chart on a display.

WASH
Well, there's Greenleaf. They'd have med help there.

MAL
Too far, more'n ten hours. Man's worse off'n that.

Inara has just entered, overheard that last line.

INARA
You know where to find what you need.

MAL
Don't recall inviting you onto the bridge.

INARA
You didn't. Mal, you know where you can find a doctor. You know exactly.

MAL
Inara—he was dumb enough to get himself grabbed in broad daylight. Don't have the time to be beatin' the trees lookin' for him now. No assurance we'd find him. Or that he wouldn't need a doctor himself.

A beat as her pain and worry for Simon and River crosses her face, then, pushing on:

INARA
I'm not talking about Simon. I'm talking about medical facilities.

A beat as Mal realizes what she means, even if we don't at the moment. He turns away from her:

MAL
That's not an option. Nor is it a discussion I much want to have at the moment.

INARA
It doesn't matter what you want. He's dying.

He looks at her. Off that eye contact—

INT. SERENITY—INFIRMARY
Kaylee enters the infirmary, joining Zoë, who is watching Book—genuinely unconscious now. Kaylee makes a move to hold his hand.

KAYLEE
(re: holding hand) Can I?

ZOE
Sure. He's out, though.

KAYLEE
He did this for me once. How's he doing?

ZOE
I cleaned it out, wrapped it up. Best I could do. I don't know.

KAYLEE
But we're headed for help, right?

ZOE
Captain'll come up with a plan.

KAYLEE
That's good, right?

ZOE
Possible you're not recalling some of
his previous plans.

After a beat:

KAYLEE
We left 'em back there.

ZOE
Yeah.

KAYLEE
Don't seem right.

Script Excerpt by Drew Z Greenberg

Mal is so bent on either ignoring or
hurting the Alliance he'll even refuse
to benefit from the technological and
medical advancements civilization has to
offer—unless it's a life-or-death situation.
This stance is further complicated by his
relationship with Simon and River Tam,
the siblings he winds up rescuing and
protecting despite his better instincts. After
all, both Simon and River are products of
the Alliance in their own way. Simon is a
gifted medical doctor, trained on Osiris in
a MedAcad, and is an unquestionable asset
to the crew. Like Mal, Simon sacrificed
everything for what he believed in, and
even went so far as to willingly leave his
comfortable, wealthy life to rescue his sister.
River, on the other hand, is a gifted student-
turned-government experiment who, at first,
is a liability due to her mental instability.

Though Mal doesn't identify with River
like he does with Simon, the girl acts as
proof that the Alliance is just as bad as
he feared. And, despite his many protests,
Mal acts as their protector several times
throughout the show.

EP. 05 'SAFE'

EXT. BACKWOODS
SETTLEMENT—NIGHT The
villagers are constructing a witch-
burning set-up... vertical pole,

kindling...you know how it goes. Men
SCURRY UP TREES, like Stark
before. They go into the high branches,
drop down dry, dead kindling.

River, being held, is calm again. But
Simon is losing it. Stark is there now,
too, looking regretful.

SIMON
Don't do this. There has to be another
way...

STARK
You asked for time, Doctor. The Patron
give you that. But you don't offer him
nothin'.

*The men holding River spirit her over to the
stake. They start to tie her to it. She doesn't
struggle. They're piling kindling there. One of
the men fires up a small TORCH.*

SIMON
(to Patron)
Take me instead! Take my life for hers!

PATRON
The witch must burn. God commands it.

*The man with the torch moves to the pile of
kindling. Is about to light it.*

SIMON
NO!

Simon manages to rip free, rush over, shoves
that guy aside.

SIMON (cont'd)
Get away from her!

*He gets hit. Hits back. More of the men come
at him. He stands between them and River.
Sees that he's woefully outnumbered. A few
show up with old, rusty rifles pointed at him.*

SIMON (cont'd)
She doesn't understand! Can't you see
what you're doing? Please...

*The mob just stares back, unmoved. Simon
sees the odds. Nothing to do now. He turns,
climbs up onto the pile of kindling—*

STARK
That's not gonna stop us, Doctor.

*He doesn't even look back to Stark. Looks
at River.*

RIVER
Post holer. For digging holes. For posts.

*She smiles at him. Doesn't seem frightened.
He smiles back, tries not to explode with the
emotion. He looks at her bonds, at the mob
converging. At the man with the torch. So he
just wraps his arms around her. She rests her
head on his chest. Then, all defiance, he turns
to the mob.*

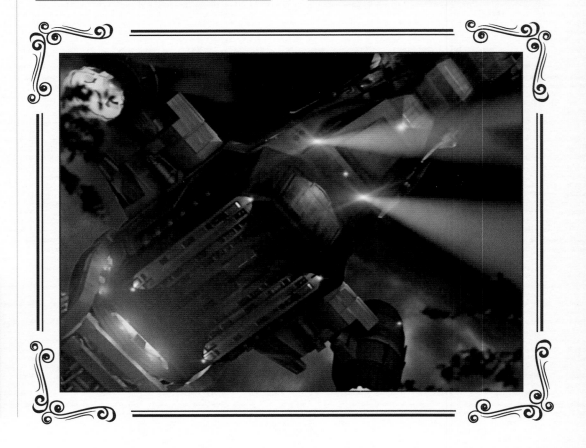

SIMON
Light it.

The Patron nods to the man with the torch. He brings it up. Touches it to the pile of kindling. It starts to SMOKE and IGNITE. Simon holds on tight.

RIVER
(clear and still) Time to go.

Then the wind picks up and it gets darker, as SERENITY RISES UP huge and gray. THUNK. The BOMB BAY DOORS open on the belly of Serenity and there's Jayne, hanging out of them, big ass rifle with a flashlight strapped to it aimed down on those assembled. He could pick off any of them at any time.

THE VILLAGERS back away, stunned.

And into the clearing strides Mal, hero shot, big ass rifle in his hands, Zoë close behind. He speaks up, for everyone's benefit.

MAL
Well, look at this. Appears we got here just in the nick of time. What does that make us?

ZOE
Big damn heroes, sir.

MAL
Ain't we just. Sorry to interrupt, people, but you all got something of ours, and we'll be needing it back.

PATRON
This is a holy cleansing. You cannot think to thwart God's will.

MAL
Do you see the man hanging from the spaceship with the really big gun? Now I'm not saying you weren't easy to find, but it was kinda out of our way and he didn't wanna come in the first place. Man's looking to kill some folk, so it's really his will y'all should worry 'bout thwarting.

He moves past the Patron, addresses Simon.

MAL (cont'd)
Gotta say, Doctor, your talent for alienating folks is near miraculous.

SIMON
Yes, I'm very proud.

Mal turns to the Patron.

MAL
(to Patron) Cut her down.

PATRON
The girl is a witch!

MAL
Yeah. But she's our witch. (cocks his gun) So cut her the hell down.

Off Mal's won't-take-no-for-an-answer look...

INT. SERENITY—INFIRMARY/ COMMON AREA Mal comes into the common area, glances into the infirmary, notes that it's empty. He turns and there's Simon.

SIMON
I've moved him to his room.

MAL
How's he fairing?

SIMON
He's going to be fine. They took good care of him.

MAL
Good to know.

An awkward beat between them. Then:

SIMON
Finally a decent wound on this ship and I miss out. I'm sorry.

MAL
Well, you were busy trying to get yourself lit on fire. It happens.

Mal starts to go.

SIMON
Captain... (Mal turns back) ...why did you come back for us?

MAL
You're on my crew.

SIMON
You don't even like me. Why did you come back?

MAL
You're on my crew. Why we still talking about this? (his back to him, as he goes) Chow's in ten. No need to dress.

As we hold on Simon:

INT. SERENITY/DINING ROOM— NIGHT The crew gathered for supper. Everyone's there except for Book. Simon appears, ushers in River. She goes across the table, takes a seat in between Jayne and Wash.

Kaylee appears carrying a bread basket, sets it on the table. She glances at Simon. He smiles at her. She smiles back. He holds a chair for her. She sits.

There's lots of chatting and laughing and arguing.

WE FOLLOW the serving dish as it's passed around. Jayne takes a big hunk of bread, puts it on his plate, passes the dish. He looks back—the bread is gone. River's got it, is eating it.

Simon takes in the communal experience happening around him. And as we pull back on this milieu—

FADE OUT

Script Excerpt by Drew Z Greenberg

And then in 'Out of Gas', where it's clear Mal directed Wash to fly under the radar:

EP. 08 'OUT OF GAS'

INT. SERENITY—BRIDGE Wash is at the helm. He's torn up with worry and anger. He's seething a bit. Mal enters. Wash doesn't even turn.

MAL
You get that beacon sent?

WASH
(much with the resentment)
Yeah, it's sent.

MAL
Good.

WASH
(under his breath)
Pointless.

MAL
What was that?

WASH
Nothing, sir. It's a brilliant plan, I'm sure we'll all be saved.

MAL
Getting a little weary of this attitude, Wash.

WASH
Are you? Well I'm very sorry about that, sir. I guess the news that we're all gonna be purple and bloated and fetal in a few hours has made me a little snippy.

MAL
It's possible someone might pick up the signal.

WASH
(pissed)
No, Mal. It's not possible. Nobody's gonna pick up the damn signal. You wanted us 'flying under the radar', remember? Well, that's where we are: out of range of anyone or anything.

MAL
Then make it go further.

WASH
What?

MAL
Make the signal go further.

WASH
Can't make it go further.

MAL
Not if all you're gonna do is sit here and whine about it, no.

WASH
What do you expect me to do, Mal?

MAL
(building)
Whatever you have to. And if you can't do it from here, then you put on a suit and get out on the side of the boat and...

WASH
(voice rising)
And what? Wave my arms around?

MAL
Wave your arms around, jump up and down. Divert the nav sats to the transmitter. Whatever.

WASH
Divert the...? Right. Because teenage pranks are fun when you're about to die!

MAL
Give the beacon a boost, wouldn't it?

WASH
Yes, Mal. It'd boost the signal, but even if some passerby did happen to receive, all it'd do is muck up their navigation!

MAL
Could be that's true.

TOP: Mal's decision to go under the radar has serious repercussions for his crew—something that Wash is not shy of pointing out to him.

WASH
Damn right it's true! They'd be forced to stop and dig out our signal before they could go anyplace!

A beat as Wash lets what he just said sink in. He snaps:

WASH (cont'd)
Well, maybe I should do that, then!

MAL
(snapping back) Maybe you should!

WASH
Okay!

MAL
Good!

WASH
Fine!

JAYNE
HEY!

Jayne has appeared, forces himself between the two of them.

JAYNE (cont'd)
What the <guay> [hell] do you two think you're doing?! Fightin' at a time like this.

A moral lecture from Jayne. They both ease off. Cool down.

JAYNE (cont'd)
(as he turns and goes)
You'll use up all the air!

WAAA! WAAA! WAAA! A KLAXON SOUNDS

Script Excerpt by Tim Minear

And again at the end of 'Ariel', during the Captain's confrontation with Jayne Cobb who tried to get a reward by turning Simon and River into the Feds. Until, finally, Mal and the crew are forced to either accept or reject River for the thinking, feeling, recovering person she is as opposed to a fragile 'object' at the end of 'Objects in Space'.

EP. 14 'OBJECTS IN SPACE'

EXT. TOP OF SERENITY—CONTINUING Early comes out the hatch, helmet on. He looks up to see his ship following perfectly, smiles.

EARLY
You made the right move, darlin'. Best for you to go with old Early.

MAL
You think so?

Early turns awkwardly (magnetic boots) to see Mal, suited up and cabled to the ship, right behind him.

MAL (cont'd)
Some of us feel differently.

Mal double palms him in the chest, an inelegant move, but the force of it sends Early flying off the ship, gone, just like that, long gone. Mal watches him go a moment, then looks up. After a long beat, River floats down to him. He steadies her as she lands. Looks at her affectionately.

RIVER
Permission to come aboard?

MAL
You know, you ain't quite right.

RIVER
It's the popular theory.

MAL
Get on in there. Give your brother a thrashing for messing up your plan.

RIVER
(going down)
He takes so much looking after...

Script Excerpt by Joss Whedon

While Inara acts as a mirror to highlight what Mal willingly abandoned, and Simon and River Tam test the limits of his convictions, Shepherd Book is a near-constant reminder of the faith Mal abandoned on the battlefield. Feelings of betrayal run so deep in the Captain's veins he turned his back on prayer as well as believing in other people. The absence of faith at the start of the *Firefly* story further highlights the Captain's sudden transformation from an idealistic, rebellious Independent sergeant to a veteran who cannot accept the fact his side lost the War.

EP. 01 'SERENITY'

INT. DINING ROOM—LATER We see a sparse but none-the-less inviting spread—Book and Kaylee have made a salad of tomatoes, and grilled up some root vegetables along with the pasta and protein/starch mush that is the usual diet of space travelers. To us, not much. To this crowd, a banquet.

People are gathering, sitting, helping themselves to things—everybody's moving and talking over each other and everyone's there save Wash and Inara.

ZOE
Oh, this is incredible.

BOOK
It's not much—I had a garden at the Abbey, thought I should bring what I could.

SIMON
It's very kind of you to share with all of us.

ZOE
I'm gonna make a plate for Wash...

BOOK
(to Simon)
Well, it won't last, and they're never the same when they're frozen.

The important thing is the spices. A man can live on packaged food from here til Judgement Day if he's got enough Marjoram.

DOBSON
(over this, to Jayne)
Can you pass me the tomatoes?

He does, after taking several slices. People settle.

BOOK
Captain, would you mind if I say grace?

MAL
Only if you say it out loud.

A beat—Mal has broken the mood. He starts eating, others follow. Book lowers his head a moment, as do Kaylee, Dobson, and Jayne, then they eat as well.

Script Excerpt by Joss Whedon

Though Mal's ties to both his crew and the former Independents are an important part of his character, he is also a captain willing to go down with his ship. As 'Out of Gas' explores, however, the Captain is not the lone wolf he pretends to be. Through several flashbacks, we see through Mal's eyes how he met Inara, Kaylee, Jayne, and Wash, and formed the *Serenity* crew.

Then, following his ordeal, Mal falters in a crucial, touching moment during an exchange with Shepherd Book.

EP. 08 'OUT OF GAS'

INT. SERENITY—BRIDGE We find Mal. He's dragging himself to the bridge. He reaches for the button to call back the shuttles. But before he can touch it...he passes out.

BLACKNESS.

UP FROM BLACKNESS.

VOICES. Familiar voices. Growing more present as Mal wakes in—

INT. SERENITY—INFIRMARY Mal blinks as he sees—

Simon, Book, Inara, Jayne... then River, then Wash, and finally even Zoë, who's sitting up nearby. No one (save maybe Zoë) is directly facing him. Various backs to him. They're in conversation, though since we're in Mal's POV we can't quite make out what they're saying. Zoë's the first to notice that Mal's come into consciousness.

ZOE
Welcome back, sir.

The others follow her look, see he's waking up.

MAL
(disoriented) I go someplace?

BOOK
Very nearly.

INARA
We thought we'd lost you.

MAL
(disconnected) Been right here.

Mal notes Wash hooked up to an IV—he's giving Mal a transfusion. Mal, in his out-of-it-ness doesn't quite understand that.

MAL (cont'd)
Wash, you okay?

WASH
(amused) Yeah, Mal. I'm fine.

MAL
Got a thing in ya.

WASH
Yeah.

SIMON
(to Mal) Try not to speak. You're heavily medicated and you've lost a lot of blood.

MAL
Oh. (then, realizing)
Thought I ordered ya'll off the ship?

The others exchange looks. Jayne glares at Inara.

JAYNE
(under his breath, accusatory)
Told ya. (points to Wash)
It was them! They come back first! Their shuttle was already here when we docked.

MAL
(to Wash, trying to remember)
I call you back?

WASH
No, Mal. You didn't.

ZOE
I take full responsibility, Captain.

SIMON
That decision saved your life.

ZOE
It'll never happen again, sir.

MAL
(to Zoë)
Good. And thank you. I'm grateful.

JAYNE
(huh?) You are?

Zoë smiles, nods.

ZOE
My pleasure, sir.

They hold the look between them. The original two. A special connection. Jayne observes that exchange.

JAYNE
Hey! That ain't... We'da been here first! But there's something wrong with 'Nara's shuttle! She done somethin' to it, Mal. Smells funny.

INARA
(heard this all day)
I've told you—that's incense.

JAYNE
Whatever.

Kaylee enters. Sees Mal's awake.

KAYLEE
(brightly) Captain! You fixed the ship! (then, a serious professional assessment) Good work.

MAL
Thanks.

SIMON
All right. I have to insist. The Captain needs to rest.

MAL
(nodding off)
Yeah. I think maybe Doc's not wrong about that. Just for a few...
(forces himself not to drift)
You're all gonna be here when I wake up?

BOOK
We'll be here.

Mal allows himself to close his eyes.

MAL
(eyes closed, smiles)
Good. That's good...

As we PUSH IN closer to his face, which, if I can say, exhibits a kind of serenity. We start to HEAR what HE HEARS...VOICES IN HIS HEAD:

SALESMAN (V.O.)
Yep. A real beauty, ain't she? Yessir. A right smart purchase, this vessel.

EXT. USED SPACESHIP LOT—DAY

SALESMAN
Tell you what, you buy this ship, treat her proper, she'll be with ya for the rest of your life.

The Used Ship SALESMAN giving Mal the hard sell.

Now WE SEE that they're standing in front of a totally different ship. Not Serenity at all.

SALESMAN (cont'd)
Son? Hey, son?

The Salesman notices that Mal doesn't seem to be paying a bit of attention.

SALESMAN (cont'd)
You hear a word I been sayin'?

He hasn't, really. Because he's looking across the lot at something else...

MAL'S POV
Across the lot sits Serenity, dirty, a bit broken down...and silently speaking to Mal. Off that—

BLACK OUT.

Script Excerpt by Tim Minear

This scene is important because Book, the preacher Mal once rejected, comforts and consoles him. Though this might be viewed as a turning point for Mal's character, he continues to protect his crew—until River Tam becomes the acting Captain to save them all from Jubal Early in 'Objects in Space'.

This reprieve is temporary, however, for Mal kicks Simon and River Tam off his boat in Beaumonde before meeting with Fanty and Rumple Mingo, intimating that the Captain's relationship with Simon continues to fray.

NEXT PAGE: **Wash and Mal make up.**

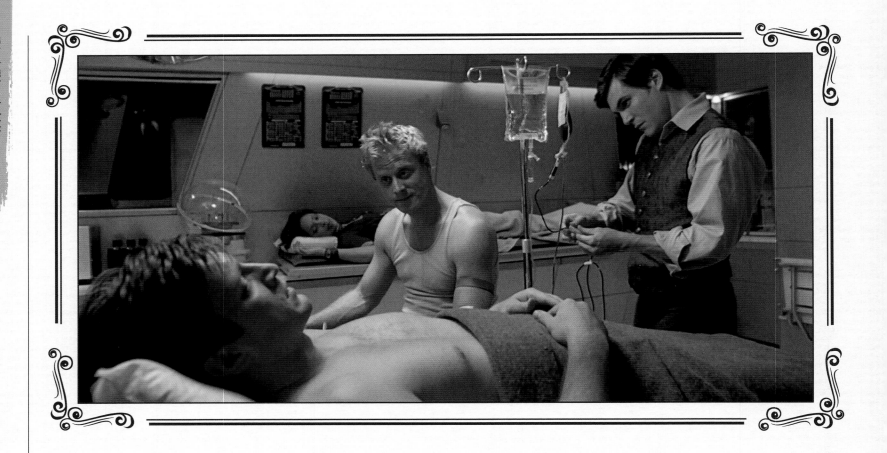

SERGEANT BEFORE CAPTAIN

Though the Tams' departure from Serenity catalyses the rest of the plot, Mal's order is not unbelievable. He is often forced to make hard decisions that either affect his crew, the jobs they take, or *Serenity* herself. This narrows the focus of Mal's responsibilities even further, to ensure the show retains a certain look and feel—and provides the audience with some comfortable predictability. Mal is Mal because of the choices he makes, and his character shines through these actions. Arguably, though Mal does experience some dynamic growth as he's forced to face his personal demons, he is an iconic character because he never completely regains his faith and does not settle down. A career soldier, Mal is a man who needs to find the next battle, and though he may open his heart to a bigger crew, he remains the same grizzled veteran of the Unification War from beginning to end.

The military side of Mal's character is reinforced by Zoë Alleyne Washburne, who served with him in the Unification War. Her character arc is tied to her relationship with her husband, Wash, and the desire to have a child ('Trash'). In 'War Stories', when Zoë takes command, it is her military training and expertise that highlights how she, like the Captain, does what needs to be done. This speaks to her capability in battle as a seasoned soldier who could hold her own in a fight, but it also shows how and why she's loyal to Mal. The war veterans share an unbreakable bond after fighting alongside one another against impossible odds.

FANCY SCHMANCY CHARACTERS

To tell a story, writers present characters in one of two ways: as iconic or dynamic. An iconic character experiences all manner of dust-ups and tragedies—but doesn't change. A dynamic character shifts and grows along with the story. In *Firefly*, each character is presented at a different point in their personal journey. This technique varies the presentations of the characters and gives the overall concept more depth. Shepherd Book, for example, stands opposite to Malcolm Reynolds because he swore off violence and embraced the life of a preacher. Though he has a mysterious past (which is explored in 'The Shepherd's Tale' from Dark Horse Comics) he continues to question his faith and his actions on board the ship. Through this examination, Book leaves *Serenity* and Mal behind, because he feared who he might become. Kaylee, on the other hand, is less dynamic. Though she has a crush on Simon Tam, which later blossoms into a relationship, her character remains largely static throughout *Firefly*.

EP. 10 'WAR STORIES'

INT. SHUTTLE II - DAY Zoë and Mal are getting her ready to go. Zoë is having trouble working the controls. Mal is securing the crate o' drugs.

MAL
Bolles is ready and waiting. Lucrative as this stuff is, I'll be glad to see the last of it. Kinda makes us a target—

ZOE
(interrupting) Did River get in here, start playing around? Ignition sequence is completely turned about. I can't even—

WASH
(entering) I can.

MAL
Get it set, okay? We got to be moving.

WASH
Here's a funny twist: no.

MAL
No what?

WASH
No sir.

ZOE
You changed the sequence?

WASH
(to Zoë)
Didn't want you taking off without me. In fact, didn't want you taking off at all. Thought maybe I'd take this run instead. Me and the Captain.

MAL
The Captain who's standing right here telling you that's not gonna happen?

WASH
Well, it's a dangerous mission, sir, and I can't stand the thought of something happening that might cause you two to come back with another thrilling tale of bonding and adventure. I just can't take that right now.

MAL
Okay, I'm lost, I'm angry, and I'm armed. If you two have something to work out
—

ZOE
It's all right. We've dealt with Bolles before, shouldn't be a problem. I wouldn't mind sitting this one out, sir.

Beat, Mal looking at both of them.

MAL
This is a <FANG-tzang FONG-kwong duh jie> [knot of self indulgent lunacy] but I don't have time to unwind it. Wash, get her started. Zoë, the ship is yours.

Wash and Zoë pass each other. She's pissed, but not overly so. They're about on a par, actually, but he smiles at her.

WASH
Bye hon. We promise not to stop for beers with the fellas.

She shuts the door behind her. Mal moves into the copilot seat as Wash whirrs her up for lift off.

WASH (cont'd)
So. You wanna sing army songs, or something?

Script Excerpt by Cheryl Cain

To further underline the bonds of military loyalty, Zoë addresses Mal as 'Sir'—even though she does, on occasion, contradict him. Her feelings for the Captain are a bone of contention that creates friction in her otherwise happy relationship with her husband, in part because Wash has never known the horrors of war.

EP. 10 'WAR STORIES'

INT. SHUTTLE II
Zoë pilots the shuttle as it lurches, indicating that it has latched onto the skyplex. Zoë steels herself, rises, moves to the door/airlock. Pushes open the door revealing—

INT. SKYPLEX—CORRIDOR

Goons and guns. Lots of them. Zoë's already got her hands in the air, one of them holding the canvas bag. Even as Goons rush her—

ZOE
I'm unarmed.

They frisk her. Take the bag, look at it.

ZOE (cont'd) I want to talk to Niska.

Off that—

INT. NISKA'S TORTURE ROOM
SCREAMS. Niska watches with
pleasure. Mal and Wash both breathing
hard from the pain of the last bit of
torture. It's a pause in the action. Dalin
appears, whispers something to Niska.
Niska listens, motions for the Torturer
to hold. Nods to Dalin, who exits.

NISKA
(to Mal) You will not mind if I pause to
do a little business?

MAL
Knock yourself out. No, really.

INT. SKYPLEX—CORRIDORS
The armed henchmen escort Zoë
through the Skyplex. Zoë paying
close attention to every detail of her
surroundings. The corridor has large
windows along the side that look out
onto the factory. They arrive at Niska's
door, where a couple more armed
henchmen await. A henchman slides A
KEYCARD near the door, opening it.
WE MOVE INTO—

INT. NISKA'S TORTURE ROOM
We're in Zoë's POV as the full horror
of it is revealed. She sees Mal and
Wash both there, restrained and in
pain. She tries to stifle her reaction.
They don't notice her yet: Mal is
whispering something to the droopy-
eyed Wash. Dalin has given the bag of
money over to Niska, who looks at it.
Takes in the amount. Now Wash blinks
through his haze, seeing Zoë there. Mal
follows his look to her—

WASH
(muttering)
No, no, no...run, run...

She ignores him, looks away, to Niska.

ZOE
It's five times what you paid us for the
train job.

NISKA
Yes. You have had, you say it, good
times...I see that.

ZOE
Should be more than enough to buy
back my men.

NISKA
This is your opinion, is it?

ZOE
It is.

NISKA
They are perhaps damaged now. Are
they worth so much to you?

ZOE
Yes.

NISKA
And to me...they are worth more. I
think it is not enough.

*Zoë clenches her jaw muscles. Fucker's not
going for it.*

NISKA (cont'd)
Not enough for two. But sufficient,
perhaps, for one.

She looks at him. Sees where this is going.

NISKA (cont'd)
So you now have a question to make
an answer. It is for you, pretty lady, and
only you, now to ch—

ZOE
(cuts him off) Him.

She points at Wash. Niska's a bit thrown.

ZOE (cont'd)
I'm sorry. You were going to ask me to
choose, right? Didja wanna finish?

*Off Niska, open-mouthed, still back at the not-
being-able-to-get-his-sentence-out moment—*

END OF ACT TWO
ACT THREE

INT. NISKA'S TORTURE ROOM
WASH FALLS INTO FRAME,
dropping hard onto his knees in front
of Zoë. She helps him shakily to his
feet. Niska eyes the money. Waves a
dismissive hand at them.

NISKA
He is yours. We are ended now.

WASH
(whispers, desperate) Mal...

*He tries to look over at Mal. Zoë takes him
gently by the chin, turns his head back to her.*

ZOE
(in his eyes) Shhh. Start walkin'.

He obeys. She turns to go, leading Wash.

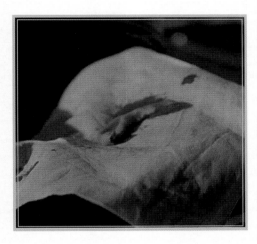

NISKA
A moment, please. This money...
Zoë stops, turns—are they going to have a problem now?

NISKA (cont'd)
There is too much. You should have some small refund.

ZOE
(tries to move) Keep it.

NISKA
No, no, no. I insist.
(to Torturer, in Czech)
They have enough for a slice.
(to Zoë, in English)
I wouldn't want the talk to be that Adelai Niska is a cheat.

The Torturer has picked up a knife, moved to Mal—and SLICES Mal's ear clean off. Mal SCREAMS in agony. Niska produces a handkerchief from his pocket. The Torturer places Mal's ear in the handkerchief. Niska then hands it to Zoë, who remains impassive, despite Mal's ROARS OF PAIN.

NISKA (cont'd)
Now we are ended.

Dismissed, Zoë and Wash move for the door, their backs turned to Mal, as his SCREAMS REVERBERATE in the small room.

INT. NISKA'S OFFICE—CONTINUOUS
Zoë and Wash move through Niska's office, away from the sound of Mal's continued HOWLING. The door to the torture room slides shut, only slightly muffling the sound. They exit.

INT. SHUTTLE II
Zoë and Wash enter. The moment the door closes, Wash basically collapses. Zoë manages to guide him down to his knees. And she sinks right along with him. He's stunned, staggered, his mind still back in that room. She looks at him with a mixture of relief, worry and, goddamn it—love.

WASH
He's insane.

ZOE
I know it.

WASH
I mean...you've told the damn stories. Saved you in the War. But I...I didn't know...

ZOE
You mean Mal?

Wash nods.

WASH
He's crazy.

She looks at him, not sure if he's in shock or making any sense at all.

WASH (cont'd)
He wouldn't break, Zoë. And he kept me from... I wouldn't have made it.

She tries to hold it together. Touches his face.

WASH (cont'd)
Niska's gonna kill him.

ZOE
He'll make it last as long as possible. Days, if he can.

A look of stoic resolve crosses Wash's face. He rises shakily but surely to his feet—

WASH
Bastard's not gonna get days.

— and moves to the pilot's seat of the shuttle.
— Off Zoë, watching her pilot husband fire up the shuttle

Script Excerpt by Cheryl Cain

Zoë is loyal to the Captain, but she's also deeply connected to her husband, Wash, which creates conflict for her character. Zoë is often expressionless because not only is she a dutiful soldier, she represents the side of Mal that remains entrenched in his psyche. When Wash dies, however, Zoë's heart breaks and she becomes vulnerable. Then, Zoë honors Wash's last request and wears a dress at his funeral.

THIS SPREAD: Wash's desire to get his hands dirty with Mal leads to a serious bout of torture.

ZOË AND WASH

Film editor/associate producer Lisa Lassek: "The relationship of Wash and Zoë is one of my favorite things in the show. And that was something that was really important to Joss. In fact, the entire episode of 'War Stories' comes from the moment where Zoë decides to choose Wash; that decision being so instantaneous is something that tells you so much about their marriage. That moment to me is a signature of *Firefly*, but, more importantly, a signature of the larger questions that are in *Firefly*. It shows that the relationship between Zoë and her husband is so different to the relationship between Zoë and Mal. It's what Joss loves to do: switch things on your expectations. It's a big dramatic moment where somebody has to make a decision, and Joss takes that completely away. And it makes perfect sense. You see Zoë's decision comes from a place of love. I mean that's just where you are when you're in that relationship.

The audience never gets the opportunity to see Zoë grow as a character on film, although her story does continue in the *Serenity* comics published by Dark Horse Comics, where we see her wish to have a child come true.

Romance, like the relationships between Mal and Inara, Zoë and Wash, and Simon and Kaylee, are only one way of highlighting how the crew feels about each other. Roles on the ship are also important to the story. Like Malcolm J. Reynolds, Zoë Alleyne Washburne is a veteran of the Unification War who stands with him even if she doesn't like his decisions. As Captain and First Mate, they form the nucleus of the crew, whereas Simon and River pair off as fugitive siblings, Book and Jayne as unlikely friends, and Wash and Kaylee as genius mechanics Mal must rely on to keep *Serenity* flying.

TARGETS AND FUGITIVES

Most television shows have an individual story present in each episode and includes a larger arc for the season. *Firefly*'s episodes are distinctive, and recurring characters that include Adelai Niska and Yo-Saff-Bridge provide a sense that the crew's actions might have consequences. Arguably, *Firefly* would still possess compelling stories without the addition of Simon and River Tam. Their presence, however, highlights the primary plot—the Alliance experimenting on innocent children—and taps into futuristic science-fiction elements like mad scientists, body horror, psychic abilities, and mysterious, inhuman pursuers.

Simon and River also add an additional threat level to ensure Mal continues to fly away from Alliance-occupied territories and cruisers. As fugitives, they also remind us that the Alliance is an active threat as opposed to a passive one. And, though Mal could afford to move on from the lessons he learns along the way, by doing so he puts Simon and River at risk.

The pursuit of Simon and River Tam is one of the few plots that isn't centered on Mal or the crew, and it's an important aspect of *Firefly* because it reinforces the Captain's worst fears. By following the Tams' story, we get a different perspective of what it's like to run afoul of the Alliance. We confirm that the government is not the bastion of peace and prosperity they profess to be, and River is our proof.

With all that's happened up to this point, it's easy to understand why 'Objects in Space' was a fitting end to the TV show. Though the story continues to this day, through a film, novels, comics, and games, these landmark episodes are undoubtedly the reason why fans keep coming back for more. Despite its flaws, *Firefly* and its memorable crew has truly earned its place amongst the stars.

RIGHT: **You can't take the sky from them.**

ACKNOWLEDGMENTS

Monica Valentinelli would like to thank both her current and former editors at Titan Publishing, her partner in life, Matt McElroy, for supporting her creative efforts and caffeine addiction, and her former teammates who put in countless hours writing, editing, and illustrating for the beloved game line. Lastly, and perhaps most importantly, she'd like to thank Joss Whedon, the cast and crew of the *Firefly* TV show and *Serenity*, and Browncoats everywhere. This book would not exist without them.

CONTRIBUTOR BIOGRAPHIES

MONICA VALENTINELLI has been flying in the 'verse since 2012. She was the lead writer and developer for the award-winning *Firefly* roleplaying game line, and wrote *The Gorramn Shiniest Dictionary and Phrasebook in The 'Verse* published in 2016. A prolific writer and editor, you can find out more about Monica and her work at **www.booksofm.com**.

MIKE BROTHERTON is a professor of astronomy at the University of Wyoming. He uses the Hubble Space Telescope, the Very Large Array in New Mexico, and the Chandra X-ray Observatory, to investigate quasars, the most luminous active galactic nuclei. He is the founder of the NASA and National Science Foundation funded Launch Pad Astronomy Workshop for Writers, which brings professional writers to Wyoming every summer in order to better educate and inspire their audiences. His science fiction writing includes novels *Star Dragon* and *Spider Star*, both from Tor Books. **www.mikebrotherton.com**

MAURICE BROADDUS is a community organizer and teacher. His work has appeared in *Lightspeed Magazine*, *Weird Tales*, *Beneath Ceaseless Skies*, *Asimov's Science Fiction*, *Cemetery Dance* and *Uncanny Magazine*. His books include the urban fantasy trilogy *The Knights of Breton Court*, and middle grade detective novel *The Usual Suspects*. As an editor, he has worked on *Dark Faith*, *Dark Faith: Invocations*, *Streets of Shadows*, *People of Colo(u)r Destroy Horror*, and *Apex Magazine*. Learn more at **MauriceBroaddus.com**.

TONY LEE is a native of Taiwan who didn't know any better than to get into the tabletop gaming industry. He's worked as a game designer, developer, translator, and editor for over fifteen years, and has lent his talents to the *Serenity* RPG and *Firefly* RPG line of tabletop games. Following the success of these efforts, Tony is a full-time Chinese-English translator specializing in mobile and computer game translations.

JENNY LYNN is a native of Southern California. She graduated from Duke University with a degree in English. She is a TV writer-producer, provided the voice of *Serenity*, and was the official translator on *Firefly*.

BEN MUND is a graphic artist who is best known for his work on the *Serenity Guide of the 'Verse* published by QMX. He has worked on the *Battlestar Galactica* and *Stargate* properties, and is also the designer/artist of *Building An Elder God* published by Signal Fire Studios.

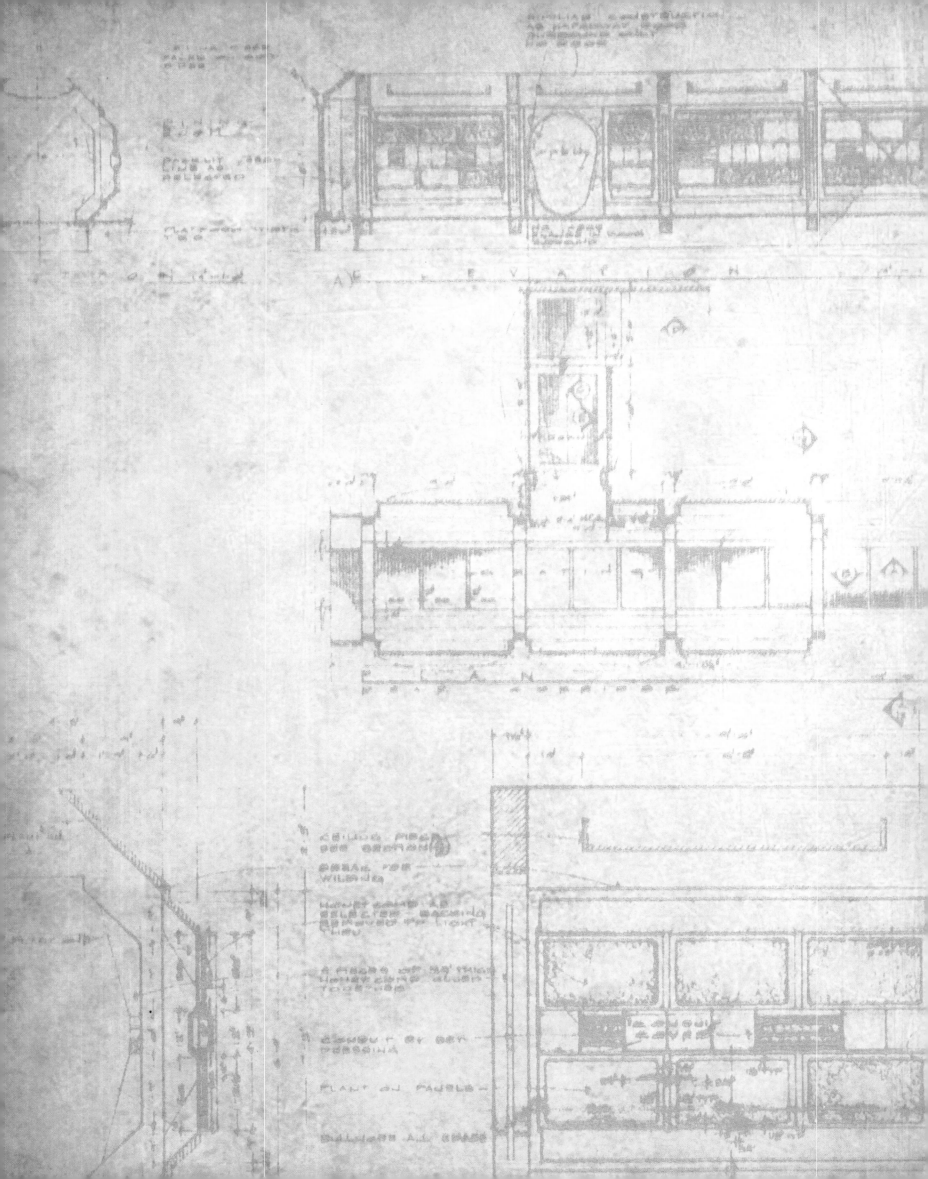